The Irony of Virtue

Other Books by Ernest W. Lefever

Ethics and United States Foreign Policy

Profile of American Politics (co-editor)

The World Crisis and American Responsibility (editor)

Arms and Arms Control (editor)

Crisis in the Congo: A U.N. Force in Action

Uncertain Mandate: Politics of the U.N. Congo Operation

Spear and Scepter: Army, Police, Politics in Tropical Africa

Ethics and World Politics (co-author)

*TV and National Defense:
An Analysis of CBS News, 1972–1973*

Nuclear Arms in the Third World: U.S. Policy Dilemma

*Amsterdam to Nairobi: World Council of
Churches and the Third World*

The CIA and the American Ethic (co-author)

The Apocalyptic Premise: Nuclear Arms Debated (co-editor)

Nairobi to Vancouver: World Council of Churches and the World

Perestroika: How New Is Gorbachev's New Thinking? (co-editor)

The Irony of Virtue

Ethics and
American Power

Ernest W. Lefever

Foreword by
William F. Buckley Jr.

Westview Press
A Member of Perseus Books, L.L.C.

The author gratefully acknowledges permission to use selections from his writing previously published in periodicals and books. The introduction to each selection notes its source and date. Several copyright holders have requested specific language for their permission, as follows:

"Cambodia Blood Bath," 1977. Reprinted with permission of *TV Guide*, News America Publications, Inc.

"A Dangerous Political Activism," 1980, ". . . But Don't Sacrifice Our Self-Interest," 1985, and "Vietnam's Ghosts," 1997. Reprinted with permission of *The Wall Street Journal*, Dow Jones & Company, Inc. All rights reserved.

Op-Ed, "Let's Help our Latin Friends," 1983, and Editorial, "Sit-in Era Had an Organized Precursor," 1993. Reprinted by permission from The New York Times Co.

"How New Will the Better World Be?" Reprinted from: *The Phi Kappa Phi Journal*, Vol. 72, No. 4, Fall, 1992.

Written permission to reprint published material has also been received from the *American Spectator*; Brookings Institution; *Christian Century*; *Foreign Affairs*; Johns Hopkins University Press; *Journal of Law, Ethics, and Public Policy*; *National Interest*; *National Review*; *Orbis*; *Policy Review*; *Review of Politics*; *USA Today*; *Washington Times*; and *World and I*.

Published in 1998 in the United States of America by Westview Press, 5500 Central Avenue, Boulder, Colorado 80301-2877, and in the United Kingdom by Westview Press, 12 Hid's Copse Road, Cumnor Hill, Oxford OX2 9JJ

Library of Congress Cataloging-in-Publication Data
Lefever, Ernest W.
    The irony of virtue : ethics and American power / Ernest W.
Lefever : foreword by William F. Buckley, Jr.
    p.   cm.
    Includes index.
    ISBN 0-8133-6881-2 (cloth)
    1. United States—Foreign relations—Moral and ethical aspects.
2. International relations—Moral and ethical aspects.   3. Political
ethics.   I. Title.
JZ1480.L44   1998
172'.4'0973—dc21   97-40895
                                                                        CIP

The paper used in this publication meets the requirements of the American National Standard for Permanence of Paper for Printed Library Materials Z39.48-1984.

10   9   8   7   6   5   4   3   2

For Margaret and our grandchildren
Paris Ann
Scott David
Alexander David
Elizabeth Joy

Contents

Foreword

William F. Buckley Jr.

The author has a story to tell, and he tells it vividly, modestly, engrossingly. Back then he was a religious pacifist. As he reflected on the challenges of the times he forsook that position and, to say it irreverently, carried God along with him. He decided that the Christian mandate required him to face problems as they existed. There was, for instance, the problem of the growing Soviet threat. Of the Berlin Wall. Of Cambodia and the bloodbath. These are events to deplore but also events against which to marshal the engines of foreign policy. Especially when such engines, like our own—unlike those of any other power—could be decisive in the struggle for peace and freedom.

So then, how should we be guided? Ernest Lefever, who calls himself a humane realist, does not go so far as to say that realism will take us to high roosts or usher in a new world order. President Reagan, acknowledging the author's contributions, many of them through the Ethics and Public Policy Center he established, nominated him to serve as assistant secretary of state for human rights, an office that could do much, quietly, to nudge history in more humane paths.

Despite his demonstrated credentials for the post, Lefever ran into solid opposition from the liberal media and their Senate counterparts. How could that body be asked to confirm the presidential choice of someone who had so eloquently and steadfastly insisted on the relevance of ethics in the formulation of policy? And who, like Jeane Kirkpatrick, had drawn the crucial moral and political distinctions between totalitarian and authoritarian regimes?

So he stayed on with his center. I acknowledge as one of the most exciting intellectual and political moments of my life serving Mr. Lefever on the occasion when he brought the two giants together for the first and only time. Not until that day in November 1988 had Dr. Andrei Sakharov met Dr. Edward Teller.

I was studiously quiet on the issue that divided the Russian and the American but now take the liberty of reflecting on the encounter. The meeting of the two men responsible for the development of the hydrogen bomb in the two great societies locked in mortal combat was freighted with tension. The reason for it was that Sakharov had been for years exiled from Moscow by the Soviet government; and there in Gorky, in virtual isolation, accompanied only by his spirited wife, he allowed himself to dwell on the terror of nuclear-tipped missiles on both sides. When finally permitted back to Moscow by Mikhail Gorbachev, Sakharov announced his opposition to any development of antiballistic missile technology and publicly criticized Reagan's Strategic Defense Initiative.

But how much did Dr. Sakharov know, after his years of isolation, about the ongoing investment of his own government in military space technology? Did he know that Moscow was spending billions of dollars a year on antimissile defenses and on its own version of SDI and had assembled tens of thousands of scientists and technicians to work on these projects? Did he know that the Soviets were spending more than the United States on these efforts?

During that dramatic evening, Dr. Teller was to hand over to Dr. Sakharov a factual report on what his own government was up to. Though this vital information was in the public domain, there was serious reason to doubt that the exiled genius was aware of it.

Both Sakharov and Teller spoke movingly, and Ernest Lefever concluded another evening illuminated by the kind of intelligent thinking he gives us in his book on the irony of virtue. Ironic indeed that during a period when the polarization between good and evil was greater than any other time in recorded history, ambiguity would prosper, even, or perhaps especially, in the high chancelleries of advanced moral reflection.

Since Lefever's writing is grounded in the timeless Judeo-Christian ethic, his words will speak to the twenty-first century as they have to the present one.

Acknowledgments

I am indebted to the teachers and colleagues who encouraged me to put my thoughts on paper and to the editors who accepted them. For this book as for earlier ones, I am also indebted to my wife, Margaret, for her understanding and patience and to my two sons, David and Bryce, for their encouragement.

I also enjoyed the moral support of my two successors as president of the Ethics and Public Policy Center, George Weigel and Elliott Abrams, and the advice of the center's vice president, Robert Royal, and its editor, Carol Griffith, both of whom I had the good sense to hire two decades ago.

My special thanks to my research assistant Daniel Lewis for his good judgment in helping to select the essays and his artful comments on the connecting tissue between them. I thank Lawrence Stratton for his timely advice and Julie DiMauro for painstakingly typing the manuscript. And a very special note of gratitude goes to Patricia Buckley Bozell for her sympathetic counsel in this and related projects where nuances count.

My greatest intellectual debt is to the late Reinhold Niebuhr, whose friendship enriched my life and whose wisdom, I trust, is reflected in these pages.

Ernest W. Lefever

An Autobiographical Sketch

Abraham Lincoln understood the irony of virtue. He acknowledged the tragic realities of war and slavery and recognized America's grave flaws as well as its substantial virtues. Yet, in the midst of a wrenching civil war, he declared that a free and united America was the "last, best hope of earth." Calling on the better angels of our nature, he believed that with the help of God we could achieve "a just and lasting peace among ourselves and with all nations."

From its auspicious beginning, America has seen itself as an exceptional nation with a real but not precisely defined mission under the "guidance of that Almighty Being whose power regulates the destiny of nations," as James Madison put it in his first inaugural address. Since then, his sense of mission has influenced the exercise of American power abroad. The men in Philadelphia were concerned for justice and freedom at home and in the larger world. But there are dangers in claiming undue virtue for ourselves or for our behavior overseas.

Rightly understood, virtue can lead to wise policies and humane consequences, but virtue untamed by facts or undisciplined by a sober understanding of man and history can lead to foolish policies and dire consequences. Arrogance, including arrogance stemming from virtue, is often a prelude to disaster.

In his seminal book The Irony of American History (1952), Reinhold Niebuhr discussed the impact of virtue on tragedy and irony. The tragic in history, he said, results from the conscious "choice of evil in a good cause" or the sacrifice of "some high value for the sake of a higher or equal one." Niebuhr cited America's nuclear dilemma—the moral necessity of threatening nuclear war in order to keep the peace and avoid capitulation to Soviet tyranny. Many highminded people have recoiled from America's possession of nuclear arms, but had any one of our presidents given in to the "virtue" of nuclear pacifism during the long Cold War years, he would have invited catastrophe.

Our post-Hiroshima presidents were in good company. In 1861, Lincoln sacrificed peace to save the Union and abolish slavery, and in 1941, Franklin Roosevelt waged war to preserve freedom. They both understood that choosing the lesser of two evils—though tragic—was the morally responsible course.

An ironic historical development, said Niebuhr, is a baffling incongruity in which the best human efforts are mocked, seemingly by chance or accident. But upon closer examination, the incongruities—especially untoward and unintended consequences—are "discovered to be the result of more than chance." The

1

outcome is ironic "if virtue becomes vice through some hidden defect in the virtue. . . . The ironic situation is distinguished . . . from tragedy . . . by an unconscious weakness rather than a conscious resolution."

The hidden defect of America's nuclear pacifists is their failure to assess the often conflicting moral claims of peace, security, and freedom. The twentieth century provides other examples of flawed virtue. Woodrow Wilson's insistence on "national self-determination" led to the Balkanization of Central Europe, and Neville Chamberlain's commitment to "peace in our time" at Munich encouraged Hitler's conquest of Europe.

Americans, with their idealism and their confidence that world peace is achievable, are more prone than other peoples to permit the "soft" virtues—idealism, goodwill, compassion, and forgiveness, which are all laudable in personal relations—to confuse or even subvert the hard decisions in the world of power politics. Most idealists fail to comprehend the persistence of conflict, chaos, and predatory power in a sinful world where sustained periods of peace are the exception. Some of them distrust American power; others feel guilty about it. Hence, idealists have frequently urged our leaders to be more trusting and conciliatory to those who would do us or our allies harm. Fortunately, the pacifist-isolationist sentiment of the 1930s was countered by common sense and by historical realists such as Reinhold Niebuhr, who warned that giving in to such sentiments could lead to war or encourage tyranny. But it took the Pearl Harbor attack to shock America out of its complacency.

*   *   *

Though this understanding of power and morality is clear to me now, I came to it gradually as I pondered the dilemmas posed by aggression and tyranny in history's bloodiest century. The story of my own development in a small way reflects the spiritual and political problems America has faced in coming to grips with Nazi Germany, Japanese aggression, and Soviet imperialism.

Like many other liberal theological students during World War II, I read Reinhold Niebuhr, America's best-known theologian, but rejected his somber view of man and politics. I was a utopian pacifist and opposed America's entry into the war. Born into a pious, working-class family in York, Pennsylvania, a year and a day after World War I ended, I came by my pacifism honestly. My parents, members of the pacifist Church of the Brethren, each came from a long line of religious dissenters. My father's forebears were French Huguenots, and my mother's were Mennonite lay preachers. I take pride in my Huguenot ancestors, several of whom were martyred for their faith, and in my maternal grandfather, a Mennonite farmer who ministered to the dying soldiers of both sides after the Battle of Gettysburg.

My mother gave birth to my four brothers and me on the third floor of our red brick duplex on the edge of town, assisted by a neighborhood doctor whose fee was $25 for each delivery. With only a sixth-grade education, my father worked for four decades in the York Corporation machine shop, where he was known as the Bible-reading foreman. Having taught school for ten years, my mother consumed Charles Dickens and historical novels and read stories from the Bible and the McGuffey Readers to her sons. Both she and my father taught and embodied Victorian virtues, from honesty and compassion to hard work and temperance.

In some ways, I was a child of the Great Depression. Our family had no car or telephone, and we got by with the bare necessities, which in my mother's view included complete sets of Dickens and Shakespeare and many other books. Early on, we raised chickens in our backyard. My father was never laid off, and we considered ourselves fortunate. My parents helped the needy in our church and beyond, but they opposed government "handouts," citing the Mormons who "looked after their own." Absorbing their Bible-centered concern for "the least of these" (biblical language punctuated our daily conversation), I believed that serving humanity was the highest calling, and I wanted to become a Christian missionary. While working my way through college and seminary, I spent part of the summer for five years in volunteer social service camps for children—from the slums of Philadelphia to a migrant workers' camp in Yakima, Washington.

My parents believed that all war was an offense against God and that problems, whether of civic order or world politics, should be resolved by nonviolent means. They were opposed to taking oaths and to state intervention in matters of religion. They never consulted a lawyer. Though essentially nonpolitical, they condemned "godless Communism" in the Soviet Union and Hitler's persecution of the Jews.

*   *   *

During my four years at Elizabethtown College, a small Brethren school in Lancaster County, Pennsylvania, my already strong pacifist views were further reinforced by two vivid events. Both took place in 1938, three years before Pearl Harbor. In March, Senator Gerald Nye of North Dakota spoke on campus, asserting that modern wars were caused by "merchants of death" who sold arms to all sides. The next day, though I had no clear idea who these merchants might be, I handed out leaflets urging fellow students to write their congressmen to oppose increased Navy appropriations.

Far more significant was a Fellowship of Reconciliation conference I attended at Bound Brook, New Jersey, that September. The FOR, a religious pacifist organization, was led by erstwhile Trotskyite A. J. Muste and included influential Protestant, Catholic, and Jewish leaders. At the gathering, my sheltered, small-town pietism clashed with the active political pacifism of sophisticated and largely New York intellectuals, some of whom were Norman Thomas socialists. Yet I felt strangely at home in this group. Around the campfire, we younger ones sang "I Ain't Gonna Study War No More," "Joe Hill," and other spirituals and labor songs, and my heart was stirred. I returned to college declaring that pacifism was more than an antiwar stance—it was a way of life. I consumed pacifist pamphlets, briefly subscribed to *The Call* (the New York Socialist Party's weekly newspaper), and later headed the international relations club and the YMCA on our campus.

Inspired by advocates of nonviolence such as Muste, Gandhi, Jane Addams in Chicago, and Muriel Lester in London, I started a peace study group. We first met on the tenth anniversary of the 1928 Kellogg-Briand Pact, which "outlawed" war as an instrument of national policy. Later, I gave a speech that opened with these words: "The Germans have just built a new artillery piece that can fire a shell for twenty miles with great accuracy. War has become unthinkable!" (Perhaps to atone for my earlier pacifism, I have been thinking about the unthinkable ever since.)

Strongly opposed to Hitler and Stalin, I held America to a higher standard. I was more immediately concerned by our "sins"—sins I could do something about (such as the chain gangs of black convicts I had seen in Georgia in 1939)—than by the monstrous crimes of the Nazis and Communists—about which I felt helpless. Unconsciously, I had fallen into the trap of what, years later, I called "moral symmetry." I naively expressed my opposition to American participation in the war in my hometown paper: "While we are waiting for Churchill and Roosevelt to get their heads together with Comrade Stalin, and before we enter the 'shooting war,' the President might well recall Churchill's scathing condemnation of America's participation in World War I."

A few months before Pearl Harbor, as chairman of the National Brethren Youth Council, I signed—along with Norman Thomas, Dorothy Day, and a dozen other pacifist leaders—a Youth Committee Against War proclamation opposing "fascism and totalitarianism" *and* American involvement in "total war."

While in college, I was ordained a Brethren minister. Later, I registered with Selective Service as a conscientious objector but was exempted from military service as a theological student. One of my brothers, a more radical pacifist, refused to register or to accept alternative civilian service. In August 1943, the day after I performed his marriage ceremony, he was picked up by the FBI, and on October 25, 1943, he was tried in the Scranton, Pennsylvania, District Court and sentenced to two years in a federal penitentiary for refusing to report for civilian service. He was not a draft-dodger but a draft-objector who kept the FBI informed of his whereabouts.

*   *   *

After the Pearl Harbor attack, it was futile to oppose our entry into the war, so I turned my energies toward another cause dear to pacifists—the fledgling civil rights movement. My seminary days—a year at the Church of the Brethren school in Chicago and two years at Yale Divinity School—coincided with America's three years in World War II. During the war, I was a part-time field-worker for the FOR. It didn't provide travel expenses, so I hitchhiked over 30,000 miles coast to coast to spread the word—opposing peacetime conscription, supporting a cooperative (as opposed to capitalist or socialist) economy, and working for a color-blind society. Thumbing my way wasn't all that easy. A healthy young male in civilian clothes competing with scads of soldiers and sailors in uniform stuck out like a sore thumb. At one Kansas crossroads in July 1944, I was the first to arrive and the eighteenth to be picked up.

In Virginia, I sat in the back of the bus (twelve years before Rosa Parks sat in the front of the bus in Alabama) to fight Jim Crow laws segregating blacks. In Chicago, I took part in one of the country's first sit-ins to desegregate a restaurant. Working with rights pioneers such as Bayard Rustin and James Farmer and with my Brethren colleagues, I arranged for the release of the first Japanese-Americans from detention camps in California, two of whom spent a night in my Chicago dormitory room. I also spoke out against anti-Semitism.

*   *   *

I spent the last two war years—1943 to 1945—at Yale Divinity School (YDS) in New Haven. The serene Georgian quadrangle was an unreal world. Cloistered with a faculty and students, half of whom were pacifist, I was living in a cozy cocoon far removed from the tragic conflict in Europe and the Pacific and, indeed, from the American people who were caught up in the massive and popular war effort. I worked for the FOR in the Connecticut Valley, including visits to conscientious objectors serving in mental hospitals. I received YDS field work credit for this activity.

In March 1944, I organized an interracial student conference at Smith College, which called for abolishing the poll tax, Jim Crow in the armed forces, Oriental Exclusion laws, and racial quotas for college admission—"the word *race* should be removed from application blanks." (At that time, quotas were used to *exclude* certain minorities, rather than to deliberately *include* them, as in later years.)

While at YDS, I sought out black students, arranged for the *Pittsburgh Courier* (a Negro paper) to be delivered to the common room, and attended a private reception for Marion Anderson. I also visited Harlem, staying with a black Episcopal rector, and on one occasion, I took some fellow students to an elaborate Sunday night dinner presided over by Father Divine, a flamboyant depression-era welfare demagogue. I may have been guilty of black preference, but I justified my behavior on the grounds that I was fighting discrimination.

*   *   *

Occasionally, I attended a Sunday service at Yale's Battell Chapel to hear celebrated preachers such as Norman Thomas or Reinhold Niebuhr. At the time, I strongly preferred the former. A month before the 1944 presidential election, I organized a debate at which three YDS professors spoke, one for Roosevelt, one for Thomas Dewey, and one for Norman Thomas. In a straw vote, Thomas got 59 votes, FDR 58, and Dewey 46—reflecting the liberal-pacifist cast of the theological students.

In March 1945, I attended a Christian student seminar in Washington, D.C. FDR had just returned from the Yalta conference. We listened to his report to a joint session of Congress from a nearby office. A dying man, Roosevelt apologized for his fatigue by referring to his heavy steel leg braces, his only public acknowledgment of his disability. I was moved by my physical proximity to the president and by the portent of Yalta.

Six weeks later—on April 12, 1945—during dinner in the refectory, I learned that President Roosevelt had been struck down by a cerebral hemorrhage at Warm Springs, Georgia. We gathered around a radio in stunned silence. I felt little emotion because I had neither affection nor antipathy for the man, who, like the Statue of Liberty, had always been there.

That night, I wrote a friend: "President Roosevelt was not a saint—but he had ideals and principles. It is easy to live up to principle when one is not faced with hard choices. It's infinitely more difficult when one must make decisions in a world of power. He will go down in history as a great statesman."

Shortly after Germany capitulated on May 7, I became convinced that Japan was on the verge of surrender. In late July, I wired Senator Kenneth Wherry, Republican whip, supporting his effort to persuade President Truman to offer "peace terms to Japan to shorten the war, save thousands of lives, and lay a better foundation for enduring peace."

On August 6, the *Enola Gay* dropped the atomic bomb on Hiroshima, a shock that reinforced my antiwar views and my determination to have a small part in postwar reconstruction. Earlier, I had opposed the allied "obliteration bombing" of Dresden, Hamburg, and other German cities, and now I faulted Truman for "unleashing this satanic force."

Looking back over my pacifism during what was surely a just war to defend freedom, I find it difficult to comprehend how morally confused I had been. My single-minded commitment to nonviolence—in my view, a preeminent virtue—had become a vice. I was self-righteous, sometimes obnoxiously so, but not fully aware of it at the time. Theoretically, I rejected the just war arguments of my Christian ethics professor Richard Niebuhr, Reinhold's elder brother, but pragmatically, I knew that a victory for Hitler and the Japanese imperialists would usher in a new dark age for humanity.

If a substantial percentage of young Americans and Britons had been conscientious objectors, Hitler might have won. Yet my fellow pacifists and I did not support the U.S. war effort. We failed to address the evil of tyranny and conquest. In our own principled blindness, we personified the irony of misplaced virtue. More concerned with clear-cut civil rights issues than with the moral ambiguities posed by tyranny and conquest, I managed to live through the war years with no conscious sense of guilt. Perhaps I was a vocational pacifist, one who could not conscientiously participate in war but who did not deny the state's right to defend itself.

My two years at Yale did not breach my pacifist armor, but they may have dented it. Occasionally, I voiced views contrary to my utopian stance, but such views did not take root until I confronted Europe's tragedy close up. I was involved in too many causes and moving too fast to permit other embryonic thoughts about God, man, and politics to come to full term. That had to await the fullness of time.

On August 28, two weeks after Japan's surrender, I accepted a one-year appointment as a field secretary with the War Prisoners Aid program of the Geneva-based World's Alliance of YMCAs (World's YMCA), with "maintenance plus $10 a month."

"I am painfully aware," I wrote friends, "that I will be merely helping to mop up the debris of an indescribably cruel war. Mopping up is necessary and right. But it is even more essential to prevent war. That is the task of everyone, not just a handful of relief workers." As one who had virtually blocked out all war news during the fighting, I was now destined to confront the war's grim consequences in Europe's bombed-out cities and in its refugee and prisoner-of-war camps.

* * *

A month after Hiroshima—young, idealistic, and armed with a B.D. from Yale Divinity School—I sailed for England on the SS *Ericsson*, a passenger ship that had been converted into a troop transport. My World's YMCA assignment was to visit POW camps—providing Bibles, other books, musical instruments, and sports gear to German prisoners, first in Britain and later in occupied West Germany.

Thus began three eye-opening years in Europe, 1945 to 1948, where I saw the physical and human wreckage of Hitler's vaunted Thousand Year Reich and the brutal tyranny of Stalin's expanding empire. Gradually, under the hammer blows of postwar realities, the political and moral irrelevance of my pacifism began to dawn on me. I never saw a blinding

light on a road to Damascus; my transformation began quietly with a series of tremors.

In London, I was shocked by the severe bomb damage in the central
city—hardly a pane of glass had been spared during the fierce Battle of
Britain in 1940. Lord Nelson still stood tall atop his column in Trafalgar
Square, but the sway of the British Empire had already passed to its erstwhile colony in the New World. Yet the London that had enchanted
Shakespeare and defied Hitler remained a proud symbol of civility and
the rule of law.

At dinner on my second day, I was jolted by the words of a fellow
Brethren minister, Andrew Cordier, who had drafted bylaws for the new
United Nations General Assembly. He told me of Stalin's brutal occupation of East Germany and his enslavement of millions of able-bodied
POWs in Siberian mines. Cordier called the Soviet Union "the world's
number one problem" and feared that Moscow would take over Europe
within the decade; he believed "there is one chance in a hundred that we
can prevent World War III." I had always regarded Communism as a virulent threat to all that was good in the West, but now I began to see that
more than words and good deeds were needed to confront it.

*   *   *

The World's YMCA and the British Foreign Office had set up a theological seminary for German POWs on the Duke of Portland's estate near
Sherwood Forest in Nottinghamshire. While assigned there, I discussed
the vexing problem of German guilt for Nazi crimes with German prisoners, including Field Marshal Erwin Rommel's chaplain and a pastor
from the Saar whose wife and five children had been killed by an American bomb.

I also talked with the controversial Pastor Martin Niemoeller, who
early on had supported Hitler but later spent seven years in Dachau for
his opposition to the Fuehrer. Subsequently, I visited the Dachau concentration camp, which had been liberated by American troops. Over the
main gate were the words *Arbeit Macht Frei* (Work Liberates), fittingly Or-
wellian words for a place where more than 30,000 persons had died. Inside, a sign near an oven for burning bodies read: "Cleanliness is your
duty. Please wash your hands"—an exquisite manifestation of the irony
of virtue.

At Bergen-Belsen, where Anne Frank was among the 50,000 Jews,
Christians, and others who had perished, I saw scattered rib bones in the
red clay. Dachau, Bergen-Belsen, and other concentration camps in Germany, together with the extermination centers in Poland, brought cruel
death to some 12 million civilians, including up to 6 million Jews. Why
had not the good Germans prevented these crimes against humanity?

Could not my government, the Vatican, or the American churches have done something?

Shortly after arriving in London, I visited Kingsley Hall, a social settlement house run by Muriel Lester. Gandhi had once stayed there, and she proudly showed me where Gandhi had kept his goats so he could drink their milk as he meditated. Although my icons were still pacifist saints, I was more bemused than inspired by Gandhi's odd habits and his naïveté about Adolf Hitler. (In 1941, Gandhi had written a "Dear Friend" letter to the Fuehrer imploring him to respect all people regardless of "race, color, or creed.") And seeing Muriel Lester close up bred further misgivings. Like other fashionable pacifists, she had survived the war with her faith in man's essential goodness and her own self-assurance fully intact.

In March 1946, I attended an FOR conference in Stockholm. The delegates from seven countries that had been occupied by the Nazis gave the conference a down-to-earth quality absent in American pacifist meetings. Several participants had suffered in concentration camps; others had been tortured by the Gestapo—harsh realities that further encouraged me to reexamine my facile assumptions about war and peace.

On my way back to London, I stopped in Oslo to see a Norwegian resistance leader who had been jailed by the Nazis. He took me to the secret place where Vidkun Quisling had been executed and to a coastal fortress holding SS and Gestapo prisoners and Norwegian collaborators. With fire in his eyes, the German camp leader repeated the warning I had heard from Andrew Cordier the year before—"There will soon be another war, and it will be between Russia and America."

*   *   *

In mid-November 1946, I arrived in Frankfurt from Paris on an American troop train for two years of YMCA service in occupied Germany. Frankfurt, the once-proud commercial center, had been reduced to rubble, except for the huge I. G. Farben office complex, deliberately spared to serve as the U.S. Army headquarters. Old women in rags pulled handmade wagons. People scrounged for food in garbage cans outside American messes. Communist and socialist posters were plastered on bombed buildings. One Christian Democrat placard read: "7,000,000 German POWs want to come home to a better Germany!" Later, I visited scores of pulverized cities—including Berlin, Hamburg, Cologne, and Dresden—and the industrial Ruhr region, a mass of rubble and twisted steel.

There was no escape from the grim reality of a great country brought to its knees by a demonic secular messiah. Yet I had come not to judge the German people but to help them. But now, as the Nazi nightmare was receding into history, a new terror was stalking Central Europe. I had seen it in the hollow eyes of refugees and POWs from the East. To better comprehend the Communist empire, I was determined to travel behind the Iron Curtain to see for myself. Thus, in June 1948, a Quaker colleague and I drove in his Volkswagen Beetle through the Soviet Zone of Austria to Hungary and Czechoslovakia—just as Stalin was tightening his grip on both countries liberated from the Nazis three years before.

Most Hungarians hated the new order, but in Budapest, we did meet one true believer. Andrew Polgar was a bright, wiry, intense student who had fought the Germans with a British unit in Italy. Like other secular Jews, he had found in Communism a surrogate religion. He called himself a humanist, idealist, and Marxist. We talked long into the night.

"How can you reconcile your ideals with Stalin's show trials and executions?" I asked.

Andrew's words, though predictable, rang with conviction. "The world struggle is *not* between the East and the West but between the rich and the poor. When you decide which side you're on, everything else falls into place. You must choose between reaction and revolution. A bloody revolution is better than a nonviolent one. The recent Labour party victory in Britain was peaceful, so it will fail before its gains can be consolidated. The people must be pushed to the point of no return by all necessary means. Human sacrifices today will yield a classless society tomorrow."

This young Leninist personified the interim ethic of the "logical revolutionary" in Arthur Koestler's *Darkness at Noon*:

> He reads Machiavelli, Ignatius of Loyola, Marx, and Hegel; he is cold and unmerciful to mankind, out of a kind of mathematical mercifulness. He is damned . . . to become a slaughterer in order to abolish slaughtering, to sacrifice lambs so that no more lambs may be slaughtered . . . and to challenge the hatred of mankind because of his love for it—an abstract and geometric love.

Andrew's idealism was as dazzling as his faith in a false god was frightening.

Another Hungarian I met was no less impressive, but his faith was in God and the church. The Communist regime had just nationalized some 4,000 religious schools, over half of them Catholic. A few days later, on Sunday, June 20, 1948, I had a private conversation with the head of Hungary's Catholics, Joseph Cardinal Mindszenty, in the royal palace at Esztergom.

"The parents' right of school choice has been taken away," the cardinal told me with deep sadness, insisting that he was "fighting not only for narrow church rights but for broad human rights." Clearly, this proud and courageous man, who had been jailed by the Nazis for five months, was on a collision course with the Soviet-installed regime. After my visit, I wrote that he would be arrested, given a show trial, and found guilty of treason. Tragically, by year's end, my prediction came true. He was imprisoned for life, but during the 1956 uprising against the regime, he found refuge in the American legation in Budapest.

My Quaker friend and I arrived in Prague in late June, four months after Moscow had established a puppet regime in Czechoslovakia. A local quip said it all: "When it rains in Moscow, Prague puts up an umbrella." Our host was Jan Kucera, a Reformed Church pastor who had opposed the Nazis and whose house was under constant and visible KGB surveillance. He showed us the window from which the distraught Czech foreign minister Jan Masaryk had jumped—or, as most believed, had been pushed. The atmosphere in the city was tense.

Pastor Kucera was troubled by Dean Josef Hromadka of Jan Hus Theological Faculty in Prague, who, in the name of social progress, had helped the Communists to consolidate Soviet control by purging "unreliable" faculty members from Charles University. I wrote Frank Wallack, a Brethren relief worker in China, that "Soviet Communism, with all its brutality, is already sowing the seeds of its own destruction."

In August 1948 in Amsterdam, I heard Hromadka tell the founding assembly of the World Council of Churches that the West had little to offer in moral leadership. Though Communism "imperiled the sacredness of human beings and the majesty of justice and love," Hromadka said, it nevertheless represented "in atheistic form, much of the social impetus of the living church." That an apologist for the most insidious secular religion of our time was given a major platform at this historic ecumenical event demonstrated the success of Communism in hijacking Christian ideals of justice and liberation. This was years before the term *liberation theology* was coined.

A decade later, Hromadka helped establish the Christian Peace Conference in Prague, an affiliate of the Soviet-backed World Peace Council. Like Niemoeller, he received the Lenin Peace Prize. It was only after he was shocked into reality by Moscow's crushing of Prague in the spring of 1968 that Hromadka saw Communism for what it was and recanted.

(As early as 1948, I wrote about the suppression of religion in the Soviet Union and portrayed Stalin as the high priest of a messianic secular faith, but it was not until 1960 that I finally visited the heart of the Soviet empire. In August of that year, I was one of perhaps three Americans [excluding the Powers family] who attended the Moscow trial of U-2 pilot Gary Powers. The Sino-Soviet split had just erupted, and Khrushchev was tightening the vice on Berlin. In 1986, I again traveled in the Soviet Union, visiting Moscow, Leningrad, and the grotesque Stalin Museum in Georgia. And in October 1991, I went to Prague, Budapest, Warsaw, Kiev, the Baltic states, and Moscow to witness and celebrate the death throes of the "evil empire.")

*   *   *

In early 1947, Erich Hofmann, a former German paratrooper whom I had met in a POW camp in England, joined me as a colleague on the World's YMCA staff in the British Zone of Germany. Because of his clear anti-Nazi record—among other things, he had kept an American flag and pictures of FDR and Churchill in his room at boarding school—he was one of the first POWs to be repatriated. We shared an intense interest in politics and a lesser interest in stamp collecting and limericks. In endless conversations, Erich enriched my knowledge of recent German history and popular culture. I arranged for him and four other German students to study at Brethren colleges in the States. In due course, he became an American citizen and served as the Peace Corps director in Ecuador.

In 1948, during my last six months in Europe, I was a stringer for the liberal *Christian Century* magazine in Chicago and the Religious News Service in New York. Working out of Erich's parental home in Hamburg, I watched the large, four-engine Sunderland amphibious planes take off from the Elbe River on their way to Berlin, part of the massive airlift launched by President Truman to rescue the city from Stalin's blockade. My understanding of postwar Europe was also deepened by traveling from Helsinki to Rome and from Paris to Berlin. Everywhere, the harsh reminders of the war, occupation, and betrayal were slowly surrendering to signs of hope.

*   *   *

Quietly but more quickly than I had realized, my worldview had been shifting under the impact of what I had seen and felt since arriving in London only three years before. Within the first year, I wrote Richard Niebuhr—my Yale professor who had gently challenged my pacifist faith—to say I had finally found his view of Christian ethics wholly relevant to what I had experienced—from my conversations with survivors of Bergen-Belsen and German clergymen who never gave the Hitler salute to my visits with Dutch children who were in detention camps because their parents had been Nazi collaborators.

In Europe, I had lost my innocence but not my hope. No longer a pacifist, I began to understand the irony of virtue—that virtue, uninformed by facts or tempered by an unsentimental understanding of human nature, could lead to disaster. At long last, I was prepared to accept the biblical realism of the Niebuhr brothers, including the Christian just war doctrine. Specifically, I was now convinced that a nation confronted by tyranny, conquest, or genocide had a moral obligation to fight back, by arms if necessary.

*   *   *

When I returned to New Haven in the fall of 1948 to pursue my Ph.D. studies in Christian ethics, the Cold War was advancing on all fronts. America had changed, and I had changed. I read George Orwell and Arthur Koestler, devoured the *New York Times*, and consulted documents such as the House Foreign Affairs Committee report *The Strategy and Tactics of World Communism* (1948), a primerlike but essentially accurate picture of Moscow's machinations abroad. I denounced Marxist dogma and Soviet tyranny in numerous conversations, letters, and articles, and I applauded the Marshall Plan, NATO, and Truman's other bold efforts to contain the Soviet Union, rebuild Europe and Japan, and stabilize the Third World.

During these three years at Yale Graduate School, my religious upbringing, my European experience, and my recently earned Niebuhrian realism blended into a working philosophy that has served me ever since. I regarded my new worldview as a fulfillment rather than a betrayal of my parental heritage. But many of my old pacifist colleagues saw me as an unprincipled turncoat and treated me with scorn and even anger. Later, I was castigated by both secular and religious liberals for my Cold War views, and I also felt the lash of the anti-anti-Communists. To make matters worse in their eyes, by the early 1950s I had serious reservations about labor union tactics and spoke up for limited government and a vigorous market economy. Unknowingly, I had become a neoconservative twenty years before the felicitous term was coined.

My concern for equal opportunity for blacks and other minorities continued, but now my major focus was the larger world struggle against totalitarianism and lesser tyrannies. Totalitarian regimes, which demanded total orthodoxy in all realms, I argued, were more reprehensible than authoritarian regimes, which permitted limited rights. And sometimes, the United States has to choose between the lesser of two evils. Vocationally, I moved from direct social service and action to the intellectual battle between opposing political forces and ideas. (Decades later, when the civil rights movement veered away from its laudable goal of equal justice under law and insisted on racial quotas and other preferences, I became deeply saddened, and I worried about the future of *e pluribus unum*.)

My new realism was reinforced by a one-to-one reading course with Richard Niebuhr that plunged me into the works of Reinhold that I had found unpersuasive during my seminary days. Now, I was prepared to accept the wisdom embodied in his *An Interpretation of Christian Ethics* (1935), which emphasized the limits and possibilities of human nature and history. Never cynical, both Niebuhrs saw man as a morally ambiguous creature endowed with both original sin and original righteousness.

As a social ethics major, I had sampled the thought of Aristotle, Augustine, Aquinas, Luther, Calvin, Machiavelli, Burke, Marx, America's founders, and Tocqueville. Among more recent works, I was intrigued by Carl Becker's *How New Will the Better World Be?* (1944), Hans J. Morgenthau's *Scientific Man vs. Power Politics* (1946), and E. H. Carr's *The Twenty Years' Crisis: 1919–1939* (1946).

In May 1949, I joined the newly formed Americans for Democratic Action, whose members included Reinhold Niebuhr, Eleanor Roosevelt, and Hubert Humphrey. In those days, most American liberals were stoutly anti-Communist. The ADA was the first postwar political organization explicitly opposed to totalitarianism of the Left *and* the Right. Concurrently, I helped organize the New York–based Christian Action, a small association of Protestant academics that I dubbed "the ADA plus God." Christian Action faded in a few years, but the ADA lived on.

While in New Haven, my understanding of America's responsibility as the "leader of the free world"—I found no fault with the designation—was deepened during two eight-week trips around the still war-shattered world in the summers of 1949 and 1950. These globe-girdling adventures, which I organized and led for Youth Argosy (an educational outfit), also served as my baptism into Third World realities. Our chartered sixty-seat DC-4 Skymaster, a piston-pounding plane that could reach 200 miles per hour with a favorable tailwind—passenger jets were unknown then—became our flying classroom. We visited Honolulu, Wake Island, Japan, Hong Kong, Thailand, India, Pakistan, Iran, Egypt (King Farouk was still on the throne), Cyprus, Israel, Turkey, Greece, and Rome.

With the help of local YMCA officials, I arranged an intense program in each capital city, including conversations with religious and political leaders such as the Anglican bishop of Hong Kong, Prime Minister Shigeru Yoshida of Japan, Prime Minister Jawaharlal Nehru of India, and the Shah of Iran. In 1949 in Israel, a year after that nation's birth, I persuaded the mayor of Jewish West Jerusalem to permit us to cross the UN truce line into East Jerusalem in Jordan to visit the Christian and Muslim holy places.

*   *   *

While in graduate school, I was married to Margaret Louise Briggs, whom I had met a year before at a student Christian conference at Natural Bridge, Virginia. The June 1951 wedding in Newton, Iowa, was performed by her father, a Methodist pastor. For a year and a half, Margaret had done social work with the Methodist mission in Algeria. After our wedding, we spent four weeks in Mexico. I insisted on visiting the villa near Mexico City where, in 1940, Stalinist agent Ramon Mercader had plunged an Alpine pickax into Leon Trotsky's skull. We were shown the couch where the evil deed was done.

(This strange side trip, on a honeymoon no less, reflected my odd inner drive to see shrines to inhumanity and to heroism, to rivet events with three-dimensional images. Over the years, I have visited such places as Pearl Harbor, the bombed shell of Coventry Cathedral, the bunker where Hitler shot himself, and his chancellery office before the red marble wall slabs had been ripped out to build the massive Soviet victory monument in East Berlin. After the Berlin Wall fell, I paid my respects at the memorial to the July 20, 1944, plotters who attempted to kill Hitler, and I visited Babi Yar near Kiev, where 33,000 Ukrainian Jews were murdered. Other sites included Paris street memorials to anti-Nazi resistance leaders who had been shot; a fortified strategic hamlet in South Vietnam; Corregidor, where 11,500 trapped Americans surrendered to the Japanese; and the North Korean invasion tunnels under the demilitarized zone dug by the late Kim Il-sung.)

My Yale dissertation, *Protestants and United States Foreign Policy: 1925–1954*, compared Reinhold Niebuhr with liberal Protestant leaders whose views were rooted in a rational idealism that tended to regard military power as morally obsolete and state sovereignty as politically obsolescent. This nonpolitical stance also characterized liberal Catholic and Jewish thought.

* * *

After completing my doctoral studies, I joined the staff of the National Council of Churches in New York as associate director of its international affairs department. There, my efforts to relate biblical realism to U.S. policy ran headlong into the liberal-idealist assumptions of colleagues still informed by the old Social Gospel movement.

In New York, I associated with Catholic and Jewish leaders who generally shared my worldview. Among them was Father Robert Hartnett, S.J., editor of *America*, who welcomed my criticism of Protestant anti-Catholicism. He, like Jacques Maritain and John Courtney Murray, had succeeded in reconciling classical Catholic social thought with the American democratic experience.

I was especially intrigued by Will Herberg, a former Marxist intellectual and atheist who had come to the Kingdom of God under the tutelage of Reinhold Niebuhr and, in 1955, wrote his seminal *Protestant-Catholic-Jew: An Essay in American Religious Sociology*.

Though it was hardly popular in ecumenical circles, I argued that today's mainline Protestants had become largely irrelevant to the major crises in Western culture and lagged behind the best secular achievements in politics and the arts. "Our greatest sin," I argued, "is not disunity, but irrelevance."

* * *

In September 1955, after three lively years in New York City, Margaret, our first son, David, and I moved to Washington, D.C. Two years later, our second son, Bryce, was born. The move was prompted by an invitation from Paul Nitze to join him at the Johns Hopkins School of Advanced International Studies and made possible by a special Rockefeller Foundation grant arranged by Nitze and Dean Rusk, then the foundation president. My intended one-year stay in Washington has stretched to forty years and counting.

During these four decades in the capital of the free world, I have been active in efforts to relate the Judeo-Christian ethic to American power—as a teacher, writer, and sometime activist. I did foreign affairs research at the Library of Congress, and in 1960–1961, I was Senator Hubert Humphrey's foreign policy staffer when he was running against John Kennedy for the presidential nomination. Later, I did research at the School of Advanced International Studies, the Institute for Defense Analyses, and, for thirteen years, at the Brookings Institution. I taught part-time at American, Georgetown, and Maryland Universities. My studies on nuclear arms, U.S. military assistance, and UN peacekeeping took me to some sixty-five countries, which added vitality and texture to my academic pursuits.

Until the early 1960s, I thought of myself as a liberal—to be sure, a Cold War liberal. At that time, most Democratic and Republican politicians supported a strong military posture against the Soviet Union. But while at Brookings, I became increasingly critical of the liberal agenda. In the late 1950s, I had been a member of the ADA's foreign affairs study group, along with Benjamin V. Cohen (a former member of FDR's brain trust), James H. Rowe, and the very liberal Joseph L. Rauh. But I soon became disenchanted with the ADA's naive confidence in arms control treaties, the UN, and foreign economic aid, and I resigned. On the domestic front, I faulted forced school busing and the tendency to emphasize the rights of criminals over those of victims.

In the early 1960s, I occasionally discussed ethics and politics with Eugene McCarthy, George McGovern, and Stewart Udall, but I parted company with them when they started to mimic elements of the counterculture. I found timely ammunition in *National Review* for my battle against the new barbarians—the uncouth precursors of political correctness. And I drew solace and wisdom from writers such as Daniel Boorstin, Herbert Stein, George Will, and later Charles Krauthammer.

In August 1968, I was unexpectedly asked to draft the foreign and defense policy planks for the Democratic Party's convention in Chicago, arguably the most turbulent in American history. Radical student demonstrators, demanding immediate U.S. withdrawal from Vietnam, descended on the city like locusts, determined to shut down the convention. My draft, including the highly controversial Vietnam Plank, was written two weeks before the delegates assembled. The plank was blessed by Lyndon Johnson, who declined to run for another term, and was reluctantly endorsed by Hubert Humphrey, who became the presidential candidate. George McGovern and Eugene McCarthy, who also ran, opposed the plank and persuaded Ted Sorenson to draft a more dovish minority version, which was defeated 60 to 40 percent by the delegates. Thus, for a brief but unrecognized moment in Chicago, the vexing Vietnam issue was joined between two groups of Americans who desperately wanted peace but differed on how to achieve it. One group emphasized firmness toward Communist North Vietnam, the other compromise. Perhaps with imaginative leadership, the convention could have been a time of healing, but emotions were too taut and the country too split for such a miracle to occur.

*   *   *

Later, I was involved in two David and Goliath encounters. In April 1973, virtually single-handedly, I persuaded the American Film Institute to cancel a scheduled showing of a virulently anti-American film in the Kennedy Center for the Performing Arts. *State of Siege*, directed by the European leftist Costa-Gavras and produced in Chile with Marxist President Salvador Allende's blessing, was a dishonest and cynical attack on U.S. public safety aid to Uruguay, where Tupamaro terrorists had tortured and murdered an American adviser. Having just been to Uruguay researching the public safety program for Brookings, I provided institute director George Stevens, Jr., with the key facts, and he promptly canceled the showing to angry cries of "censorship" from the radical chic arts community.

The second and less successful encounter addressed bias in the elite media. In 1974, the Institute for American Strategy published my study *TV and National Defense: An Analysis of CBS News, 1972–1973*. This comprehensive content analysis of Walter Cronkite's evening news show revealed a statistical slant that strongly favored dovish critics of U.S. defense policy. The study drew considerable press attention and a protracted rebuttal from CBS News, and it endeared me to traditional conservatives with whom, until then, I had had little contact.

Increasingly concerned by Moscow's growing military might, I joined Paul Nitze's Committee on the Present Danger in 1976 and later Midge Decter's Committee for the Free World.

*   *   *

During George McGovern's campaign for the presidential nomination in 1972, Jeane Kirkpatrick invited me to join the hawkish Committee for a Democratic Majority. I immediately declined: "There is not enough health in the Democratic Party." That's interesting, she said, Irving Kristol also declined with a similar comment. I voted for Richard Nixon and every Republican presidential candidate since, but like Jeane, I didn't formally resign from the Democratic Party until 1981, after we both had been nominated for foreign policy posts by Ronald Reagan.

With almost no debate, Jeane was quickly confirmed as U.S. ambassador to the United Nations. But despite the near identity of our views, especially toward the Soviet Union, my nomination as assistant secretary of state for human rights drew a sustained and tightly organized attack from the liberal Left, which was only then recovering from its initial shock over Reagan's landslide victory.

The *Washington Post* led the attack in a February 5, 1981, "news" story, calling me one of the "harshest and most persistent critics of the human rights ideas" of President Carter. The next day, a *New York Times* editorial called my nomination "altogether alarming" and described me as an "ultraconservative who sneers at existing policy as sentimental nonsense and believes it is profound error to embarrass allies, however repressive."

Overseas, I was hit by *Tass, Izvestia,* and the *Voice of Cuba. Tass* got it half right by dubbing me a "rabid reactionary and Soviet-hater." Syndicated cartoonist Pat Oliphant portrayed me simply as a skull and crossbones. Jack Anderson implied that I was a racist, and Mary McGrory called me "a human rights wrecking ball and a proven red-baiter."

Behind the assault was a group of liberal-Left lobbyists who claimed the support of fifty members of the Coalition for a New Foreign and Military Policy, including the American Friends Service Committee, National Council of Churches, Americans for Democratic Action, and other groups insisting that the Cold War was caused more by American paranoia than by Soviet behavior. The *Christian Century, Christianity and Crisis,* and the *National Catholic Reporter* joined the feeding frenzy. NCC president William Howard called me "an outspoken opponent of both public and private" human rights efforts. A pro-Castro group charged that I repeatedly visited Guatemala under the aegis of a group linked to death squads! In fact, my one brief field trip to that country was under the aegis of the Brookings Institution.

Clare Boothe Luce called the attack a campaign of "calculated falsehoods, errors, and innuendo that would make some KGB disinformation scribblers look like pikers." After a negative vote by the Senate Foreign Relations Committee, I phoned President Reagan at Camp David and withdrew my name from consideration. He expressed his dismay with Republican committee chairman Charles H. Percy, who had sided with my critics from the outset.

To this day, I am still astounded by how my entire life, particularly my human rights record, could have been so distorted, but I recognize that the fury of the attackers was really aimed at Reagan. I was both a symbol and a scapegoat. Rowland Evans and Robert Novak wrote that no other presidential appointee "symbolized the Reagan Revolution so purely" because I "passionately believed in the ideas of American democracy and passionately hated Communism."

In the Left's determination to recoup its losses and strengthen its grip on the culture, I became a small-time pawn in a growing ideological war over what America stood for. In a real sense, the assault against me in 1981 foreshadowed the ideological campaigns against Robert Bork and Clarence Thomas for the Supreme Court. The post I was nominated for was trivial compared to that of a Supreme Court justice, who could influence American society for decades. Yet each of us was subjected to a barrage of false charges that distracted attention from the real issues in the raging cultural war.

*   *   *

During my early years in Washington, I ran a series of private consultations on ethics and foreign policy issues at the Cosmos Club for policymakers, theologians, and academics. Regular participants included Paul Nitze, Arnold Wolfers, Robert Osgood, Charles Burton Marshall, and Paul Ramsey. Dean Rusk, Senator Humphrey, and other political figures occasionally took part. These and similar extracurricular efforts eventually led to my major visible achievement—founding the Washington-based Ethics and Public Policy Center in 1976.

From the outset, the center's purpose was to "clarify and reinforce the bond between the Judeo-Christian moral tradition and domestic and foreign policy issues." To this end, I invited to its advisory board Paul Ramsey, Irving Kristol, Michael Novak, Carl F.H. Henry, Seymour Seigal, Richard John Neuhaus, George Will, and others. In all modesty, the center has become a respected place for serious reflection and writing. And predictably, it has honored for their courage and integrity such champions of freedom as Vladimir Bukovsky, Lech Walesa, and Edward Teller.

When I, a Protestant, retired as president in 1989, I was succeeded by George Weigel, a Catholic lay theologian, and in 1996, he was followed by Elliott Abrams, a Jewish scholar-attorney—symbolizing the center's interfaith approach to culture and politics. All three of us could be called Niebuhrian realists, a perspective that I trust will continue to inform the center as it grapples with timeless truths and timely issues.

*   *   *

In sum, my spiritual and political pilgrimage has had three phases—from a pietist pacifism to an active liberal political pacifist stance and then on to a humane realist understanding of political accountability. To put it another way, I moved from a rational idealist to a historical realist position or from liberalism to neoconservatism. In some ways, my development parallels Reinhold Niebuhr's in the 1930s and Irving Kristol's in the 1950s. Both of these influential giants, however, had one burden I was spared—they had to shake off their early socialist assumptions and the lingering and sometimes esoteric Marxist lingo that has afflicted so many New York intellectuals.

*   *   *

The forty essays in this volume were selected from more than five hundred published over the past half century in a score of periodicals. They were gleaned from *Foreign Affairs, The National Interest, National Review,* the *New York Times,* the *Wall Street Journal,* the *American Spectator, USA Today, TV Guide,* and several academic and religious journals. Two are excerpts from out-of-print books. The pieces have been edited for stylistic uniformity. Most have been shortened and occasionally paraphrased to eliminate redundancy and transient references. To spare the reader annoying intrusions, I have omitted footnotes (which scholars may check in the original articles) and used ellipses only in quotations from other sources.

Lacking the discipline to write fewer and better articles for consequential journals, I squandered my energy on a range of topics—the Soviet threat, nuclear arms, the KGB, the CIA, human rights, UN peacekeeping, tribalism, and the wayward press—and in widely scattered places. Well over half the selections rebut what I consider ill-advised foreign policy advice from persons professing to speak in the name of virtue. They express my views at the time, but rereading them in 1997, I am surprised by their consistency since the late 1940s, when my utopianism finally surrendered to reality.

Virtually all selections reflect both my political science training and my theological views, though usually the latter are assumed rather than made explicit. Many also have a reporter's sense of time and place. And throughout, they reveal the irony of virtue expressed in secular and religious utopian thought. In the face of prophesies that we are living in the last days of Rome, the book concludes with a moderately hopeful assessment of America's capacity to shoulder its unsought imperial burden well into the twenty-first century.

PART ONE

Utopian Beginnings

Reared in a Protestant pacifist home and proud of my dissenting Huguenot heritage, I became an active religious objector to war and remained so through college and Yale Divinity School—and World War II. Six months before Pearl Harbor, I expressed my views on the European war in a letter to my hometown paper in York, Pennsylvania:

> *While we are waiting for Churchill and Roosevelt to get their heads together with Comrade Stalin, and before we enter the "shooting war," the President might well recall Churchill's scathing condemnation of America's participation in World War I. After the real issues of World War II are unearthed, will it again be said that U.S. participation was responsible for the loss of millions of human beings and another vindictive peace pregnant with the seeds of World War III?*

I was appalled by the brutal and messianic regimes in Nazi Germany and Communist Russia. Having read portions of Mein Kampf *in 1938, I saw Hitler as a demonic figure, a conviction deepened by my friendship with Oliver Foss, a Jewish refugee student. I opposed the Nazis, the Soviet Union, and U.S. participation in the war, but I was not an isolationist. I was a utopian internationalist, convinced that America had a responsibility to work for peace and freedom in the world.*

As a theological student, I was exempted from the military draft. Though opposed to U.S. military involvement, I did not actively urge young men to become conscientious objectors, much less draft-dodgers. I respected conscientious participants. Wrapped in my utopian cocoon, I was virtually immune to the moral issues in the world conflict and managed to survive a popular and, in retrospect, a just war without conscious feelings of guilt.

Since I could do little about the war or the Axis barbarians, I spent my energy tackling domestic problems, mainly discrimination against blacks and the internment of Japanese-Americans.

I was a civil rights activist twelve years before Martin Luther King, Jr., joined the movement. And I sat in the back of the bus twelve years before Rosa Parks sat in the front of the bus and for the same reason—to challenge the racist Jim Crow laws in the South. In Chicago, I took part in one of the first sit-ins to desegregate a restaurant.

As a Church of the Brethren minister, I also participated in volunteer summer work camps, from the slums of Philadelphia to the hop fields of Yakima, Washington.

Spared the dangers faced by my male peers who were conscripted to serve their country, I volunteered to give equal time in postwar reconstruction. For three years, from 1945 to 1948, I worked among German prisoners of war in Britain and West Germany for the World's YMCA. Before leaving for Europe, my verse appeared in the journal Progressive Education:

> We are the war children, born in a world of fear.
> We are small and frail, but upon our slender backs
> Must rest the burdens of tomorrow's world.
> Permit the children to come unto me; we ask no more.
> We are the war children.

In Europe, my lingering utopianism gave way to a more realistic ethic. When I visited a London session of the UN General Assembly in early 1946, I had not yet fully appreciated the realities of world politics and the irony of virtue.

The selections in Part One clearly reveal my utopian views and demonstrate that at that time, I was more activist than academic, more reportorial than reflective.

1 One God, One World, One Blood

While in seminary, I worked for racial justice by writing, lecturing, and direct action. I joined the new Committee on Racial Equality, whose best-known leader, Bayard Rustin, years later organized the March on Washington where Martin Luther King made his historic "I Have a Dream" speech. My "credo of racial brotherhood"—using the editorial we—was published in a church youth paper in July 1944. It declared that "all racial quotas should be abolished and the term race *should be removed from application forms." In those days, quotas were used* to restrict *minorities! My call for a "National Fair Practices Act" anticipated the civil rights legislation of the 1960s.*

*   *   *

In the face of rising racial tension in the world today, we cannot remain silent about our faith in the unity proclaimed by Saint Paul before a crowd of cynical and self-righteous Athenians over nineteen hundred years ago. His conviction that all men were made of *one blood* to live together in *one world* under the sovereignty of *one God* pronounces a devastating judgment upon us.

We cannot close our eyes to the plight of India, where thousands of freedom-seeking patriots have been imprisoned without trial by a foreign white power engaged in an alleged fight for democracy. Of more immediate concern is our own nation, where after more than three hundred years of white domination, our Negro countrymen are still forced into a status of second-class citizenship. We cannot lightly dismiss the fact that congressmen elected by a very small percentage of the population of certain poll tax states hold key positions in our legislative halls. The forcible uprooting of more than 100,000 persons of Japanese ancestry, most of whom are American citizens, from the West Coast, without trial or investigation, is a dangerous precedent. These are but symptoms of our pattern of discrimination and segregation that is deeply embedded in every area of our society, in both the North and South. In the presence of increasing racial conflict, we reaffirm our faith in the unity of all mankind.

Of One Blood

Affirming that all men were made of one blood to live together as one family, we declare these principles:

1. Although there are superficial differences among races, such as color of skin or shape of head, we believe that all races are equal in intelligence and in the capacity for moral development. This is not only a tenet of our Christian faith and an established fact of science, but also a basic assumption of democracy.
2. We believe that equality of opportunity should be extended to all persons, in every area of American life; this cannot happen as long as we maintain our present pattern of segregating racial groups. Political and economic equality cannot be realized without the practice of social equality.
3. Fully recognizing the value of political, educational, and economic means for eliminating racial tension, we also affirm our faith in the principle and efficacy of nonviolent direct action as a method for achieving racial justice and for establishing brotherhood. Although this method has not yet been widely used in the United States, we believe that it has tremendous possibilities for more extensive application now and in the immediate future.
4. We recognize that racial discrimination is but one expression of the larger social problem, and that its complete solution depends upon the fundamental reorganization of our social and economic life. Although we seek "to make all things new," we hold that any contribution to the solution of racial difficulties will be a contribution to the solution of the total problem.
5. We believe that no person is truly free as long as any minority is suppressed, and that liberation from the bonds of racial prejudice will mean freedom for the privileged as well as for the oppressed.
6. Recognizing the urgency of present developments in the interracial scene, we believe that immediate and decisive action is imperative. We must take such action not only to prevent race riots which are increasingly imminent, but we must also work unceasingly to accelerate those processes which by peaceful means are breaking down the old barriers of discrimination and segregation.

In One World

In harmony with the above affirmations we must address the task of abolishing racial discrimination from every area of American life, and we must seek to make the same principles operative in the international sphere. Specifically:

1. We urge the support of all existing legislation that guarantees racial equality.
2. We advocate the abolition of the poll tax, which disenfranchises millions of Negro and white citizens and is responsible for placing our most reactionary congressmen in positions of influence.
3. Segregation in all branches of the armed forces and in all departments of government, local, state, and national, must be abolished.
4. Industrial democracy demands a permanent Federal Fair Employment Practices Act with funds to carry out effective enforcement.
5. We urge the adoption of a national Fair Racial Practices Act which will make all discrimination illegal, in public places and conveyances, in housing, in community activities, and in churches.
6. We advocate the abolition of all forms of discrimination in our colleges and other educational institutions. All racial quotas should be abolished and the term *race* should be removed from application forms.
7. We urge the immediate repeal of the remaining Oriental Exclusion legislation, and the prompt release of Japanese-American internees into communities of their own choosing.
8. We believe that all colonial peoples should be granted the right of self-determination at the earliest possible moment, and should be assured of equitable representation at the peace table. We are especially concerned about the welfare of India, Puerto Rico, and the African colonies.

Under One God

As Christians who believe in the unity of mankind under one God, we cannot escape the tremendous personal responsibility that falls upon each one of us in this hour. Reconciling man to God and man to his fellows is not a task for our leisure moments, but one that demands our allegiance in every relationship of daily living. In recognizing this:

1. We commit ourselves to the implementation of the above principles in our own lives, in our churches, in our communities, and in our nation. This will require a thoroughgoing educational program undergirded by appropriate action.

2. We call upon all persons of goodwill to join hands with us in this task. We are deeply encouraged by much that is being done. The unflinching dedication of Lillian Smith, editor of *The South Today*, has moved the nation. We are heartened by the gains of the National Association for the Advancement of Colored People, and view with anticipation the dynamic March on Washington Movement under the able leadership of A. Philip Randolph.

3. Finally, we commit ourselves to the difficult and painful task of rooting out of our own lives any vestiges of race prejudice or superiority that remain. This requires genuine fellowship with persons of all racial groups in our homes, schools, churches, and social activities. In thus identifying ourselves with all groups we will seek to become sensitive to their problems. We will patronize only those places where brotherhood can exist, and attempt to change those that discriminate. Recognizing that the practice of brotherhood in a world like ours will bring suffering, we will attempt to take that suffering upon ourselves rather than inflict it upon others. This will require courage and fearlessness of a high order. We commit ourselves to those spiritual disciplines that will prepare us effectively for the ministry of reconciliation. We will place our trust in God, who "hath not given us a spirit of fearlessness but of power and love and discipline."

2 Sit-In at a Chicago Restaurant

The 1963 protest at a Greensboro, North Carolina, lunch counter is usually considered to be the first sit-in to desegregate eating places, but several such demonstrations occurred twenty years earlier, during World War II. My letter to the New York Times *(November 14, 1993) recalled a 1943 interracial sit-in I participated in. Two of my three references to "Negroes," the usual term for blacks in those days, were changed by the politically correct* Times *editor to "African Americans."*

*   *   *

Permit me to add to "How My Aunt Charlie Pioneered the Sit-In Era" (letter, October 31, 1993) by Barbara T. Wilson. She is right in asserting that her aunt's sit-in occurred a good fifteen years before the one in Greensboro, North Carolina, at the Woolworth lunch counter in 1963, recently celebrated as the first sit-in.

Not to take anything away from her aunt's laudable and pioneering witness against racial segregation, but there was an earlier, and organized, sit-in in Chicago, perhaps one of the very first, in which I participated as a seminary student.

It took place on Saturday, June 5, 1943. Our target was Stoner's Restaurant, the only one in the Loop that refused to serve blacks. I had joined the newly formed Committee on Racial Equality, whose leaders, Bayard Rustin and James Farmer, organized the demonstration.

About forty of us gathered at an African-American church, divided ourselves into six small groups (five all white and one black and white), walked in eight-minute intervals to the restaurant, and entered. We had been instructed to dress appropriately for a "first-class" restaurant and to act with courtesy. Apprehensive and excited, I felt I was on the cutting edge of dramatic change.

For more than an hour, we waited until the mixed group was seated. In flustered desperation, Mr. Stoner, a Methodist layman, called in the police, who promptly left, saying they saw no disturbance. We were all then served, but the blacks only with empty grapefruit shells. None of us ate until all were properly served. Then our group burst into song—a spiritual. Other patrons joined in.

Our 1943 peaceful demonstration—we were civil and broke no law—was regarded as drastic in those pioneering days. It had, moreover, been undertaken only after a year of friendly but fruitless persuasion, including talks with Mr. Stoner and his pastor.

Ten years later, on June 2, 1953, the Supreme Court barred restaurants from refusing to serve African-Americans, and thirteen years later the Rev. Dr. Martin Luther King Jr. joined the civil rights movement in connection with the Rosa Parks bus incident in December 1955.

And twenty years later, in 1960, the Greensboro sit-in took place with the authority of the Supreme Court behind it.

3 Conscience Behind Bars

During World War II, the Selective Service Act provided alternative civilian service for conscientious objectors to military service. I visited many objectors in civilian camps and corresponded with several in prison, including my older brother, who refused civilian service. The essay that follows (from a Methodist student monthly, Motive, *in December 1944) reflects my admiration for pacifists and other dissenters. Gandhi's nonviolent crusade for India's independence inspired me to march in front of the British Consulate in Chicago, carrying a sign that read "Free Gandhi—Free India."*

* * *

> *While there is a lower class, I am in it, while there is a criminal element, I am of it, while there is a soul in prison, I am not free.*
> —*Eugene V. Debs, 1918*

In his autobiography *Toward Freedom*, the often-imprisoned Jawaharlal Nehru makes this statement about an India National Congress meeting in which bold decisions were made: "Every vote that we gave became a message of farewell to ease, comfort, domestic happiness, and the intercourse of friends, and an invitation to lonely days and nights, and physical and mental distress." This heroic farewell to personal freedom applies to America's more than 4,300 conscientious objectors (COs) who have been placed behind the bars of our twenty-three federal prisons between October 1940 and August 1944. Every sixth man in U.S. federal prisons is a CO who violated the Selective Service Act.

In Britain, despite the terror of constant air attacks, there are approximately three times as many COs (including non-combatants) per 10,000 as there are in the United States. Owing to London's more liberal policy, a much smaller percentage has been sent to prison—only 302 as of March 1943. The sentences there are considerably lighter, usually from three months to a year. The absolutist objector who convinces the civilian tribunal of his sincerity is granted complete exemption. Such a policy here would practically empty our prisons of COs.

Already there have been more than nine times as many COs imprisoned in this country as there were in World War I. Of the 450 convicted in the First World War, 17 were sentenced to death, 142 received life terms, the remaining sentences ranged from 99 years to less than one year. No death sentence was carried out, and in November 1920 the last COs were released, two years after the signing of the armistice and fifteen months after the last British objectors were freed.

Why Men Go to Prison

COs are sent to prison for several reasons. Nine percent expressed their inability to cooperate with Selective Service by refusing to register, by failing to return their questionnaires, or by not reporting for their physical examinations. Twenty-eight percent refused their assignment to Civilian Public Service. Three percent walked out of CPS camps because they could no longer accept conscription or because of insufficient work of national importance, denial of civil rights, lack of pay for services rendered, or the failure to provide truly civilian control.

More than 3,000 of the COs are Jehovah's Witnesses. There are also some 150 Moslems who will have nothing to do with this "Christian war." The overwhelming majority of the men are religious objectors in the broadest sense of the term; a tiny minority are classified as "philosophical, political, and rational" objectors. COs from recognized religious groups include: Methodists, 54; Catholics, 46; Friends, 41; Mennonites, 22; Presbyterians, 20; Baptists, 20; Episcopalians, 14; Jews, 14; Brethren, 6.

Life Behind Bars

Most COs have been sent to "moderate custody" correctional institutions. The prison community presents an entirely different world, pregnant with numerous problems as well as with opportunities for education and service. Refusal to work is a grave offense, punishable by being sent to the "hole" (cell stripped of everything but a hole in the floor). COs have encountered difficulty at this point because they have on occasions refused to do war work. The prison attempts to give men work that will not violate their consciences.

There appears to be little visible physical violence in federal prisons, but there is enough mistreatment and brutality to merit investigation and correction. Racial discrimination practiced in most institutions, both North and South, has been constantly challenged by the COs. Charles Walker, a Methodist teacher who walked out of CPS, writes: "None of us takes part in church services because of segregation; likewise in sports for the same reason."

Rigid censorship of personal mail, periodicals, and books is practiced in many prisons. Each inmate is permitted only seven outside correspondents. Incoming and outgoing letters are censored. *Fellowship*, the pacifist journal, is permitted in prisons, but *The Conscientious Objector* is not. The Jehovah's Witnesses *Consolation* cannot enter, but their *Watchtower* can.

In attempting to rid the prison of these and other evils, at least six major non-violent strikes—refusal to eat and refusal to work—have been launched by the COs resulting in definite improvements and awakening the public to the great need for penal reform.

No prisoner can withstand the impact of a prison experience without being changed. It may serve to harden him or to refine his spirit, as in the lives of Saint Paul, George Fox, and Eugene V. Debs. Charles Swift, a pacifist imprisoned in World War I, wrote: "Except in war, there is probably no human institution that inflicts suffering as prison does upon the average inmate. The CO has his faith or convictions to sustain him; most other prisoners have nothing."

Despite the Bureau of Prisons' stated policy of *rehabilitation*, the sources for this article without exception emphasize that released prisoners are less able to make a contribution to society than they were before they were subjected to this "rehabilitating" experience. Don Royer writes: "One of the prison officials respected by the inmates said that for the majority of men, the prison can hope to effect only a *negative rehabilitation*."

Behind prison walls society hides the evidence of its own weaknesses. Today, as in ages past, society imprisons those who fall below its standards and those who rise above.

4 Barbed Wire, Sand, and Tears

Critical of President Roosevelt's February 1942 order to intern 110,000 West Coast Japanese-Americans, I helped several young internees from Manzanar Camp in California to move to Chicago and visited three internment camps, officially called relocation centers.

By September 1944, some 30,000 internees had been resettled in the civilian economy. But it was not until after the war that all Japanese-Americans were released. Forty-three years later, in August 1988, President Ronald Reagan signed a law to "right a grave wrong" by compensating surviving detainees.

The following selection, written at the time but adapted for a piece in the Washington Times (March 3, 1983), recalls my visit to an internment camp in Nebraska in August 1944.

*   *   *

Ulysses said we are part of all we have met, but some encounters become more active parts of our memory than others. An experience I had nearly four decades ago confirmed my lifelong interest in people deprived of their freedom or denied their rights—the 110,000 West Coast Japanese-Americans who were interned in detention centers three months after Pearl Harbor in the name of "national security." Today, most Americans believe the detention was unnecessary and was a violation of their basic rights. This was my view at the time and still is.

In 1942, a friend in California wired me, asking if I could help secure the release of several "residents" of the Manzanar Camp by providing temporary accommodations in Chicago, where I was then a theological student. I said yes, and shortly thereafter two young men arrived and for a few days stayed in the seminary dormitory. To my knowledge, they were the very first to leave any of the detention centers. Subsequently, a hostel for them and others was established near the University of Chicago.

In August 1944, I visited the Amache Relocation Center for Japanese-Americans in Nebraska and wrote an article, "Barbed Wire, Sand, and Tears," about the visit. A slightly edited version follows:

I hitchhiked (my normal mode of transportation during my student days) with a friend from Colorado who wanted to visit her Nisei high school friend at the camp. The driver who took us to our destination asked why we wanted to visit "that Jap camp," adding that "they gave these yellow slant-eyed rats the best land around here. And new tools too; we can't even buy 'em. I wish I had my way with them."

The early afternoon sun beat down relentlessly upon the feathered sand dunes as we trudged up the slope toward the temporary barrack city of more than 6,000 residents. At the main gate, guarded by armed military police, was a large sign: "585 Japanese Americans in Service From Amache." Just a few days before, a memorial service had been held in the camp for six evacuees who had been killed in action in Italy.

The new $285,000 school employed fifty teachers, the white ones received standard salaries, but the evacuee teachers were paid $12 to $19 a month. One teacher said it was difficult to teach "democracy" to innocent victims of racism who were forced to live in desert "concentration camps." She acknowledged, however, that residents were treated well and had the basic material necessities. The Amache Co-op store had more than 2,000 members and did a $40,000-a-month business.

Our hosts, Mr. and Mrs. Tanaguchi Tanda, lived in a 16-by-20 foot barrack room furnished with three canvas cots, a small stove ("Space Heater, U.S. Army, No. 1"), a bench, a box used as a chair, a small cupboard, and a table. Running water and cooking facilities "were not needed," they said, because there was a common dining hall, latrine, and laundry equipment for every twelve barracks.

The Tandas had four sons. Henry was in the Army in Florida, and Tad already had spent four months with U.S. forces in Italy. Jim and Charles were both working in Michigan, the former in a garden nursery and the latter in an aircraft factory. Before the evacuation, the Tandas lived in Salinas, California, where Mr. Tanda was a hard-working farmer. They were moved to Poston, Arizona, on July 4, 1942, and transferred to Amache in May 1943. Mrs. Tanda had come to the United States thirty-seven years before. Their sons were good enough to spill their blood for the United States, but their Japanese-born parents were not able to become citizens because of the Oriental Exclusion Act.

5 The UN Meets in London

In September 1945, a month after Hiroshima, I arrived in London to begin work for the World's YMCA among German POWs in Britain. Then a neo-Wilsonian, I believed that the new United Nations organization could help fulfill the dream of a warless world. In January 1946, I observed the first session of the UN General Assembly, then convening in London. My naive observations were published in the Church of the Brethren's Gospel Messenger, *March 9, 1946.*

*   *   *

Looking down from the "distinguished visitor's gallery" in Church House near Westminster Abbey, I observed the delegates from fifty-one member states gather for the first session of the UN General Assembly. There was Mrs. Franklin Roosevelt chatting with newspapermen. Seated nearby were the representatives from the Soviet Union. Across the central aisle were the Chinese representatives. Toward the back was the delegate from Liberia.

The hall was simply and attractively decorated for the great conference. Behind the platform there was a background of blue and tan sweeping up to the ceiling. In the center hung the UN symbol—a world embraced within an olive-branch wreath. The delegates sat on plain blue-backed chairs behind long natural-finish tables. On the platform there were three chairs: one for the French-speaking president, one for the Secretary General, and a third for the parliamentary adviser.

In the first-floor audience were newspapermen, soldiers from the various battle fronts of the world, and just plain persons, all hoping that the UN would eventually become an effective force for peace.

There was nothing exciting about the business transacted. The British representative's proposal for international control of drugs and narcotics was adopted without dissent, and so it went. The session prompted several observations.

1. Although all nations regardless of size had one vote, the equality was superficial. Behind all decisions were the big three—the United States, Britain, and the USSR. Out of sheer necessity the little nations have, in effect, already surrendered their sovereignty, and the great powers show little willingness to submit to international decisions.
2. Despite the fact that two-thirds of the world's population is nonwhite, approximately ninety percent of the delegates were white.
3. Certain nations were not represented. Sweden and Switzerland as neutrals could not be invited. And who represented the millions in Germany and Japan? Eventually, it is to be hoped all peoples, regardless of race or nationality, will be democratically represented.
4. In addition to the spectators and delegates, there were the unseen guests. The prisoners of war, the displaced persons wandering over Europe, the starving babies, the homeless, the wounded, the little people who always suffer because of war— all these look in desperation to this "town meeting of the world" to prevent the scourge of war. The blood of millions is crying for peace.

But I am not cynical about the UN. I will support its constructive endeavors and will help to correct its weaknesses. It may be the UN against the atomic bomb. The UN is quite imperfect, but with support and improvement it may grow into a true international body. The delegates want peace and we must see to it that they are prepared to pay the price for it. Realistically, this means that their governments must define their interests broadly enough to include the legitimate interests of other states.

After the session adjourned, I went across the street to Westminster Abbey, where lie the bones of kings, poets, and saints who have dreamed of the dawn of peace. I paused by the tomb of Lord Tennyson, who looked forward to the day when there would be a "parliament of man" and a "federation of the world." I bowed my head and breathed a prayer that the UN might become the realization of Tennyson's prophecy.

PART TWO
Toward a Realistic Ethic

My transition from a utopian worldview to what I immodestly called a "humane realist" position was not a road-to-Damascus experience. It took place gradually during my three postwar years in Europe. The grim legacy of World War II was evident in a thousand ways. I arrived in bomb-shattered London on September 27, 1945, three weeks after the Japanese had surrendered. Europe's wartime agonies were compounded by hundreds of thousands of POWs and millions of refugees from the East. In November, the Nuremberg war crimes trials began.

As a voluntary field secretary for the World's YMCA, I provided educational, recreational, and religious supplies to German prisoners of war, first in Britain and then in the British Zone of Germany. I worked closely with religious leaders and British military officers and attended international meetings in London, Stockholm, Geneva, and Amsterdam. I also visited camps for Nazi prisoners in Norway and Germany and the children of Nazi collaborators in Holland.

Determined to understand both political developments and everyday life, I hitchhiked in Britain, Sweden, and Germany and traveled in my trusty Volkswagen Beetle throughout Western Europe and behind the Iron Curtain—in Soviet-occupied Germany, Austria, Czechoslovakia, and Hungary. In Budapest, a conversation with Cardinal Mindszenty in June 1948 convinced me that this eminent religious leader was bound to clash with the Communist regime.

The evil of Nazi Germany and the Soviet Union—embodying the two demonic political religions of our century—was etched in my conscience and made vivid in a slogan I saw in Brussels: Hammer and Sickle = Swastika.

My return to New Haven in September 1948, this time to Yale Graduate School, coincided with the intensifying Cold War. Within the reflective atmosphere of the Sterling Divinity Quadrangle, I refined my new realistic worldview and related the "biblical realism" of Richard Niebuhr and his brother Reinhold to the struggle between the West and the Soviet Union and between Christianity and Communism. Thereafter, I expressed these views as a foreign policy specialist at the National Council of Churches and during my forty years in Washington as a teacher, writer, and founder of the Ethics and Public Policy Center.

6 Moral Consistency and Political Clarity

During my European experience, the unacknowledged contradictions in my utopian stance gradually gave way to a more realistic approach as I groped, largely unconsciously, for political and moral clarity. What I had seen and heard, rather than what I had read, prompted a letter to my Christian Ethics professor, Richard Niebuhr. By June 1946, after only nine months in Europe, I was beginning to see the irony and error of an ethic that gave primacy to the virtue of nonviolence and failed to recognize the wisdom of the classical just war doctrine. I apologize for the pompous prose in the letter.

* * *

When I was a student at Yale Divinity School, there was no professor with whom I disagreed more than with you, but today there is no professor whose teachings are more helpful as I wrestle with the ethical and theological imponderables of the Christian faith.

I have talked with the victims of Belsen and listened to stories from the lips of Jews and Christians whose lives have been wrecked by Gestapo and SS men. I have seen the wanton devastation of great areas in Holland and visited Dutch children in special camps because their parents were collaborators.

I have talked with leaders of the Dutch Reformed Church who fervently defended their church's call for the return of the death penalty for war criminals. I have talked with Germans in more than sixty POW camps in three countries; they ask why they are being kept behind barbed wire one full year after the European war ended.

I have talked with a German clergyman who lived in his country during the reign of terror, never giving the Hitler salute. I have seen Christians hate—even transferring their hatred to the language spoken by the enemy.

All this I have heard, seen, and felt. I know that man is a sinner, capable of cruelty that beggars description. I know that men's evil lives after them, for I have seen the aftermath of war. I have seen the debris of man's insatiable inhumanity. I have seen hell.

But, I have seen more. I have seen men rise above hate, blessing those who have tortured them.

I know that man is a sinner and that I am a man and a sinner. But I believe that God's grace is sufficient to bestow the gift of salvation, the fruits of which will be at least partially realized in this life.

7 Religion and Communism in Hungary

As a stringer for the Religious News Service, I visited Budapest in June 1948, my first experience behind the Iron Curtain. The Soviet-installed regime had just nationalized all religious schools, so I interviewed Joseph Cardinal Mindszenty and Pastor Albert Bereczky, a leading Calvinist theologian, for their views. Mindszenty, a proud and blunt man who had been jailed by the Nazis, was highly critical of the new order, fully aware that his views were anathema. Pastor Bereczky's attitude toward the Communist regime was more guarded and conciliatory. The church-state issues they addressed are still relevant in today's world. (The piece that follows is reprinted from the New Century Leader, *April 1949.)*

*   *   *

Arriving in Budapest on June 15, 1948, the day before Hungary's Communist-dominated Parliament voted to nationalize the religious schools, I had an opportunity to study the immediate reaction of Protestant and Catholic leaders to this new order. Despite the colorful posters and billboards throughout the country hailing the merger of the Communist and Social Democratic parties and the nationalization of factories, the highly controversial school issue was the first topic of conversation.

Under the School Nationalization Act, the Hungarian State took over 4,474 religious schools, of which 2,797 are Roman Catholic, 1,097 Reformed, and 579 Jewish or Greek Orthodox. The teachers became state employees. Approximately 20 percent of the religious secondary schools and several colleges were exempted from the nationalization program. The new school bill embraces valid educational reforms long overdue and implements the principle of separation of church and state which is taken for granted in America.

The Hungarian government is determined to ease out the churches, and particularly the Roman Catholic, from their positions of privilege and power, but has shown a readiness, for obvious reasons, to make concessions. Under the bill, two hours of religious instruction remain compulsory and in the hands of the clergy. The state will continue to subsidize the teaching activities of the churches, but will gradually withdraw this support over twenty years.

New textbooks from kindergarten to university, written from the Marxist viewpoint, will be introduced. This has already happened in other "People's Democracies" and in the Soviet Zone of Germany. Teachers who don't follow the approved curriculum may be dismissed as "fascist" or "reactionary."

The three major religious groups in Hungary have reacted to the school reform in different ways. The position of the Roman Catholic Church, with 65.7 percent of the population, is one of fighting opposition. On June 24, Cardinal Mindszenty is reported to have excommunicated members of the government and the parliament who voted for the nationalization of schools. In July, priests were arrested for "agitating against Hungarian democracy." A long fight lies ahead.

The Reformed Church (Calvinist), the second largest denomination with 20.8 percent of the population, has taken a position of guarded cooperation with the new school program. The Lutheran Church with a membership of 6 percent of the population has taken a position of opposition and non-cooperation. The Communist-controlled press has charged Lutheran Bishop Lajos Ordass of Budapest as being "anti-democratic" because of his opposition to the nationalization.

The Roman Catholic and Reformed Churches represent the polar positions. Without pronouncing judgment, I will permit two leading spokesmen of these denominations to clarify their own positions in their own words.

On Sunday morning, June 20, Cardinal Mindszenty, Prince Primate of Hungary, granted me a forty-five minute audience in his palace at Esztergom from which even his secretary was excluded. Speaking in German, the Primate answered my questions, giving me permission to quote him directly.

I put the same questions in writing to the Reverend Albert Bereczky, pastor of the Pozsonyi Street Reformed Church in Budapest. A leading theologian, Pastor Bereczky was Hungary's senior delegate to the 1948 Amsterdam Assembly of World Council of Churches.

The contrast between Cardinal Mindszenty and Pastor Bereczky on the Hungarian school issue illuminates the worldwide church-state issue. Below are the verbatim answers of the two churchmen to my three questions:

Question 1: What will be the immediate and long-term effects of the School Nationalization Act on the churches and their educational work?

Cardinal Mindszenty: This act is a thorn in the heart of the Roman Catholic Church. The natural rights of parents and the right of God's church to educate will be wounded. Religion in the very old Roman Catholic institutions will be cast out. The Christian Weltanschauung develops not only from formal religious instruction, but also from literature, national and world history, and the natural sciences.

When religious instruction is reduced to two hours a week in an atmosphere of twenty-eight or thirty hours of materialistic teaching, that religious instruction is as much as nothing. The forces of materialism seek not only to place parochial schools under license, but to abolish religious instruction altogether. In Hungary, ninety-five percent of the people want religious schools. With all legal means we will fight for the right of God's church to educate the children.

Pastor Bereczky: The act has created a completely new situation. The Reformed Church believes that Christians must obey the authorities ordained by God, but that the final limit of this obedience is defined in the Book of Acts, "We ought to obey God rather than men." As we see it, the nationalization of schools does not go beyond this limit. The Reformed Church is to retain the four historic colleges; this proves that the right of churches to maintain schools has not been abolished.

There are three possibilities open for our church: (a) Develop in these four Reformed colleges the most modern and best type of Christian education. (b) Pursue with the greatest missionary zeal religious instruction during the two hours granted in the state schools. (c) Use all opportunities granted by the state to continue home mission activities, especially Sunday School work among youth.

Question 2: To what extent does the present Hungarian government guarantee freedom of religion in general and freedom of religious instruction in particular?

Cardinal Mindszenty: According to the law books, freedom of religion is granted, but in practice, this is not the case. The celebrations of Mary's Day, for example, were made difficult and in several instances totally forbidden. The means employed in hindering these observances were not democratic.

The difficulties of holding the jubilee procession at the 200-year-old Mary Shrine here in Esztergom, scheduled for today, is another case in point. Three times it was officially forbidden. Only yesterday a telegram came from the ministry stating that we could hold it. In addition, threats of deportation, arrests and dismissals for those who

would participate came from Communist Party sources. About forty
Hungarian railway workers were demoted for participating in the
800th anniversary celebration of the Virgin Mary Shrine on June 6.

We have no daily Catholic newspaper while the government and related organizations have 60 daily papers and 140 weeklies. The
Catholic Church has only one weekly paper, but without paper and
with censorship. Pastoral letters from my office, from the Board of
Bishops, and from individual bishops are subject to censorship before
printing. At least three have been confiscated. Our radio programs are
also censored.

Pastor Bereczky: An agreement between the Reformed Church and the
government states: "The Hungarian Republic hereby declares that it
guarantees full religious liberty and pledges to underwrite this guarantee with all possible and necessary means." The government has assured and defended religious freedom thus far and has made possible
the continuation of normal church life by granting essential financial
appropriations for salaries and material support to church institutions.

The government has abolished the difference among the so-called
established, accepted, and tolerated churches which means that since
1947, the Methodists, Baptists and smaller Protestant churches have
the same rights and privileges as the so-called historic denominations
like the Reformed and Lutheran churches. This is an extension of religious liberty.

The government assures the compulsory teaching of religion in the
schools. Now, every religion, even the smallest, has the opportunity to
give its children religious instruction in the schools.

Question 3: Do Western churchmen misunderstand the position of the
churches in Hungary and other states within the Soviet sphere of influence? If so, what misconceptions on the part of Westerners can you
list?

Cardinal Mindszenty: You in the West do not understand our position. In
the school question, for example, the church is fighting for freedom,
not against it. When a school monopoly comes, the right of parents to
choose between schools disappears. The Roman Catholic Church is
fighting not only for narrow church rights, but for broad human rights
as well. In Hungary, human rights and church rights are bound together.

Pastor Bereczky: There are churchmen in the West who do not have a clear
picture of the situation in Hungary because they are ignorant of the
past when all Christian groups were greatly affected by the extraordinarily privileged position of the Roman Catholic Church. People in the
West refuse to admit that the resistance on the part of high Roman

Catholic leaders against the Hungarian government is a purely political matter and has nothing whatsoever to do with religion.

Consequently, everyone who has this Western viewpoint places a high value on the purely political struggle of Hungarian Catholicism against the new socialist state. It is becoming increasingly clear to Protestants here that this political struggle is not a contention between the Christian Church and a state hostile to Christianity, but a fight between two antagonistic political tendencies which has nothing to do with matters of faith and religion.

8 Ethics and World Politics

As the Cold War moved into the mid-1950s, I was preoccupied with relating the Judeo-Christian ethic to the world struggle and was urged to write a primer on the subject. The result was Ethics and United States Foreign Policy *(1957), my first systematic statement of the issues. The book ran into eight printings and was sent to U.S. Information Agency libraries abroad. I called it a poor man's Reinhold Niebuhr; Niebuhr said it was "excellent in every respect." Here are some excerpts from chapter 1.*

*   *   *

There is a widespread and profound confusion among religious and political leaders regarding the relation of ethics to international politics. Religion is often a source of confusion rather than understanding. "Power politics" and ethics are often thought of as mutually exclusive and morally incompatible poles or political alternatives. There is no foreign policy, however noble, that does not include "power politics," or, however cynical, that does not include moral considerations.

*   *   *

When Prime Minister Chamberlain negotiated with Hitler at Munich in September 1938, his intention was "peace in our time," but the immediate effect of his unwise statesmanship was the encouragement of further German expansion and the long-term consequence may well have been World War II. That good intentions often lead to evil results is ironic. An ironic situation is one of incongruity in which the best efforts of men are mocked, seemingly by chance or accident. Upon closer examination, says Reinhold Niebuhr, the incongruity of irony is "discovered to be the result of more than chance." The situation is ironic, he continues, "if virtue becomes vice through some hidden defect in the virtue; if strength becomes weakness because of the vanity to which strength may prompt the mighty man or nation; if security is transmuted into insecurity because too much reliance is placed upon it; if wisdom becomes folly because it does not know its own limits. . . . The ironic situation is distinguished . . . from tragedy by the fact that the responsibility [for it] is related to an unconscious weakness rather than to a conscious resolution."

*   *   *

American citizens often insist upon contradictory goals like peace *and* security when the historical situation presents only the alternatives of a peace of tyranny or security through war. This was the case in 1940 and 1941 when most Americans wanted President Roosevelt to keep the United States out of war. These same Americans wanted other things such as prosperity and national security. But the world between Munich and Pearl Harbor did not offer the luxury of both peace and security. American security could be maintained only by risking and eventually engaging in war. The contradictory demands of the public, which made life so difficult for our policy makers, were decisively resolved by the surprise Japanese attack on December 7, 1941.

Many Americans regard it as immoral to use the national interest as a guide to foreign policy. President Woodrow Wilson said: "It is a very perilous thing to determine the foreign policy of a nation in terms of the material interest. It is not only unfair to those with whom you are dealing, but it is degrading as regards your own actions." The difficulty with Wilson's statement is that the "material interest," which includes such mundane objectives as the maintenance of territorial integrity, is inextricably bound up with such trans-material objectives as the preservation of religious liberty and freedom of assembly.

The pursuit of national interests is wrong only when these interests are not true to the central national purpose or when the national policy is itself morally unjustifiable. It is one thing for Germans to support national objectives as defined by the Nazi regime, and quite another for them to support the national interest as understood by the Bonn Government of 1957. If the national purpose of the United States is conceived in terms broad enough to take into account the interests and rights of other peoples and nations, and if our more specific interests are appropriate to this purpose, it is morally right for our government to pursue a foreign policy based upon the national interest.

Biblical Religion and Politics

One's understanding of international politics and foreign policy is not only drawn from the study of history, political science, and current affairs, but is a reflection of what one basically believes about the nature of man and history. Biblical religion is expressed both in the imperative and declarative mood. Its imperative "thou shalt" is always accompanied by the declaration of who God is, what man is, and what God has done for man. The Bible declares what *is* and what *ought to be*. It asks and answers two questions of central concern to our understanding of ethics and politics— "What is the human situation?" and "What is the duty of man?" An understanding of what *is* is a prerequisite for understanding what *ought to be*. An understanding of who God is and what God has done for man is the basis for understanding what God requires of man.

*   *   *

The long road from Versailles to Pearl Harbor and beyond is cluttered with the whitened bones of crusades that failed—the League of Nations, peace through economic planning, the Kellogg-Briand Pact, and peace through the renunciation of war, to name but a few. These crusades, in which American religious leaders invested so much energy and devotion, failed not for lack of good intentions or enthusiasm, but because the crusaders tended to believe that morally desirable goals were, for the mere fact of their desirability, politically possible. They misread current history because they failed to understand the tragedies and contingencies of the whole realm of history. They misunderstood history because they did not understand the limits and possibilities of human nature.

Biblical religion affirms that God is the Lord of history, the creator, sustainer and redeemer of mankind, the judge of men and of nations. God, not man, is the measure of all things.

Reason is not an independent agency that transcends the self, but is rather a servant of the self. It can be enlisted in man's rebellion against God as well as in his obedience to God. At times some men are able, by the grace of God, to overcome narrow self-interest and to act on behalf of a larger and nobler self or of a community of selves. Man's nature, capable of good or evil, is morally ambiguous. This gives us hope without illusion and humility without despair.

The Limits of Theology in Politics

Human beings seek moral justification precisely because they have a moral sense. But their interests, acknowledged or unacknowledged, often tempt them to clothe their vices in the garments of virtue, to pursue narrow interests in the name of humanity, to make moral principles the servants of self-interest. As John Adams expressed it: "Our passions, ambitions, avarice, love and resentment . . . possess so much metaphysical subtlety and so much overpowering eloquence that they insinuate themselves into the understanding and the conscience and convert both to their party."

How can religion be made a source of wisdom rather than of confusion? There is no easy answer. It is too simple, although partially true, to say that a false theology leads to confusion and that the "right" theology leads to understanding. Most Americans approach politics pragmatically, rather than theoretically. Explicit political doctrine or theory is not a part of the working equipment of the majority of our political leaders. Yet all of us do have certain acknowledged assumptions about the nature of man, history, and politics that do influence our understanding of international politics and foreign policy. It is useful to examine critically one's implicit assumptions to see if they help or hinder one's effort to relate ethics to foreign policy. It is quite possible, of course, for a statesman or an ordinary citizen to have a profound and morally sensitive understanding without subscribing to any explicit theological creed. Yet I believe that a recognition of the central affirmations of the Judeo-Christian faith will deepen one's awareness of the complexities and ambiguities, as well as the opportunities, of international politics and will help deliver one from utopian illusions on the one hand and cynical despair on the other.

9 Moralism and U.S. Foreign Policy

In response to the increasingly bitter and confused debate over American involvement in Vietnam in the early 1970s, I contributed an essay, "Morality Versus Moralism in Foreign Policy," to Ethics and World Politics *(1972). In a* Commentary *article, Daniel Patrick Moynihan called my analysis of rational idealism and historical realism "the best writing yet on this subject."*

*   *   *

It is too simple to attribute the pervasive moral confusion in America to our involvement in Vietnam, though that protracted trauma doubtless has brought to a head our growing weariness with the burdens of power and disenchantment with what Denis Brogan once called "the illusion of American omnipotence." Even before Vietnam our earlier and more naive national self-confidence had been shattered by a series of disappointments and reverses—the "fall of China" in 1949, the inconclusive Korean War, the loss of Cuba to the Communist camp, and the divisiveness and conflict in the wake of decolonization. Most Americans have finally learned that even the mighty United States cannot shape the destiny of peoples in the larger world, at least not without violating our profound moral inhibitions against the exercise of unabashed force to aggrandize our power or nourish our vanity. Since Pearl Harbor, few spokesmen have advocated that we shed our cherished scruples in the quest for an American imperium.

Underlying the moral awakening and confusion has been a continuing struggle between two different ways of looking at history and politics, two streams of American thought that have vied for ascendancy, especially since the mid-nineteenth century. The late Reinhold Niebuhr called these inclinations "rational idealism" and "historical realism," each manifesting itself in diverging political attitudes, expectations, and behavior.

Rational idealism in essence is the child of the Enlightenment and in its pure form it affirms the perfectibility, or at least improvability, of man and the possibility, if not inevitability of progress in history. The diverse schools within this approach are united in their ultimate faith in the nobler nature of man. The earlier idealists saw reason as the redemptive agent that would save man and politics and eventually inaugurate an era of universal peace and brotherhood—the socialist paradise or the Kingdom of God on earth. The natural goodness of man, they believed, can be translated into the structures of politics. Poverty, injustice and war can be eliminated. The rational idealists were supported by the views of men such as Tom Paine, Walt Whitman, and Walter Rauschenbusch, the articulate spokesman of the Protestant Social Gospel movement. Wilsonian idealism, the manifestation of rationalism in the international sphere, reached its zenith in 1928 with the signing of the Kellogg-Briand Pact outlawing war as an "instrument of national policy."

Historical realism, in contrast, emphasizes the moral limits of human nature and history and has its roots in St. Augustine, John Calvin, Edmund Burke, James Madison, and most other classical Western thinkers. Rejecting all forms of religious and secular utopianism—including fascism and Communism—the post-Versailles realists have included men as varied as Niebuhr, Carl L. Becker, Winston Churchill and Dean Acheson. Noting that the extravagant expectations of the Wilsonians were not ratified by subsequent events, the self-designated realists hold that all political achievements are limited by man's dogged resistance to drastic reconstruction. With this recognition of "original sin," they argue that perfect peace, justice, security, and freedom are not possible in his world, though approximations of these lofty goals are not beyond man's grasp. To the rational idealist, the "impossible ideal" is achievable because it is rationally conceivable. To the historical realist, the "impossible ideal" is relevant because it lends humility without despair and hope without illusion.

In the real world there are few wholly consistent adherents to either approach. Were Jefferson and Lincoln rational idealists or historical realists? Obviously, they were a combination of both—Jefferson leaning toward the idealist view, and Lincoln toward the realist. Like most Americans, they tended to be optimistic about the more distant future and at the same time practical and realistic about immediate problems and possibilities.

Rational idealism and historical realism are not complete moral systems, but two different perspectives coexisting uneasily within the Western commitment to a political order of justice and freedom. As approaches, they are subject to certain limitations and weaknesses. In one sense each tends to balance and correct the other. Most moral philosophers, political theorists and statesmen tend toward one view or the other. On the practical level, virtually all political leaders have been realists, regardless of how idealistic their rhetoric may have been. I believe that the historical realist approach is a more adequate reading of the Judeo-Christian tradition and a sounder guide to politics than its post-Enlightenment rival, but recognize that it, like rational idealism, is subject to corruption.

Idealists vs. Realists

Both of these respectable philosophical approaches have been demeaned and distorted by emphasizing certain of their virtues to the neglect or exclusion of other elements in the larger body of Western normative thought. Each is vulnerable in its own way to the vices of political aloofness on the one hand, and crusading arrogance on the other. Rational idealists, frustrated by stubborn political realities, sometimes degenerate into sentimentalists whose strident demand for perfection becomes a substitute for responsible behavior. When personal purity becomes more important than political effectiveness, the resulting aloofness is virtually indistinguishable from that of cynical Machiavellians who insist that might alone makes right. The historical realist becomes irresponsible when his preoccupation with man's baser nature cuts the taproot of social concern and permits him to become a defender of injustice or tyranny.

A lopsided realist can come to hold that what is good for America is good for the rest of the world and that it is our "manifest destiny" to make other peoples over in our own image, by force if necessary. An equally lopsided idealist can support efforts to reshape other societies by more subtle, but not necessarily less reprehensible, means. Members of each approach can degenerate into cynical isolationists or overbearing crusaders. Seen in this light, the extremists in both groups have more in common with each other than with the mainstream of their own tradition.

The corruption of realism or idealism can be called moralism—the most popular rival and impostor of genuine morality. Morality or ethics (the Greek derivative with the same meaning) has to do with right or wrong behavior in all spheres. It is the discipline of relating ends and means. However primitive or sophisticated, all moral systems define normative ends and acceptable rules for achieving them. Moralism, on the other hand, is a sham morality, a partial ethic. Often it is expressed in self-righteous rhetoric or manipulative symbols designed to justify, enlist, condemn, or deceive rather than to inform, inspire, or serve the cause of justice. The moralism of the näive and well-intentioned may be sincere. The moralism of the ambitious and sophisticated is likely to be dishonest. Intellectually flabby and morally undisciplined, moralism tends to focus on private interests rather than the public good, on the immediate at the expense of the future, and on sentiment rather than reason. Morality is a synonym for responsibility. Moralism is a conscious or unconscious escape from accountability.

Soft and Hard Moralism

The varieties of moralism flowing from the corruption of the two approaches always subvert honest political dialogue and responsible behavior, but at the present point in American history *soft moralism* of the sentimental idealists is a greater threat than *hard moralism* of the power realists. The views of the hard cynics—the extreme Machiavellis and gung-ho imperialists—find little hospitality in the university, the church, the mass press, or in the public generally. Few Americans call for the reconquest of the Philippines or the military "liberation" of Cuba or Eastern Europe. The small voice of the hard moralists is barely audible. In sharp contrast, the soft moralism of the rational idealists has had increasing appeal because many Americans are wearied by the burdens of power—the cost of nuclear deterrence and the perplexities of helping to keep the peace in distant places. Senator George McGovern in significant respects is a soft moralist, though his more extreme views have been chastened by his attempt during the 1972 presidential campaign to develop a broad base of support among the American people.

Today, the rational idealistic approach—in its religious and secular versions—and the various corruptions of this stance find wide acceptance among certain articulate leaders in the church and university, and are actively promoted by a segment of the mass media. Given the high level of moral turbulence and uncertainty, it is important to take critical note of this more pervasive manifestation of American moralism, acknowledging that some of its attributes are also similar to those of hard moralism.

Moralism, soft or hard, tends toward a single-factor approach to political problems, while mainstream Western morality emphasizes multiple causation, multiple ends, and multiple responsibilities. Many Americans have demanded peace (often simplistically defined as the absence of war) with insufficient regard for the other two great social ends, justice and freedom. Some have urged the United States to withdraw immediately and totally from Vietnam or to stop building nuclear arms without weighing the probable impact of their advice on the prospects for justice in Southeast Asia, freedom in Western Europe, or global stability. Others have insisted that U.S. involvement in the Third World has thwarted the march toward justice. If one of the valued goals—peace, justice, or freedom—becomes the supreme political end, the other two are bound to suffer. Peace (or order) without justice and freedom is tyranny. Justice without freedom is another form of tyranny.

The statesman has a mandate to use the resources at his command to maintain a tolerable balance among the competing claims of order, justice, and freedom, though in grave crises he may be compelled to sacrifice one temporarily to save the other two. Confronted with the infamy of Pearl Harbor, the American people sacrificed peace in the interests of security and were prepared to accept limitations on their freedom for the same end. Any political community must enjoy minimal security before it can develop the discipline of justice and the safeguards of freedom.

Preoccupation with a particular value, such as "the right of self-determination" (one expression of freedom), can have dire consequences. A single-minded emphasis on self-determination insured the Balkanization of Eastern Europe after World War I. In the 1960s, when the Katanga and Biafra lobbies marched under the same banner, the effect was to prolong conflict and suffering in the abortive secessionist attempts in the Congo and Nigeria. The pro-Biafra crusade, a dramatic example of the moral confusion of single-issue causes, was led by an improbable conglomeration of the New Left and Old Right, humanitarians and hirelings, churchmen and secularists, isolationists and interventionists.

The Sovereign State

The soft moralistic view tends to distrust the state, especially its coercive power, while Western ethical thought affirms the necessity of the state and insists on the responsible use of its power. Absolute power may corrupt absolutely, as Lord Acton asserted, but less-than-absolute power may or may not corrupt those who exercise it. There is little evidence that Lincoln, Churchill, or Truman were corrupted by power; they may even have been ennobled by it. Hitler, Stalin, and Mao were doubtless corrupted before they gained power. Power is amoral. It can be enlisted to liberate or enslave, to guarantee security or take it away. There is a vast difference between the Germany of Adolf Hitler and the Germany of Willy Brandt.

A state government must possess a monopoly on the legitimate use of violence within its domain. As the sovereign authority over a given territory—whether city, country, or empire—the government is the ultimate agency for resolving internal conflicts of power and interest. Were it not for the state, St. Augustine said, men would devour one another as fishes. Martin Luther asserted that the central task of the state was to protect the innocent by restraining evildoers. Of the modern democratic state, Reinhold Niebuhr wrote: "Man's capacity for justice makes democracy possible; but man's inclination to injustice makes democracy necessary." The problem is not to eliminate the state, the professed goal of Marxists and anarchists alike, but to make political power accountable to its citizens by a system that permits them peaceably to give or withhold consent and if necessary to throw the rascals out. If a government becomes tyrannical and all peaceful means for redressing grievances have been exhausted, the people, said Lincoln, have the right to rebel by violent means. The acceptance of Lincoln's view on the right of revolution does not negate the essential character of the responsible state. It is the fundamental agency for "insuring domestic tranquillity, providing for the common defense, promoting the general welfare, and securing the blessings of liberty." In serving these central social objectives there is no substitute for the state, the sovereign political community. In a democratic and pluralistic society, however, other agencies, such as the university, the church, and economic organizations, have a positive role to play.

American Military Power

Soft moralism is highly critical of the exercise of American military power, except in self-defense, and even this is often narrowly defined. America has been criticized for throwing its weight around, and even for repressive policies toward the Third World, though solid evidence is seldom adduced to buttress these charges. On the other hand, a few hard zealots have called for a stronger exercise of power to impose an American order in one part of the world or another. Classical moralists reject both the arbitrary abstention from power and its unrestrained use, and insist that the United States has a responsibility for international peace and order commensurate with its capacity to affect external events. Our military power—as a deterrent, a threat, or an active force—should be limited to dealing with real and present dangers to world peace. A workable international order can only rest on a propitious balance of forces with each of the two superpowers inescapably playing a vital role. U.S. military might, including its nuclear arsenal, is an essential factor in preventing a shift in the balance of forces that could lead to war or the capitulation of friendly states to nuclear blackmail.

The international security system led by the United States—involving NATO, other mutual defense arrangements and military assistance—has gone a long way toward protecting the weak against the ambitions of the strong. What would have been the fate of Western Europe, Greece, Turkey, Iran, Thailand, Taiwan, South Korea, and Japan if the United States had not extended its protection? Since the balance sheet on Southeast Asia is not yet completed, it is not certain that U.S. involvement has set back the long-range prospects for stability, order, and freedom. American security assistance to some fifty Third World states in the past two decades has helped to maintain in many of them the minimal stability essential to constructive political and economic development.

To affirm an indispensable American burden for reinforcing peaceful change is not to define the specific disciplines of that role. How, when, and under what circumstances Washington should threaten or use how much coercion poses a perplexing political and moral question. It can be resolved only by statesmen who understand both the limits and possibilities of American power in situations where the United States has little control and an uncertain moral mandate. Because of these complexities and uncertainty about its own responsibilities, the United States has on occasion used too little or too much power or exercised it too early or too late. The Bay of Pigs comes to mind.

Intervention and Reform

Some soft American moralists actively call for interventionist foreign policies designed to reshape the internal customs and institutions of other states. At the same time, they often degrade or even deprecate the primary security role of foreign policy. This strange combination of reform-intervention and security-isolation turns foreign policy on its head. In the classical view, the first task of domestic policy is order and justice. The reform interventionists, soft or hard, blur the salient distinction between what can and ought to be done by a government for its own people, and what can and ought to be done in the vast external realm over which it has no legal jurisdiction and where its moral and political mandate is severely limited. The insistence that the U.S. government employ extraordinary and sometimes coercive means to reshape the internal political, economic or social structures in other sovereign communities is morally arrogant; it flies in the face of the most basic international law which, in the words of the UN Charter, prohibits intervention "in matters which are essentially within the domestic jurisdiction of any state."

Western morality respects the right of each political community to develop in its own way at its own pace, as long as it does not impinge coercively on other political communities. President Nixon's words in Rumania in 1969 were a refreshing restatement of this principle: "We seek normal relations with all countries, regardless of their domestic systems"; each state has the right to "preserve its national institutions." His trip to China underscored his words. Ignoring this self-constraint, moralistic voices keep urging the government to withhold security or economic aid in order to force domestic changes within Brazil, Greece, and other friendly states whose structure or policies do not accord with the critic's preferences.

This peculiar American penchant to export our virtue reached a high-water mark, at least in rhetoric, under President Kennedy and found belated legislative sanction in 1966 in Title IX of the Foreign Assistance Act.

This act declared that all U.S. economic aid programs should encourage the development of "democratic private and local governmental institutions" in the recipient countries by using their "intellectual resources" to stimulate "economic and social progress" and by supporting "civic education and training skills required for effective participation in governmental and political processes essential to self-government." Still, this intrusive sally into other people's affairs, however näive or wrongheaded, does not compare to the breathtaking sweep or moral pretension of the Communist Manifesto with its strident call to the workers of the world (read self-appointed elect) to redeem societies everywhere without regard to state frontiers. Arrogance is the chief sin. Civilized human beings, observed Leopold Tyrmand, should "agree not to burden each other" with their "excessive humanity."

Viewing U.S. foreign policy as an instrument for reform rather than of stability is not only arrogant; it also overlooks the severely limited capacity of any external agency to influence and reshape alien cultures. Any government has the right to request American or Soviet technical assistance. By the same token, Washington and Moscow have the right to accept or turn down the request. The provision of economic or military aid that serves the interests of both parties presents few problems. It is wrong, however, for the donor government to give, withhold, or modify aid to force significant domestic changes unacceptable to the recipient regime and unrelated to the efficient use of the assistance.

The crusading impulse to reform should be clearly distinguished from the humanitarian motive that has prompted the U.S. government over the years to do more for the foreign victims of famine, earthquake, and war than any other government in history. Earthquake relief is not designed to restructure institutions, overthrow regimes, or promote "free elections."

The Weak and the Powerful

Soft moralism tends to associate virtue with weakness, just as it associates vice with power. Western morality affirms the fundamental worth of the poor and the weak and recognizes that they are less able to defend their rights than the rich and powerful. Further, under the rubric of noblesse oblige, men privileged by wealth or station are duty-bound to protect and assist the lowly. But this does not automatically endow the weak with innocence or virtue, whether they are deprived by nature, sloth, exploitation, or other circumstances.

The behavior of all states, great and small, must be judged by the same moral yardstick, recognizing that the degree of responsibility is commensurate with the capacity to act. "He who has much given to him will have much required of him." Yet, there is a widespread tendency among moralistic Americans to regard the fledgling new states with a kind of perverse paternalism that excuses childish, demanding and otherwise irresponsible behavior, such as that of the delegates who applauded the expulsion of Taiwan from the UN in 1971 or those who charged Washington and Brussels with "deliberate genocide" and "massive cannibalism" for rescuing more than 2,000 innocent foreign hostages of nineteen nationalities in the Congo in 1964.

Neither the weak nor the strong are immune from error or corruption. The celebrated and much confessed "arrogance of power" should not blind us to the arrogance of weakness, which may express itself in simple claims of virtue, insistence on unjustified "reparations," or demands for minority control, all calculated to exploit a pervasive sense of guilt in the American character. As Churchill pointed out, we Anglo-Saxons tend to feel guilty because we possess power. Prime Minister Nehru and other Third World spokesmen often assumed an air of moral superiority, insisting that they were uncorrupted by power and therefore possessed an innocence and humanity denied the leaders of the powerful, and hence guilty, states. In a UN speech in 1960, Premier Saeb Salaam of Lebanon said: "We, the small, uncommitted nations, can perhaps take a more objective view of the world situation. We can judge international issues with comparatively greater detachment and impartiality; in a sense, the small uncommitted nations can be said to represent the unbiased conscience of humanity."

Recent official Swedish statements reflect this moralistic tendency. Though espousing neutrality, Swedish officials have been quick to condemn the behavior of the big powers, particularly the United States, and to take "moral" stands on a variety of international issues. Stockholm has supported Hanoi and the Viet Cong against America and has given moral and material aid to the Communist-assisted guerrilla fighters seeking to overthrow Western-oriented regimes in southern Africa. It is morally easy for politicians or religious leaders to cheer or condemn from the sidelines when they have no responsibility and are unwilling to become committed. With studied hyperbole John P. Roche makes the point: "Power corrupts. And the absence of power corrupts absolutely."

Preoccupation with the Present

The prevailing moralistic approach tends to be preoccupied with the present, neglectful of the past, and nonchalant about the future. Impatient with imperfection, the new romantics indulge in what Elton Trueblood has called the "sin of contemporaneity." It may be argued that enchantment with the chronological now represents a positive contribution drawn from the existential emphasis on the present tense imperative, but evidence suggests it is usually an escape from the eternal now that binds the past and future in an endless chain of responsibility. Man is a creature of history, a product of the past, an actor in the present, and an influence for the future. To reject the past, as so many radicals do, is to reject the fabric of human continuity that gives moral meaning to the present.

Many students today show no interest in the developments that had the most dramatic impact on the political outlook of their parents. If events like Pearl Harbor, the Korean War, and the Budapest uprising are not known or have no common meaning, how can the two generations communicate? The understanding of recent history is vital, even if earlier eras must be shortchanged. This suggests the advisability of teaching history backward, starting with today's newspaper and covering the past decade before moving to the more distant past.

Moral and Political Calculation

In their disdain for history, ancient and recent, and their insistence on achieving quick solutions, many romantic idealists sell the future short by neglecting the disciplines of moral and political calculation. The principal practical test of any political decision is not the intention of the actor or the means he uses, but its immediate and long-range consequences.

Moral choice demands calculation—an assessment of multiple causes, multiple alternatives, and multiple consequences. Many critics of U.S. defense policy condemned the announced underground nuclear test that was carried out in Alaska in November 1971. Some said it would trigger a devastating earthquake or tidal wave or otherwise damage the natural environment. Other critics insisted that the test was a giant step in accelerating the strategic arms race. After careful calculation, President Nixon decided to go ahead, convinced that the natural risks had been exaggerated and that the probable consequences were on balance good for U.S. security and world peace. Following the test there was no indication of a radioactive leak and the damage to the environment appeared to be slight. It did demonstrate the feasibility of the Spartan warhead, an essential component in any viable ABM system designed to protect America's land-based Minuteman missiles, which in turn are designed to deter a nuclear attack against this country. Further, the test may well have strengthened the U.S. position at the Strategic Arms Limitation Talks with the Soviets, which produced agreements in May 1972 on nuclear weapons. These and many other factors were considered in the calculus preceding the president's decision. Critics do not bear the burden of decision, but are they not obligated to consider all the major issues at stake before they pronounce final moral judgment?

The Devil-Theory

Some of the more extreme American moralists, baffled by complexity and impatient with the untidy state of the world, sometimes adopt what amounts to a devil-theory of politics. They attempt to identify the central flaw, the fatal error, the demonic force underlying our present plight.

The earlier rational idealists discovered a series of plausible devils that, separately or in combination, were held responsible for war, injustice, poverty, and many other afflictions of mankind. Each was fatally vulnerable to its rational and righteous counterpart. The prince of darkness, capitalism, could be slain by socialism. The confusion of tongues, the cause of international misunderstanding and conflict, could be cured by education and Esperanto. Nationalism could be exorcised by internationalism and world government. The military and the "merchants of death" could be abolished by the renunciation of war. The idealists and their ideal solutions failed. The Wilsonians, it has been said, reached for utopia and gave us hell.

The targets of present-day devil-theorists bear a striking resemblance to those of earlier decades. Now it is the military-industrial complex, the establishment, the system, the corporate structure, technology, or greed. For many of the radical dissenters the chief demon is "decadent liberalism," a menacing Mephistopheles embracing all the vices of gradualism, reform, due process, and peaceful evolution—benign bourgeois beatitudes that blur the necessity to "destroy the system" and thus subvert revolutionary zeal. Some zealots prefer more personal devils, such as Lyndon Johnson, Dean Rusk, or Richard Nixon. By the same token, some have personal messiahs such as Mao, Ho, and Che.

The devil-theory approach lends itself to an apocalyptic interpretation of the political situation. The whole world is polarized and the golden mean, the vital center, and orderly change are thrown to the winds. The forces of good (read progressive or revolutionary) at home and abroad are arrayed against the forces of evil (read status quo or reactionary) and there is no compromise. The "establishment" will be crushed and "the people" will prevail. It is only a matter of time and dedication. Here one sees the rhetoric of the Maoists and Marxists being used loosely and without discipline by the soft romantics.

Limits of Moral Reasoning

Most American moralists have an inadequate understanding of the limits and possibilities of logic, rationality, and calculation. According to classical Western norms, moral reasoning is a possibility, indeed a necessity. Man is a reasoning creature. Within the limits of circumstance, he can plan, devise, calculate, though he can rarely control or determine events. Circumstances are too complex and intractable and human emotions too unpredictable to come up with full solutions. Precise prediction is impossible and risk is never absent.

To acknowledge the serious limits of rational calculation is not to deprecate reason, or the necessity to marshal relevant facts, or the desirability of projecting the probable consequences of competing lines of action. Politics is more an art than a science, but the scientific discipline of weighing evidence is a compelling moral obligation. To ignore evidence, to disdain logic, or to overlook empirical data is to retreat into blind emotion which spawns illusions. If the romantics fail to discipline their desires with data and persist in their illusions, they become almost indistinguishable from cynics or nihilistic troublemakers.

Just as the contemporary sentimentalists expect too little from reason, the earlier rational idealists expected too much. Reason provides the capacity to behave responsibly. Reason is not an independent human agency that transcends the self, but rather a servant of the self with all its pride and prejudice. A morally sensitive statesman can enlist reason in the pursuit of wise and prudent policies. A morally corrupt politician can likewise enlist reason for his ignoble ends. The old utopians believed that reason and goodwill, unaided by power, would transform politics, but the new romantics seem to despair of reason altogether.

Western morality, in sum, affirms the dignity of man and the necessity for the state. It is precisely because man is finite and inclined to pursue his selfish desires at the expense of his neighbor that structures of order and justice are needed. The responsible state alone is capable of insuring that basic human rights will not be trampled underfoot.

The great majority of American people, by temperament and their respect for law, are committed to a domestic order rooted in a prudent balance of justice and freedom, and to an international order that is safe for diversity and peaceful change. Movement toward these political goals at home and abroad requires a working combination of the "impossible ideal" and an appreciation of political limitations. A man's aim should exceed his grasp, but not by too much. Our times call for idealism without illusion and realism without despair.

10 Reinhold Niebuhr's Enduring Legacy

Reinhold Niebuhr, teacher, theologian, prophet, and pamphleteer, is perhaps the most influential American political philosopher and moralist of the twentieth century. In a doctoral dissertation at Yale, I compared Niebuhr's thought on world politics and U.S. foreign policy to that of mainline Protestant leaders. This article appeared in the American Spectator, *April 1986.*

*   *   *

"Anyone can become angry," wrote Aristotle. "That is easy, but to be angry with the right person, to the right degree, at the right time, for the right purpose, and in the right way—that is not easy." Reinhold Niebuhr (1892–1971)—self-styled biblical realist—was quick to anger and did not always direct his anger at the right person or in the right way. He was not a precisely calibrated man but a dynamic and turbulent bundle of ambiguity.

His celebrated contradictions have led sympathetic observers to contrast him with the systematic and more disciplined older brother, H. Richard Niebuhr, who "thought before he wrote." Reinhold's ambiguity enabled an ideologically mixed bag of persons—from Arthur Schlesinger, Jr., Robert McAfee Brown, and Harvey Cox to Michael Novak, Richard John Neuhaus, and the late Will Herberg—to claim that they are true Niebuhrians. Among some of his followers, notably Harvey Cox, there is the tendency to downplay Niebuhr's fundamental and enduring contribution to Western moral and political thought. And selective interpreters, whether of the extreme left or right, trivialize Niebuhr's biblically rooted insight into the tragic yet hopeful nature of man and history, and his commitment to human dignity, justice, freedom, and the survival of the West. By focusing on his angry outbursts against contemporary actors in the political drama, they often overlook his fundamental rejection of Nazi and Soviet totalitarianism. He did occasionally vacillate on the specific means for championing justice and freedom, but on the central issue of freedom versus tyranny Niebuhr was never ambiguous.

His larger consistency, rooted in his belief in "original sin" and "original righteousness," was elaborated in his most systematic work, *The Nature and Destiny of Man* (1943). Even in his early pacifist-socialist years in the 1920s, Niebuhr railed against both secular and religious utopians who thought they could build the Kingdom of God on earth. This central theme became stronger as the brutalities of Hitler's and Stalin's secular utopias impinged upon him. On several occasions, he said that it took Hitler and Stalin to force him to accept the logic of his earlier premises.

As early as 1932, the essential thrust of Niebuhr's thought could properly be called neoconservative, if one earns that designation by throwing off pacifist, socialist, and other illusions in the face of harsh realities and embracing more modest approaches to grappling with injustice and tyranny. In 1928, he declared himself a "realist" and disavowed his former utopian confidence in man, automatic progress, and social engineering. From the early 1930s until the mid-1960s, he supported the fundamental direction of U.S. policies for defeating Hitler and containing the Soviet Union. Though he spoke out on domestic issues, Niebuhr was preoccupied with international politics and U.S. responsibility for confronting the new barbarians.

Two new books attempt to revive interest in Niebuhr to a generation that has not known him. Richard Fox's *Reinhold Niebuhr: A Biography* (1985) provides a thorough portrait of the man and his thought, but its thoroughness is also its flaw: Fox tends to obscure the essential Niebuhr under an avalanche of intriguing detail, concluding that Niebuhr "was not a man for all seasons," and that it "is futile to wonder what he would have said today about Central American revolutions, about 'free enterprise,' and about the women's movement."

Robert McAfee Brown's *The Essential Reinhold Niebuhr: Selected Essays and Addresses* (1986) is a fine collection of largely theological pieces. In the introduction Brown says, "We must be careful not to assume that a particular analysis, eminently valid for the time," is "necessarily valid for another time," though as he properly notes, "the amount of Niebuhr's thought that transfers from one age to the next is impressive."

Yet Brown goes on to violate his warning by invoking Niebuhr in support of his own liberal view that tends to equate the brutality of the Soviet regime with the imperfections of the American society. He rightly reflects Niebuhr's views that all political communities are under God's judgment and that the United States is not perfect, but wrongly asserts that the "patent evils of Stalinism" are "latently (and sometimes not so latently) present" in America. Niebuhr, he says, deplored "the Vietnam tragedy" as "an example of American imperialism" (Brown's words). But he fails to mention Niebuhr's undiminished confidence in American democracy and his consistent support for a strong military to undergird our Free World responsibilities.

To avoid the pitfalls of using Niebuhr selectively, one must distinguish the essential Niebuhr from the socialist-pacifist Niebuhr of the 1920s and also from the failing and confused Niebuhr of the late-1960s—the last five years of his life. This confusion prompted Professor Paul Ramsey of Princeton, perhaps the most authentic incarnation of the essential Niebuhr, to say in sorrow: "Reinhold Niebuhr signs petitions and editorials as if Reinhold Niebuhr never existed." Other students of Niebuhr, myself included, remain perplexed by his comments on the Vietnam war. Many of Niebuhr's statements during his last five years were profoundly at variance with his repeated insistence that America must use military means to stop the expansion of messianic Marxism, whether Soviet or Chinese.

The essential Niebuhr emerged and flowered in a highly productive period of thirty-five years, roughly from 1930 to 1965. In these vintage decades he developed this century's most compelling critique of "rational idealists," "liberals," "utopians," and "sentimentalists," as he variously labeled his adversaries. He called for a "historical realism" that recognized both "man's limitations and possibilities."

In 1928, Niebuhr recalled that when the First World War started, "I was a young man trying to be an optimist without falling into sentimentality. When it ended, I became a realist trying to save myself from cynicism." He did not join the disarmament movement and he defended the right of states to use violence in the interests of justice. He condemned the naive confidence in the Kellogg-Briand Pact and criticized idealists for glorifying the League of Nations. Early on he warned against the menace of Hitler. When Mussolini invaded Ethiopia, Niebuhr urged the revision of U.S. neutrality laws so we could invoke sanctions against Italy. In 1937 he condemned Japanese aggression against China and shortly thereafter urged a U.S. embargo against Japan. "Tyranny," Niebuhr wrote, "is worse than war" because it is "a 'cold war' which destroys life, liberty and culture" and "must inevitably lead to war."

His shrewd analysis did not immediately prompt him to support U.S. military intervention in World War II, but by early 1940 he said that America needed a "navy big enough to defeat all the fascist powers." A few months later he admitted that he had been wrong in his earlier criticism of President Roosevelt's "preparedness program," noting that FDR had "anticipated this peril . . . more clearly than anyone else." In July 1941, six months before Pearl Harbor, he called for the immediate use of the American navy and air force."

At the same time, Niebuhr maintained a running criticism of the mainline Protestant churches for their perfectionism and neutralism: "If modern churches were to symbolize their real faith they would take the crucifix from their altars and substitute the three little monkeys who counsel men to 'speak no evil, hear no evil, and see no evil.'" Anticipating the current debate over moral symmetry, Niebuhr charged the Christian perfectionists with blurring the moral distinction between tyranny and democracy, and with espousing "perfectionism without pity, goodness without discrimination and responsibility, and loveless love." He condemned the churches for giving advice that, if followed, would ensure "an easy Nazi victory" and for escaping the war issue by spinning "utopian plans" for the postwar world.

Lingering socialist postulates clouded Niebuhr's view of the Soviet Union through the 1930s. Though he had been critical of certain Soviet practices since the early 1920s, as late as 1936 he called the Soviet Union "the most thrilling social venture in modern history." By 1938, however, he was comparing Stalin's "dictatorship" to Hitler's, and in 1940 he predicted the possibility of postwar Russian expansion into Europe. He was especially critical of the "subservience" of overseas Communist parties to "Russian diplomacy, in all its tortuous turnings," adding that the "trouble with all the comrades and semi-comrades" was that they had "made Communism their Christ and Russia the Kingdom of God." (Before Pearl Harbor, Niebuhr was a member of both Norman Thomas's Socialist party and William Allen White's Committee to Defend America by Aiding the Allies. When a Socialist ideologue informed Niebuhr of his inconsistency, saying that "this war is a clash of rival imperialisms," Niebuhr agreed: "So is a clash between myself and a gangster." He promptly quit the Socialist party.)

In a 1953 essay often overlooked by liberal revisionists, "Why Is Communism So Evil?" Niebuhr castigated Marxist arrogance, Soviet brutality, and the "timid spirits" who will not acknowledge "this universal evil of Communism. . . . Communist dogmatism creates an ideological inflexibility" that reinforces "the monolithic political structure" of the Soviet Union. A decade later he declared that Soviet Communism was far more dangerous than any authoritarian regime—it was "a pretentious scheme of world salvation, a secularized religious apocalypse."

Niebuhr was impatient with the idealistic planners for the postwar world. In 1943 he said that any viable postwar settlement would require the continuing commitment of U.S. power and that an Anglo-American alliance "must be the cornerstone of any durable world order." The United Nations, like the failed League before it, was at best a frail reed and at worst an illusion. In 1945 he said that if the divisions between the Soviet Union and the Western allies continued to widen, the UN might become "irrelevant." He repeatedly attacked "the illusion of world government" and in 1949 wrote an article by that name in *Foreign Affairs*

which remains a testament to his profound understanding of world politics. A war against Russia, he said, was possible; the Western allies
should be prepared for it. Convinced that Soviet expansionist policies
were the major threat to freedom and world peace, he became an unabashed Cold Warrior, agreeing with Churchill that U.S. superiority in
nuclear arms was the "chief deterrent of a Russian venture to conquer
Europe."

This remarkably consistent affirmation of political realism and responsibility persisted until the mid-1960s, marred only slightly by the not
fully examined assumptions of his Marxist past. He acknowledged this
flaw in a 1952 essay, "The Triumph of Experience Over Dogma," in which
he said that he clung to shreds of Marxist dogma long after he supposed
himself free of such illusions. He embodied Churchill's provocative assertion that "facts are better than dreams."

This record adds up to a profile of a thoughtful neoconservative, a liberal mugged by reality. One must allow for foibles, contradictions, and
ambiguities in any seminal thinker, especially one as turbulent and torn
as this preacher turned political philosopher in the crucible of a world
menaced by the totalitarians. Niebuhr drew his wisdom from the Judeo-
Christian moral tradition—from the Hebrew prophets, Saint Paul, Saint
Augustine, and Martin Luther—and, less consciously, from American
statesmen like James Madison and Abraham Lincoln. Will Herberg, a former leading intellectual in the Communist Party USA who was converted by Niebuhr into a Judeo-Christian realist, asserted that one could
establish a kinship between Niebuhr's conservatism and that of Edmund
Burke.

Vintage Niebuhr, then, is indeed a man for all seasons. He directed his
anger against the evils of Nazi Germany and the Soviet Union, and
against the idealists, utopians, and rationalists who could not comprehend tragedy and evil in the world, and the cynics who didn't care about
the fate of freedom.

PART THREE

Christianity and World Politics

In August 1948, shortly after visiting Communist Hungary and Czechoslova-kia, I attended the founding assembly of the World Council of Churches in Amsterdam. The East-West struggle was a major issue, and the overwhelming majority of delegates believed that the gulf between the Christian and Communist worldviews was unbridgeable. John Foster Dulles spoke for the Christian West, and Josef Hromadka, a theology professor from Prague, apologized for the Communist East. The WCC was still clearly on the side of democracy and peaceful change. Dulles condemned Soviet Communism's rejection of moral law, denial of basic rights, and expansion into Europe, and he spoke of the social and economic achievements of Western democracy.

In rebuttal, Hromadka declared that the West had little to offer in moral leadership. He acknowledged that Communism "imperiled the sacredness of human beings and the majesty of justice and love" but asserted that it nevertheless represented, "in atheistic form, much of the social impetus of the living church." Even then, Communist efforts to influence Christians dedicated to justice and human rights were evident.

Throughout my career, I have supported efforts to achieve Christian unity and wisdom on social and political issues. For three years (1952 to 1954), I was on the executive staff of the U.S. National Council of Churches as an international affairs specialist.

Part Three deals primarily with the political ethic of the World Council of Churches as it gradually changed under the impact of the socialist worldview that emphasizes egalitarianism over freedom. The WCC moved from its anti-Communist and antistatist position in 1948 to a "liberation theology" that tended to equate the compassion of Christ with the Marxist class struggle. The U.S. National Council of Churches made an almost identical pilgrimage.

The first four essays reflect my views of the WCC from 1948 to the present. The final selection is a critique of the reckless rhetoric that all too often characterizes statements on foreign policy by American religious leaders.

11 *The World Council of Churches*

From its beginning in 1948, the World Council of Churches was committed to forging a unified Christian position on pressing economic, social, and political issues. This selection, excerpted from my book Amsterdam to Nairobi: The WCC and the Third World *(1979), summarizes the evolution of the council's increasingly radical stance on Communism, capitalism, and the world struggle from the WCC's founding to 1980, as reflected in its pronouncements and conferences. My controversial book, published when I was president of the Ethics and Public Policy Center, was welcomed by evangelical Protestants and drew favorable columns from Ronald Reagan and William F. Buckley—and harsh criticism from mainline Protestant leaders. In the book's foreword, George F. Will wrote: "Readers can decide for themselves the extent to which bad sociology, bad theology, bad faith, and, yes, sin feed on one another and are to blame for what the WCC has been doing." The book was used as the basis for a CBS-TV 60 Minutes program.*

*   *   *

The inaugural assembly of the World Council of Churches in August 1948 convened in Amsterdam in a festive mood of postwar reconstruction, renewal, and high expectations. The Dutch capital had been spruced up to celebrate the jubilee of Queen Wilhelmina and the investiture of Princess Juliana. For the first time since the Nazis were driven from the Netherlands, Dutch citizens and foreigners alike were able to view the magnificently restored collection of Rembrandt paintings in the Royal Museum.

The Amsterdam Assembly was the most representative gathering of Christian churches in history. It drew 350 delegates from 150 churches in 43 countries, representing nearly all the Protestant denominations in the world as well as the Anglican, Greek Orthodox, and Old Catholic. The Roman Catholic and Russian Orthodox churches were not represented.

"Man's Disorder and God's Design" was the Assembly's theme, but political disorder was more evident than God's design. The anti-German hostility of Christians in formerly occupied lands had abated, though not disappeared; a rally of 10,000 Dutch young people gave a standing ovation to Pastor Martin Niemoller (who had spent years in the Dachau concentration camp) after he delivered a stirring speech, the first public address in the German tongue given in the Netherlands since the war's end. But as old wounds were healing, new and deeper conflicts were beginning to emerge. The familiar labels of victor and defeated, liberated and neutral, were giving way to the new language of the East-West conflict—Western democracy vs. Communism, Marxism vs. capitalism. The emerging Cold War was symbolized by two speakers, John Foster Dulles, a Presbyterian lawman who later became U.S. secretary of state, and Professor Josef L. Hromadka, a churchman who was then a member of the Central Action Committee of Communist Czechoslovakia; each of them spoke on "Christian Responsibility in Our Divided World."

Western Orientation

At Amsterdam and for a decade and a half thereafter the dominant themes, concerns, and leaders of the WCC were Western, primarily European and North American. Its chief concerns in 1948 included reestablishing ties between church leaders in the Allied and Axis states, helping with reconstruction in Europe, aiding refugees and prisoners of war, and defining responsible nationalism. From the beginning, there was a small and growing interest in the "younger churches" of Asia and Latin America, and later of Africa.

The Assembly addressed the ideological, political, and moral conflict between the Communist East and the democratic West but took a modest view of the church's ability to shape political or economic systems:

> The Church cannot resolve the debate between those who feel that the primary solution is to socialize the means of production and those who fear that such a course will merely lead to new and inordinate combinations of political and economic power, culminating finally in an omnicompetent State. . . . Property is not the root of the corruption of human nature [and] ownership is not an unconditional right. . . . The Christian churches should reject the ideologies of both Communism and *laissez-faire* capitalism, and should seek to draw men away from the false assumption that these extremes are the only alternatives. Each has made promises which it could not redeem.

The Assembly refrained from defining an acceptable halfway house between socialism and capitalism and declined to recommend any specific political or economic structures, though it clearly came down on the side of peaceful and constitutional change. Its basic political message was embraced in its definition of a "responsible society"—"one where freedom is the freedom of men who acknowledge responsibility to justice and public order, and where those who hold political authority or economic power are responsible for its exercise to God and the people whose welfare is affected by it."

This definition was clarified by the Second Assembly, held in Evanston, Illinois, in 1954: "Responsible society is not an alternative social or political system, but a criterion by which we judge all existing social orders and at the same time a standard to guide us in the specific choices."

Colonialism and the Third World

Amsterdam's condemnation of colonialism and racism was measured: "We protest against the exploitation of non-self-governing peoples for selfish purposes; the retarding of their progress toward self-government and discrimination or segregation on the grounds of race or color." The WCC assumed that the Western colonial powers would grant self-determination and would promote constructive political and economic development by encouraging constitutional democracies, providing technical assistance, and transferring resources. Early statements clearly opposed the expansion of Communism, Soviet or Chinese, and saw no reason to expect any good from a totalitarian system.

The Assembly in Evanston (1954) showed a growing concern for the "underdeveloped countries" and acknowledged the revolutionary upheaval in Asia, Africa, and Latin America. The principal focus, however, continued to be on the East-West conflict, particularly the question of strategic arms control in view of the Soviet Union's explosion of a hydrogen bomb in 1953. It advocated international controls to bring about "the elimination and prohibition of atomic, hydrogen, and all other weapons of mass destruction, as well as the reduction of all armaments to a minimum." These sweeping goals and specific demands reflected a confusion between aspiration and political achievement. (See Chapter 12.)

Evanston went far beyond Amsterdam in condemning colonialism and racism, two issues of considerable interest to the Third World. By 1954, India, Pakistan, Burma, Ceylon, and Indonesia had been granted independence. The Mau Mau rebellion raged in Kenya. Ho Chi Minh was fighting the French in Indochina. At the same time, peaceful plans for independence were under way in Nigeria, Ghana, Sierra Leone, Somalia, and other parts of Africa. Evanston called on the colonial powers to "remove the yoke which now prevents other nations and people from freely determining their own government and form of society." The report on international affairs noted that "the older types of colonialism and imperialism are surely dying out," but that "new forms of imperialism call for vigilance," an oblique reference to Communist expansion. It expressed admiration for efforts by the "more developed countries" to give technical assistance to newly independent states.

"Rapid Social Change"

A theme of the New Delhi Assembly in 1961 was "rapid social change" which invested "the responsible society" with a more revolutionary meaning. The major Third World issue was Portugal's role in Angola. During 1961 there were several insurrections by nationalist groups against Portuguese policies or rule. After the first revolt, in northern Angola, its leader, Holden Roberto, deplored the "extreme violence" of his followers, which had led to the killing of perhaps 750 Portuguese settlers. These excesses set the stage for severe military action by Portuguese authorities in which thousands of Africans were reportedly killed. The WCC Executive Committee criticized Portuguese policy and endorsed political self-determination for Angola's black majority.

Two embryonic ideas emerged at New Delhi that would later influence the WCC's stance toward the Third World. The first was an implicit acceptance of "temporary authoritarian regimes" as guarantors of social order and economic development. Second was the concept of what later came to be called the New International Economic Order. It dealt briefly with economic cooperation, UN development aid, fair trade policies, price stabilization of major commodities and manufactured goods, training and research in development, and population control.

Toward a More Radical Stance: 1966–1968

During the seven years between the New Delhi Assembly in 1961 and the Uppsala Assembly in 1968, the WCC virtually moved from a "theology of order" and peaceful change to "theology of revolution." From Amsterdam (1948) through New Delhi, the Council asserted that the disordered world was to be transformed into "the responsible society" by accepting God's design. As the familiar foundations were shaken by the hand of God, Christians celebrated the tremors from which a new humanity would be born.

The adoption of radical and rapid change by the WCC was the product of both external and internal forces. In part, the council was caught up in the revolutionary ferment in Western intellectual circles and thus both reflected and stimulated a similar outlook among its representatives from the Third World. Black militants in Watts and Washington made common cause with European student activists in speaking out on Third World grievances. They all were persuaded that economic and political "repression" south of the equator could not end short of revolution at home and abroad. For them, the Third World was not simply a geographical area or an economic problem but fundamentally a symbol of universal "repression." Richard John Neuhaus later accused the WCC of practicing "a kind of colonialism, or neocolonialism, of the Left in selecting the voices it wishes to hear from the Third World."

During the latter part of the turbulent decades between 1948 and 1968, the World Council of Churches became increasingly receptive to the growing and controversial "liberation theology" movement that was then under way among Roman Catholics in Latin America. Even before their doctrinal foundation was ratified in Nairobi in 1975, WCC "liberation theologians" had become involved in Third World politics. This was manifest in the Council's vigorous Program to Combat Racism, which from 1970 through 1978 gave over $3 million to Marxist and other "liberation" groups and supporting organizations in Asia, Latin America, the Caribbean, Europe, and North America.

12 *An Absence of Moral Seriousness*

The second assembly of the World Council of Churches, which I also attended, was held in Evanston, Illinois, in 1954. Its report on "international affairs" was virtually devoid of serious political analysis or moral reflection. My critique, published in Reinhold Niebuhr's Christianity and Crisis *(November 29, 1954), drew fire from my former colleagues at the National Council of Churches, who implored Niebuhr to withdraw his already written editorial supporting me. Under pressure and weakened by a stroke, he yielded but later wrote me, "I thoroughly agree with your article."*

*　　*　　*

An authoritative ecumenical pronouncement has two essential elements—it must reflect a consensus which has emerged from an intensive dialogue of Christians from many lands and traditions who seek to discover God's will on a particular problem, and the dialogue must have taken into account all relevant sources of insight in and outside the churches. The Evanston Report on "Christians in the Struggle for World Community" emerged from a dialogue that had not been sufficiently intensive or extensive. Central insights from the academic disciplines of history and political science were conspicuous by their absence.

The report reflects the strengths and weaknesses of the most vocal spokesmen of the churches' concern for international affairs among WCC communions. Perhaps the main contribution of the report is its restatement of the universal goals of peace and justice which stand in judgment against the provincial loyalties of men and nations. It makes some contribution to the understanding of world affairs and foreign policy, but it does not begin to measure up to the best secular or Christian writing in the field.

The mediocrity, distortion, and error that creep into ecumenical documents are in part the inevitable concomitants of the process by which they are written, but basically these faults reflect the theological contradictions in the traditions that contribute to the dialogue. The report's confidence in man and in the possibility of "earthly justice, freedom and peace for all men" would have shocked the Reformers.

Faulty assumptions about the nature of man, history, and world politics lead to a faulty analysis of the world situation and to unrealistic and irrelevant recommendations for bettering it. The drafters, for example, asserted that the "Council of Europe and the Organization of American States provide the major examples . . . of regional organizations for collective self-defense," while NATO was not even mentioned. Further, the report said nothing about the relation of military power to diplomacy, the necessity for negotiating from strength, while three paragraphs were devoted to the promotion of human rights through international action.

Faulty assumptions lead not only to bad analysis and irrelevant "solutions," but to irresponsible and ineffective behavior. In short, bad theology leads to bad politics and bad ethics.

Rival Power Blocs

The present situation, says the report, is characterized by a conflict between social and political systems, ideologies, and "rival power blocs," and by the massive "revolt against economic deprivation, political bondage and social inequality. . . . Underlying the more obvious barriers to genuine world community is the lack of a common foundation of moral principles."

The brief analysis of the world situation is vague, incomplete, and two-dimensional. The report speaks of the "clash of national interests, social systems, and ideologies" as "current tensions" when they are really current manifestations of the unending struggle for power among men and nations, which in turn springs from man's age-old rebellion against God. The report seems to assume that if we work and pray hard enough, the power struggle will one day give way to an "international order of truth and peace."

The lion's share of the report is devoted to restating the familiar goals of world peace long accepted by most "ecumenical" Christians and other liberal democrats. We must work to eliminate war, totalitarian tyranny, aggression, and imperialism, and to establish a "lasting peace" of freedom, justice, truth, and love. Although measures short of these ultimate goals may be "frail expedients" we are morally obligated to work for such partial objectives.

On the struggle between the Soviet and non-Soviet worlds, the report advocates six "minimum conditions to be met by both sides" which can serve as "a transitional stage or point of departure" on the road to "an order of genuine cooperation." The conditions are: (1) a belief that peace is possible, (2) the unwillingness of either bloc to use force beyond its present sphere of influence, (3) a vigorous effort to end injustices that might lead to war, (4) "a scrupulous respect for the pledged word," (5) "a continuous effort to reach agreement on . . . peace treaties and disarmament," and (6) a "readiness to submit all unresolved questions of conflict to an impartial international organization and to carry out its decisions."

The trouble with these "minimum requirements" is that they are not minimal at all, and at least one of them is completely beyond the realm of possibility. If it were politically possible for the Soviet Union or the United States to submit "all unresolved" conflicts to an international agency and accept its judgment without question, that state would forthwith cease to be a state. Its effective political power (sovereignty), the central characteristic of a state, would have passed to the international agency. Thus, this "minimum requirement" is no less than a demand for world government now. Its utter unrealism is illuminated by the fact that the UN member states after four years of consideration cannot even agree on a definition of "aggression."

The writers tend to ignore two elementary facts: the decisions of war and peace are made by the governments of states, especially the superpowers; and the foreign policy alternatives open to these governments are highly limited by the power and unpredictability of actual or potential enemies, by the restraint of allies, by the reluctance of uncommitted powers, by public opinion at home, and by the inexorable vicissitudes of history in general.

The failure of the report to submit to the discipline of the achievable is due in part to its confusion of what is desirable with what is politically possible, and, on a deeper level, a confusion of "social progress" with biblical hope. The constant reiteration of lofty goals without coming to grips with the limitations of the human situation leads to social ineffectiveness and moral irresponsibility. Modest goals can lead to effective and responsible action. Grandiose blueprints end in disaster. Someone has said that the 1920s reached for utopia and gave us hell.

"Men's Hearts Must Be Changed"

In a revealing understatement the report warns that world peace "will not be easily or quickly attained." But its recommendations seem to ignore the few barriers it mentions, to say nothing of the formidable difficulties that go unacknowledged. Basically, "men's hearts must be changed." Many of the report's recommendations require considerable heart changing, and few of them come to grips with a world of unchanged hearts. "Christians must pray more fervently for peace, repent more earnestly . . . and strive more urgently to establish world contacts for reconciliation, fellowship, and love." We must work for "a common foundation of moral principles," and must "help remove . . . the causes of war." The churches should develop "an enlightened and effective public opinion on international affairs."

The report says nothing about how changed hearts, fervent prayers, or Christian opinions are brought to bear at the points where the decisions of war and peace are made. What can the Christian as a citizen do to influence the foreign policy decisions of his government? This crucial question goes unanswered. Instead, the report bypasses the effective unit of power and decision in international affairs, the state, and concentrates on international covenants and agencies that are little more than reflections of the underlying struggle for power and security. The drafters tend to place excessive hope in international law, covenants, and agencies, overlooking their own mild warning that "international law is more often the fruit than the source of community."

The report's overconfidence in international machinery is best illustrated in its view of the United Nations. Recognizing that the UN necessarily reflects the "divisions of the international community," the report attributes the inability of the UN to deal with the bipolar conflict in part to its "brief history" and to constitutional limitations. The UN must be strengthened and one way to strengthen it is Charter revision when the "moral" climate permits. The drafters seem to ignore the fact that the issues of peace and security are not determined by words in a charter or by imperfections in international machinery, but by how governments use their power.

The UN "has made significant contributions to order and justice," says the report, but it is far more cautious about the political possibilities of the agency than many American zealots. Nevertheless, it tends to view the UN as an active agent with power in its own right, rather than as an arrangement with no effective restraint on the use of state power. The UN, like the League of Nations, is essentially a continuing conference of sovereign states. It has no political power, and indeed no existence apart from the existence of its members. The UN can solve no problems. Conflicts can be resolved only when the governments of the nations involved are willing to make the necessary concessions. Further, as many scholars and statesmen have pointed out, public diplomacy, UN style, is often less effective than old-fashioned private diplomacy.

The report has special praise for the far-flung non-political work of UN agencies. Here it is on firmer ground, as long as it does not assume that such social and humanitarian work necessarily contributes to world peace. There is little evidence that wars would cease if poverty, disease, and illiteracy were wiped from the face of the earth, Karl Marx notwithstanding. Wars and threats to the peace are caused by the existence of a state powerful enough to impose its will on peoples outside its domain and with a ruling elite willing to attempt it. Making two blades of grass grow where one grew before has little effect on threats to the peace, but a regional defense alliance like NATO has a great effect. The marvelous humanitarian work of UN agencies and similar bilateral programs are worthy in their own right even if they do not contribute to peace.

The report reflects an unjustifiable confidence in the rationality and goodness of man and in historic "progress," as well as an inadequate understanding of world politics. To be morally responsible, ecumenical conversations must take into account the insights of historians, political scientists, statesmen, depth psychologists, and even journalists, for as Saint Augustine said, "Truth by whomever spoken is of God."

13 A Dangerous Political Activism

As the World Council of Churches became increasingly committed to liberation theology as a remedy for Third World ills, I continued to speak out. One example was this widely reprinted piece that first appeared in the Wall Street Journal (May 21, 1980).

*   *   *

"While saints are engaged in introspection, burly sinners run the world," said John Dewey.

The leaders of the World Council of Churches have never accepted this division of labor. And they are right. Throughout the history of Christianity its saints and sinners have insisted that the church, and in a large sense religion, should serve the conscience of society and that Christians should have some responsibility for the quality of the social, economic, and political order. But they have disagreed on what this responsibility is and how it should be expressed.

Today, hardly a week passes without a headline about church and state, Christianity and politics. A new secretary of state pledges to invigorate the human rights policy of his born-again Christian President. Pope John Paul II forbids priests from holding elective office in secular government. Leaders of the National Council of Churches, long active in pro-choice politics, condemn 200,000 fellow Christians who gather in Washington "to pray for America" because many of them have contrary views on these and other controversial issues.

A Desire to Be Relevant

Christians of various political persuasions here and abroad will continue to wrestle over the proper relation of the City of God and the City of Man precisely because most of them hold that they as citizens and the church as a community of believers should be concerned about the quality of earthly life. But when this concern is informed by bad theology and a shallow understanding of history, and is driven by a desire to be "relevant," it can lead to a dangerous political activism.

A striking example was the $85,000 grant given in August 1978 to the Patriotic Front guerrillas in Zimbabwe-Rhodesia who by terror were seeking to overthrow the interim regime there. Though the money was ostensibly for "humanitarian" assistance, no effort was made to monitor its use and Council leaders admitted that it was intended as a "political statement." As if to underscore its political intent, the Council then gave $125,000 to the SWAPO guerrillas in South West Africa (Namibia) who by terror tactics were seeking to prevent an orderly transition to majority rule.

These grants were made under the WCC's Program to Combat Racism, which between 1970 and 1979 gave $3,063,545 to more than a hundred organizations in nearly thirty countries. (This represents a small portion of the Council's budget, and since 1971 the program has been funded only by contributions designated for it.) About 65 percent of these grants went to organizations seeking radical political change in southern Africa. Among the recipients in the United States were the American Indian Movement, Coalition for Concerned Black Americans, Free Southern Theater, Malcolm X Liberation University, National Conference of Black Lawyers, and the Puerto Rico Solidarity Committee. The WCC grants to the guerrillas in southern Africa precipitated a lively controversy in religious and secular circles and raised two basic questions: For whom does the Council speak? Why does the Council side with radical forces in the Third World?

The World Council of Churches is a many-splintered thing. It is not a superchurch but a deliberative body of 195 Protestant and Eastern Orthodox denominations in a hundred countries. Like the UN General Assembly, it operates democratically, and, as in the Assembly, the voting power has shifted from a Western political orientation to a particular version of Third World interests and demands.

From its founding in 1948, the WCC has sought to create greater Christian unity, promote evangelism, and strengthen Christian influence in the social and political sphere. The first two tasks as well as the Council's non-political welfare activities have produced little controversy. But its political pronouncements and programs have provoked a storm of protest.

As in any large bureaucracy, the WCC's decisions emerge from a complex process in which its headquarters staff—approximately 275 people with offices in Geneva—plays a key role. On the major controversial issues, however, there has been a solid working consensus among senior staff, its Central Committee (135 members), the six regional Presidents, and the General Secretary (currently Philip Potter, who last year defended aid to Marxist terrorists on the grounds that God's rule demands "a radical change of economic, social, and political structures").

Though the WCC is formally a representative organization, this does not mean that it speaks for its member churches. Much less does it mean that the Council speaks for millions of members of those churches. The WCC reflects some diversity, but in addressing social concerns it speaks primarily for an activist minority consisting of top staff and officers plus most members of the Central Committee.

There has developed a kind of self-perpetuating "social action curia," as Professor Paul Ramsey of Princeton has called it, whose views on social change have over the past fifteen years shifted sharply to the left. As a result, the majority of WCC-affiliated church members, at least in North America and Western Europe, feel unrepresented or misrepresented by the Council's social stance.

The WCC has gradually moved from its original, largely Western concept of political responsibility to a more radical ideology. By 1975 it had embraced the concept and practice of "liberation theology," whose diagnosis and prescriptions bear a striking resemblance to those of the most powerful secular utopianism of our time, Marxism. The positions of this "revolutionary" theology on Third World and other issues have often been indistinguishable from those expressed in Moscow and Havana.

The WCC has been deeply influenced by a concept of the Third World that describes the wretched of the earth (whether in Asia, Africa, Latin America, or the United States) as victims of four oppressive forces: racism, capitalism, neocolonialism, and multinational corporations, all of which are buttressed by official U.S. policies. Third World peoples must be "liberated" from their poverty and bondage by the secular revolutionaries and their Christian supporters. Consequently, "temporary" authoritarian control by leftist regimes is justified and even advocated, while authoritarian rule of the right is roundly condemned.

WCC pronouncements often show more tolerance for totalitarian regimes than for authoritarian ones, despite overwhelming evidence that the chances for justice and freedom are far greater under the latter than under the former—far greater in authoritarian South Korea, for example, than in totalitarian North Korea; far greater in Chile than in Cuba, where tens of thousands of persons are attempting to flee Castro's paradise. The Council's reluctance to criticize massive violations of human rights in Communist countries while condemning lesser breaches of freedom in non-Communist states further illustrates this split-level morality and political confusion.

The WCC's approach to the economic problem has also undergone a radical transformation. In its early years, the Council urged Western governments and private enterprise to export technology and capital to the Third World, but by 1975 it was warning of the perils of such policies. The major culprits were the multinational corporations, whose essential aims, according to a 1975 WCC pronouncement, are "to take advantage" of cheap labor and to "draw out profits," making use of "the immense control they exercise over world trade and prices." The "type of goods they produce is meant invariably to satisfy the needs of an elite class, the technology they use is ill-suited for the needs of these countries," and their operations benefit only "the higher income groups in the host countries."

Since the multinationals are brutal exploiters with few redeeming virtues, the WCC initiated a critical investigation of them to find a better way of "organizing the earth's resources and human skills." The unstated better way is apparently government ownership or control.

Misplaced Sense of Guilt

Why have World Council leaders lost confidence in the classic teachings of Christian social responsibility and in the efficacy of democratic and constitutional change? Conversely, why have they found the secular utopians' call for revolution more appealing? Certainly a misplaced sense of Western guilt about Third World poverty, as P.T. Bauer of the London School of Economics has pointed out, has something to do with it. Some WCC leaders also find Marxist views attractive because they hope to recapture moral authority in an increasingly complex and secular world by running with the radical-chic pack.

Other Council leaders have mixed feelings of infatuation and fear toward Marxism. Their ambiguity stems from a profound confusion between ends and means; the ends of justice, freedom, order, and plenty and the appropriate means for moving toward these goals.

Christianity offers no simple cure for poverty, injustice, or lack of freedom. And concerned Christians are often confused about how best to mitigate these ills. The democratic and peaceful way seems too slow, undramatic, and unfashionable. But empirical evidence suggests that prosperity and respect for human rights within the Third World are more likely to result from adapting a Western, democratic, market model than from adopting the rigid and often harsh Marxist models of the Soviet Union, Cuba, or China.

14 *Redeeming the Third World*

For four decades, World Council of Churches leaders have been preoccupied with the "developing world," as it came to be called. In their view, inevitable revolutionary change can be combined with Christian redemption. This conviction became abundantly clear with their praise of Marxist regimes in Cuba and Nicaragua and their assistance to Communist Vietnam. The following selection, "Backward Christian Soldiers!" appeared in The National Interest *(Winter 1988–1989).*

*   *   *

The World Council of Churches, the largest existing ecumenical organization, addresses questions of faith, worship, evangelism, and Christian unity, but its notoriety derives from two things: the ardor with which it espouses social and political causes; and in the process of doing so, the clear and consistent preference it shows for radical solutions and elites. Both in its eagerness to subordinate the sacred to the profane and in its affinity with quasi-religious, messianic political movements, the WCC is very much a creature of its time.

Its leaders participate in international conferences, organizations, and movements committed to revolutionary and violent change. They are active in a global network of radical academics, scientists, journalists, and politicians that provides training and money for "liberation" efforts driven by Marxist-Leninist fervor and frequently supported by the Soviet Union. Taken together, these hundreds of radical organizations and movements have a significant impact on the intellectual and psychological climate in which statesmen must make fateful decisions about war and peace, tyranny, and freedom, and poverty and plenty.

The Council operates by ostensibly democratic procedures, but is hostage to the strong influence of its permanent executive staff. The WCC's most authoritative body is the Assembly made up of delegates from the member churches. Between Assembly meetings, held every six or eight years, WCC decisions are made by a Central Committee of about 135 members, which meets annually. Since 1975, Committee members from Third World and Communist states have outnumbered those from Western countries. Between the annual Committee meetings, its Executive Committee of some twenty-five members acts on its behalf.

In Geneva, Switzerland, its headquarter's staff of about 275 runs the entire social action program. They are supported by the seven presidents and the Executive Committee, most of whom see the world through revolutionary lenses. Even when the WCC deals with humanitarian relief, evangelism, liturgy, and Christian unity, these matters are often distorted by revolutionary fervor. In practice, the ideological stance at various levels of the WCC, including its conferences, delegations to problem spots, and publications, has differed little since the advent of "liberation theology" in the 1960s. In this worldview, the United States is the chief villain in the struggle between the old "oppressive order" and a "new just order." Capitalist states in Western Europe and the Pacific rim also come in for their share of criticism.

The Sandinistas: "Transmitters of Hope"

Nowhere is the ideological slant of the WCC's politics more apparent than in its stance towards Central America. In July 1979, several Christian leaders in Nicaragua played a significant role in toppling the corrupt regime of President Anastasio Somoza de Bayle. Many of the "revolutionary Christians" who had joined the alliance led by the Sandinista National Liberation Front viewed the merger of religion and Marxism as "a sign of hope for all of Latin America." Subsequently, several Catholic priests joined the Sandinista government.

Far from being a radical departure, such activism was consistent with the "liberation theology" which flowered in Central America in the early 1970s. Liberation theology invokes such biblical concepts as the "Kingdom of God," "justice," and "salvation" to justify Marxist revolutionary aims and methods, including violence.

Most liberation theologians regard the poor much as Marx regarded the proletariat—as the source of revolutionary liberation from feudalism and other traditional social and political structures. In their writings, religion and revolution have become intertwined to such a degree that Christian participation in revolutions is deemed all but obligatory.

This marriage of religion and revolutionary politics found widespread sympathy among World Council leaders, as initially it did in many democratic circles. When subsequent events showed that Sandinista Marxism was incompatible with the stated democratic goals of the Nicaraguan revolution, and when a number of former revolutionary leaders like Eden Pastora and Alfonso Robelo testified to that effect, much of that Western sympathy drained away. But not that of the WCC. The Council, for example, did not respond to the Nicaraguan Commission of Jurists' report that 8,655 persons had been killed in Sandinista prisons between 1979 and 1983. Charles R. Harper of the WCC's Human Rights Resources Office on Latin America blandly said that the Council would withdraw its support for the Permanent Commission for Human Rights in Managua since human rights had been guaranteed by the Nicaraguan government.

Though the Sandinistas had censored the press, tortured prisoners, forcibly relocated Indian minorities, and burned some churches, the WCC in 1983 pronounced the Nicaraguan people as "life-affirming" and "commended the Nicaraguan Christian community for its active participation in the building of national institutions and reconciliatory processes leading to peace and justice." In its context, that language could hardly be construed as anything but a blessing on the Managua regime.

Many Christians had supported the guerrillas in their struggle against Somoza, but once in power the Sandinista government launched a campaign of harassment against the churches. It supported a "popular" or "people's" church to lure Catholics away from the traditional or "reactionary" church. This blatant threat to the Catholic Church's authority compelled Pope John Paul II, in August 1982, to accuse the so-called popular church of yielding to political ideologies and sowing discord. The WCC, nonetheless, continued to sympathize with the state-sponsored popular church.

Despite a spate of arrests of Catholic priests and Moravian Church ministers, a WCC team in 1981 could find "no recognizable persecution of the Church" in Nicaragua. After all, the team's report contended, the "Institute of Nicaraguan Cinema, under the Ministry of Culture, has produced a film called *Gracias a Dios y la Revolution* ("Thanks to God and the Revolution") about Christian participation in the revolution."

Three years later, ten Catholic priests were expelled from Nicaragua for what the Sandinistas termed "anti-government activity." The expulsion followed a march by more than three hundred people (five of the ten expelled priests were among them) led by Archbishop Miguel Obando y Bravo of Managua, in support of Father Amada Pena, who was accused of aiding anti-Sandinista rebels. The archbishop said: "This is evidence that Marxism is trying to eliminate the church in Nicaragua because Marxism is the enemy of the Church."

Amnesty International found that the Sandinistas had fabricated the evidence against Father Pena. The WCC Central Committee ignored Father Pena's arrest, and Emilio Castro of Uruguay, who became the new WCC general secretary in January 1985, said that "it is totally unfair to talk about clamping down on religious freedom in Nicaragua."

Nicaragua's Miskito Indians

Shortly after they took over, the Sandinistas began to integrate the indigenous people of the Atlantic coast into the "revolutionary process." Most of the Miskito Indians in the region were Moravian Christians who were living on their ancestral lands. Because they had been ill-treated by Somoza, many of the Miskitos had initially sympathized with the Sandinistas. But during their forced relocation and subsequent persecution, the Indians resisted, and the Managua regime responded savagely. The Indians' civil rights were seriously violated. There is evidence that one-fourth of the 165,000 Indians either have been relocated or are in refugee camps; one-half of the Indian villages have been destroyed; and one thousand Indian civilians are imprisoned, missing, or dead. The Sandinistas insist that the relocation was necessary because of guerrilla activities in the area where the Indians lived, but it began well before there was any anti-Sandinista resistance there.

When the WCC finally took notice of the Sandinistas' war against the Indians, it accepted Managua's explanation of its brutal practices. The Council said that the Nicaraguan government "had demonstrated its openness in acknowledging the inappropriateness of some policies related to the Miskito Indian and other ethnic groups of the Atlantic Coast and is moving toward reconciliation." A "Progress Report" on the Miskito Indians, published by the WCC's Commission of Inter-Church Aid, Refugee, and World Services, suggested that the Indians should cooperate with the government as much as possible.

This is a far cry from the WCC's stance toward the American Indians or their equivalents in other lands. In June 1982, for example, the Central Committee's statement on "Land Rights for Indigenous Peoples" criticized Australia, Brazil, Canada, Chile, Columbia, Guatemala, Mexico, New Zealand, Paraguay, the Philippines, Puerto Rico, and the United States for mistreating ethnic minorities. There was no criticism of Nicaragua.

After a WCC delegation visited Nicaragua in September 1983, it acknowledged that the relocation of the Indians had caused great resentment and that Indian leaders and pastors who protested the policy had been jailed for opposing the revolution. Yet the delegation concluded that "the leadership of the Church supports the revolutionary process and insists that official action taken against its institutions and employees are [sic] not a case of religious persecution."

Indeed, when a WCC delegation visited Nicaragua in September 1983, its report was extremely favorable. The delegation was impressed by "the pluralism in the government, the service of Christians, lay and clergy, at every level of government." As for the media, "Though we are supporters of a free press, we can understand some of the particularities of Nicaragua that argue for present press censorship." The Sandinistas' more oppressive policies could be forgiven because their government was seen as "a sign and transmitter of hope." The WCC delegation recommended that the "churches world-wide . . . learn from the unique experiment being lived by the Nicaraguan sisters and brothers in the Christian communities."

In July 1985, another WCC delegation visited Nicaragua, Honduras, Guatemala, and El Salvador. In Nicaragua, it contacted only government and pro-government groups and some delegates admitted that they had paid little or no attention to opposition groups, such as the Catholic archdiocese led by Cardinal Miguel Obando y Bravo, a critic of the Somoza dictatorship who had become a stern critic of the Sandinistas.

The 1985 Central Committee expressed sympathy with the Sandinistas and noted that the United States was involved "in support for the present government in El Salvador; in promoting the militarization of Costa Rica and Honduras; in economic and diplomatic measures as well as constantly increasing military threats against Nicaragua." Such positions earned the WCC praise from the East German Communist newspaper *Neues Deutschland* for "chastising U.S. policy in Central America."

El Salvador and Cuba

The 1982 elections in El Salvador drew 70 percent of the electorate to the polls despite the leftist guerrilla campaign of harassment and intimidation, and the 1984 elections, which won the presidency for Jose Napoleon Duarte, seemed ample justification of U.S. policy in that wartorn country. Soon after Duarte's victory, right-wing death squad killings dropped off sharply and civilian casualties in the civil war also diminished, if more slowly. American aid to the former military regime in El Salvador had made elections feasible, and thus advanced the cause of democracy there.

The WCC thought differently. In 1983, it made a point of not including the Salvadoran 1982 elections in what it termed "promising signs of life" in Latin America. It also declined to note the failure of the anti-government guerrillas' call to Salvadorans for a "final offensive" in January 1981.

In repeated statements, the WCC has praised the Sandinistas and Fidel Castro and condemned "American imperialism" in Central America. The WCC in May 1980 urged President Carter to "stop support and military aid to military regimes, and to respect the right of the people of Latin

America to seek a new social order that is more just and humane." And in 1981, Washington was again asked "to desist from all direct or covert, present, or planned intervention in the countries of Central America and the Caribbean."

Occasionally, there were hints that countries other than the United States were involved in Central American conflicts, but the WCC's preference for the revolutionary alternative prohibited it from naming Cuba, the Soviet Union, or other Soviet bloc countries as Sandinista allies and active supporters of revolutionary violence in El Salvador and elsewhere in Latin America.

Therefore, in its condemnation of "American imperialism" in Central America, the WCC never mentioned the great disparity between U.S. and Soviet military and economic aid to the region. Moscow subsidizes Cuba to the extent of $12 million a day. There is no comparable subsidy by Washington to any country in the area. In 1983–85, Soviet bloc economic and military aid to Cuba and Nicaragua was $15.85 billion, while U.S. aid to all of Central America was $3.14 billion. By the end of 1984, Moscow was providing ten times as much military assistance to Nicaragua and Cuba as Washington was to all of Latin America. From 1981 to 1986, Soviet military aid to the Sandinistas approximated $1 billion, including $600 million in 1986 alone. In sharp contrast, Washington in 1987 provided $70 million in military aid to the democratic resistance in Nicaragua.

By 1985, the Sandinista army of seventy-five thousand was supported by more than ten thousand military "advisers" from Cuba, the USSR, East Germany, Libya, and the Palestine Liberation Organization. As of early 1987, there were fifty-five U.S. military advisers in El Salvador and about one thousand troops in Honduras to support joint exercises. There were no other U.S. forces in Central America, except for ten thousand troops stationed in the Southern Command in Panama to safeguard the canal and other U.S. interests throughout Latin America, an area ten times larger than Western Europe, where there are 300,000 American troops.

Such easily accessible facts about comparative U.S. and Soviet military and political influence in Central America had little impact on WCC thinking. Nor did reports and books by former victims of Cuban oppression, such as *Against All Hope* by Armando Villadres, published in 1986, which revealed Castro's abuse of prisoners and the persecution of Christians. WCC staff members who visit Cuba are apt to return as enthusiastic about Cuban policy as they were before. Villadres, a Cuban Christian and poet released in 1982 after twenty-two years' imprisonment in Cuba, wrote: "Incomprehensibly to us, while we waited for the embrace of solidarity from our brothers in Christ, those who were embraced were our tormentors." Yet a member of the WCC's Commission on the Churches' Participation in Development had earlier said "that Cuban society shows a lot more signs of the Kingdom of God than many other societies."

Words and Deeds

Unlike the Vatican, the World Council does not base its foreign policy pronouncements on a careful, systematic, or historical study of the issues it addresses. It tends to respond spasmodically to headlines or more steadily to the agenda of the secular Left. Its biblical and theological references are superficial and often contrived. Hence, the statements lack the depth and the coherence of Catholic encyclicals and pastoral letters, or the studies of responsible journalists and secular research centers. Nevertheless, WCC views reflect a dogged consistency in repeating and acting on revolutionary rhetoric.

The WCC's left-wing perspective is not limited to Central America. For example, it insists that Western capitalism and the profit motive are major causes of militarism and war. The U.S. "military-industrial complex" threatens to provoke nuclear war. NATO's doctrine of deterrence is called "as unmitigated an evil as an actual war," though the WCC has conceded that deterrence may provide an "interim assurance of peace."

Thus, the WCC condemned NATO's deployment of medium-range Pershing II and cruise missiles while making no comparable condemnation of the Soviet SS–20s already in place, nor of the relentless Soviet drive to achieve preponderance in conventional forces. The Council opposed the U.S. Strategic Defense Initiative. The posture, advice, and wording of WCC statements on nuclear arms since the mid-1960s closely paralleled that of the secular nuclear freeze movement and the peace campaigns supported by Moscow.

The Council statements on Afghanistan also took Moscow's side, virtually blaming the Soviet invasion on U.S. imperialism, and suggesting that the Soviet occupation of that country could be equated to the deployment of U.S. missiles in Western Europe.

When dealing with Africa, the WCC has attributed the continent's problems to Western capitalism, militarism, imperialism, and racism. It has focused almost exclusively on the sins of "white racism" and shown little or no interest in black dictatorship, violence, or genocide.

In East Asia and the Pacific, the pattern is repeated. The WCC condemns the relatively democratic and market-oriented countries of South Korea and Taiwan for human rights abuses while remaining silent about the much more extensive violations in North Korea and the People's Republic of China. In 1977, when Hanoi's brutal repression (and religious persecution) was forcing hundreds of thousands of boat people to risk their lives to escape, the general secretary of the WCC described the Communist victory as the "most dramatic manifestation of hope in our time."

The revolutionary rhetoric of the WCC is often reinforced by deeds, which have included financial support and operational advice to radical groups in Asia, Africa, and Latin America. From 1970 through 1986, its Program to Combat Racism supported more than a hundred like-minded groups in thirty countries. The outstanding feature of the Program has been its selectivity. Aid has been available for aboriginal organizations in Australia, the National Indian Brotherhood in Canada, and the Malcolm X University in the United States—but not to persecuted minorities in Communist countries, whose existence is conveniently overlooked or unacknowledged.

Almost 65 percent of the Program to Combat Racism grants went to SWAPO, the ANC, and other groups supporting their objectives in southern Africa. The WCC has overlooked the far more brutal and widespread racial/tribal violence elsewhere in Africa (e.g., Nigeria, Uganda, Burundi, Zaire, and Ethiopia), suggesting that it is more interested in promoting radical politics than human rights.

The WCC's financial support of revolutionary groups has not been as influential as the more difficult-to-document participation of WCC staff and consultants in dozens of radical propaganda and pressure groups around the world, including efforts seeking to "raise the consciousness" of peasants in South America, Moscow-sponsored front groups such as the Christian Peace Conference and the World Peace Council, and well-staffed American "think tanks," such as the Washington-based Institute for Policy Studies (IPS).

For a quarter of a century IPS has been the most effective organization in America in providing ideological direction and organizational skills for the New Left. IPS fellows and WCC staff members have close ties over the years in their support for radical causes. Their ideological and action agenda are virtually interchangeable. The Council has reportedly made financial contributions to the IPS and to its Washington Office on Latin America. The WCC was a co-founder with IPS of the Transnational Information Exchange whose members have included these and other left-wing groups: Institute for the Study of Military Problems, Multinational Cooperations in Latin America, World Information Service on Energy, Research Group on Electronics, South African Communist Party, and the African National Congress. There are numerous other informal ties between the WCC and the IPS.

North Korea and Vietnam

Two examples of WCC activity in Asia illustrate the organization's more direct support of Communist regimes or objectives. Its criticism of human rights abuses in South Korea and its silence in the face of far more egregious violations in North Korea have recently found expression in a "peace and justice" offensive in Korea. It should be recalled that the brutal persecution of Christians under the Stalinist Kim Il Sung regime is almost without parallel. In the mid-1950s after the Korean War, most

Christians fled to the south. The regime slaughtered thousands of those remaining. The church was wiped out. Undeterred, in the mid-1980s, the WCC along with the U.S. National Council of Churches (NCC) contacted a recently-established and state-sponsored "Christian Federation of North Korea" to advance "peace and justice in Northeast Asia."

In November 1985, two WCC executives visited Pyongyang to discuss ways to facilitate reconciliation between the churches of North and South Korea and to promote the political reunification of the peninsula. They also visited Seoul and helped persuade the South Korean Council of Churches to advocate, as a first step, the dissolution of the U.S. Military Command and the expulsion of some 38,000 American forces that have been in South Korea since the end of the war to deter a second invasion from the North. The Council also called for the United States to recognize the Pyongyang regime. In short, the WCC effort supported the long-held objectives of the Communist North.

In Indochina, the WCC, again in cooperation with the NCC, also supported Communist objectives. After the fall of Saigon in 1975 there was an exodus of boat people fleeing Vietnam, Laos, and Cambodia. Thousands who could not escape faced a bitter existence. Communist authorities persecuted Christians and Buddhists. City dwelling "undesirables" with no farming experience were herded into New Economic Zones in the countryside. These zones were used for punitive re-education and were virtual concentration camps.

In 1979, Communist authorities in Vietnam and Laos asked the WCC and officials of the NCC to provide material assistance for two New Economic Zones. Operating through the Christian Conference of Asia, the WCC established a $2 million budget for the two projects. Contributions from American churches and other sources were estimated to total $500,000. To avoid the appearance of Communist control over the funds, the grants were channeled through the "Vietnamese Committee for Friendship and Solidarity with American People," an agency authorized by the Hanoi government. The motivation of the WCC and others in this bizarre transaction aside, it is clear that the objectives of a brutal Vietnam regime were served and the needs of many genuinely deserving people were neglected.

The Liberal-Left and Zeitgeist

On virtually every international issue, the WCC has condemned the United States and the West and has advocated, justified, or remained silent on policies of the Soviet Union. And it has backed up its words with deeds. This posture is a far cry from the stance of the WCC when it was founded in 1948. For its first decade, it affirmed Western values and democratic institutions and opposed Nazi and Marxist totalitarian regimes, strategies, and pretensions.

Why has the WCC strayed so far? Why, despite this century's tragic experience with Communist rule, does it consistently employ a yardstick by which the West falls short and the Marxist is seen as promising? Has the WCC become a witting or unwitting pawn of the Communist movement, or worse, a pliant instrument of Moscow? Why has it materially supported the ANC, the Sandinistas, Hanoi, and North Korea?

The two chief reasons for the left-wing lurch are the changing membership of the Council and the triumph of liberation theology in the ecumenical movement. Since the Russian Orthodox Church was admitted into the WCC in 1961 there has been increasing Soviet influence and pressure on Council bodies and deliberations. The more than one hundred Soviet bloc delegates at the assemblies in Nairobi (1975) and Vancouver (1983), along with Third World and Western sympathizers or apologists, were active both in the open and behind closed doors. Evidence suggests that key Soviet delegates were under orders to press the Soviet view on all major issues. WCC leaders knew that each Russian Orthodox delegation included at least one KGB officer. The late Cynthia Wedel, a former Council president from North America, acknowledged this, arguing that it was better to have Soviet delegates in the WCC than outside.

Once inside, Russian Orthodox representatives pressed successfully to increase the number of Soviet bloc staff in the Geneva headquarters. The development of the WCC parallels that of the UN General Assembly and Secretariat, as well as bodies such as UNESCO. In each, the influence of the Soviet bloc states and their Third World friends has dramatically increased since the 1950s.

But this changing geographical composition does not explain the WCC's direction. For the truth is that in recent years the majority of Western delegates have also supported Soviet views. This reflects the impact of an ideological Zeitgeist which has captured many Protestant and Catholic leaders during the past two decades. The Zeitgeist has various names—liberation theology, Third World ideology, the New Left, coercive utopianism, socialism, or—more old-fashioned—Marxism-Leninism. Uncertainty over U.S. involvement in Vietnam and its larger role in the world, and a sense of guilt about America's inability to eradicate discrimination at home combined to produce a resurgence of romanticism and utopianism in the 1960s and early 1970s. Those most affected were intellectuals in the "new class," including academics, the media elite, and mainline liberal Protestant leaders.

It is a frame of mind typified by such writers as Garry Wills, who find that the real United States—its society, culture, economy, political system, and foreign policy—fails to measure up to the critic's vaguely articulated ideals. In his review of Wills's *Reagan's America: Innocents at Home*, published in 1987, Irving Kristol describes the book as "an indictment of

Ronald Reagan, or the American people who elected him, of the American history that shaped him and them. It is an act of revenge by a homeless sophisticate against all those innocents at home in America. Garry Wills no doubt considers himself a patriotic American, but it is a patriotism directed toward some ideal, never existing, still-to-be-born America." Many American ecumenical leaders share this strange alienation from their own political culture.

This largely American-bred ideology both influenced and was influenced by similar trends in Western Europe. In fact, it is no exaggeration to say that Third World ideology was imported from the First World. While decisions within WCC bodies did reflect geographical and cultural differences, there is now a remarkable concurrence in outlook among the delegates from the Soviet bloc, the Third World, and the West. Occasionally, there is some debate and tension, but radicalism now prevails, usually by a substantial majority. Many within this majority passively accept the judgment of the articulate few. But half-hearted votes count as much as those cast by the "true believers," to use Eric Hoffer's telling phrase.

The capture of the WCC by the Left cannot be remedied by organizational changes. Each member denomination has a quota of delegates proportionate to its size and they are chosen by a representative voting device. Within each denomination, political activists are more articulate and hence more often elected to WCC policy-making bodies. These delegates work closely with the permanent staff. They know one another and usually share similar outlooks. So the WCC has become a self-perpetuating community of like-minded people. Members who have different views tend to be cut out. Those who oppose the reigning ideology can challenge it by educating themselves and by running for election to represent their denomination. But the stranglehold of the present social action establishment—the elected delegates, the permanent WCC staff, and the staff-selected consultants and writers—will not be easy to break.

In sum, the WCC has been and is actively engaged in a global network of militant, left-wing groups that give aid and comfort to the Communist cause and run counter to the legitimate objectives of the United States and the West. Perhaps more than any other organization, the WCC is able to provide left-wing totalitarian movements with a cloak of moral sanction and legitimacy. Departing from the great and realistic Judeo-Christian moral heritage, and acting in the name of "justice" and "liberation," the WCC now seeks to advance key elements of the Marxist-Leninist worldview, forsaking any solidarity with the millions who live oppressed under Communist rule, and instead embracing or apologizing for their oppressors. Ironically, it does so even as that worldview is being substantially discarded in the Kremlin itself.

15 Reckless Rhetoric and Foreign Policy

As the debate over our involvement in Vietnam heated up, Martin Luther King made common cause with extreme opponents of U.S. policy in Southeast Asia. Leaders of Clergy and Laymen Concerned About Vietnam, a group of left-leaning activists "who are angry and hate [American] corporate power," persuaded King to sign their radical manifesto and to give an irresponsible speech—which they wrote—at Riverside Church in New York on April 4, 1967. In it, King charged that America was primarily responsible for the Vietnam conflict and that President Johnson and Wall Street were inciting "racism, materialism, and militarism" in a "society gone mad on war." Our government had become "the greatest purveyor of violence in the world today," King stated, testing "our latest weapons on [the Vietnamese], just as the Germans tested new . . . tortures in the concentration camps."

My critique of King's speech and other irresponsible statements appeared in Worldview *(November 1970). Among the many published letters criticizing the article was one from Lutheran Pastor Richard John Neuhaus, then a radical activist who called LBJ a murderer and suggested that the Cold War was a fiction to disguise American imperialist ambitions. Today, after a singularly eventful pilgrimage, Neuhaus is a Catholic priest and an eloquent and wise voice of Christian realism and responsibility.*

* * *

The reckless attack on United States foreign policy by the more extreme American critics during the past few years has far exceeded in shrillness and volume the irresponsible outbursts of the Joe McCarthy era. There has been an alarming deterioration in the quality of dialogue and debate on the vital issues of war and peace. This disquieting development cannot be explained, much less justified, as a plausible response to occasional imprudent official statements that sectors of the press delight in exploiting. The virulent critics who attack the motives of President Nixon and other high officials without substantiating evidence subvert civility and fair play and appear to reflect a profound and perhaps unconscious alienation from the mainstream of Western morality.

The problems confronting the president in Southeast Asia and the Middle East were never more perplexing. The need for rational and responsible criticism was never greater. The president needs and wants the honest criticism or support of all citizens who seek to make their consciences felt by voice or vote. Mr. Nixon's plea that dissenters lower their voices and strengthen their arguments by facts and logic has gone largely unheeded. The dialogue between people and president and between the Executive and Legislative branches continues to be poisoned by inflammatory rhetoric and impassioned code words that confuse the issue, distort the options, undercut the majesty of the presidential office, and erode the president's capacity to act effectively for peace and justice.

The reckless use of the English language is not confined to the libelous and obscene assaults by the Black Panthers, the Weathermen, and other semi-revolutionary or nihilistic groups that explicitly reject majority government, rule of law, peaceful change, and our other cherished democratic practices as "reactionary." Nor is it confined to the increasing number of confused adolescents and junior academics who have adopted with little change the revolutionary rhetoric and abusive epithets of the elitist and authoritarian Left.

The new verbal assault on the character of our political leaders and the integrity of our democratic institutions has made serious inroads on hitherto responsible and rational circles that stood fast against the crude, and by comparison mild, rantings of Joe McCarthy. Today, small but significant sectors of the church, the university, and the mass media have wittingly or unwittingly fallen prey to the demagogic slogans of the new revolutionaries and the catch phrases of the nihilists, though the rhetoric of those with liberal leaning is often more polished and subtle. Yet these learned leaders frequently use emotive terms like imperialism, repression, systemic violence, white power structure, military industrial complex, racism, and mercenaries—terms calculated to condemn rather than to inform. Since these words convey no coherent or accepted meaning, they confuse rather than clarify responsible discourse on Vietnam, civil rights, or the allocation of federal resources. It is tragic when academic and religious leaders lay aside rational argument in favor of the inflammatory code words of an Angela Davis, a Rap Brown, or a Jerry Rubin.

Sweeping pejorative terms are almost always employed without factual evidence to support their use. The *New York Times*, other influential media, several Senators, and some religious leaders have accused the U.S. Government of subsidizing "mercenaries" in Southeast Asia, with the clear implication that this practice is immoral. There are honest differences about the wisdom of our material support of Korean or Thai volunteer units in South Vietnam to fight aggression (i.e., organized military forces that violate an international border to forcibly overthrow an existing government) from North Vietnam, but the introduction of the pejorative term "mercenaries" hardly clarifies the problem. In simple English, a mercenary is one who volunteers his military services against reimbursement. The term, of course, takes on a different meaning when the volunteer fights on alien soil. But even here the *Times* supported the mercenary units from two dozen countries who performed military service in the UN expeditionary force in the Congo in the 1960s. Perhaps for the *Times* and Senator William Fulbright the volunteers they don't like are mercenaries and the mercenaries they do like are "volunteers"! Is this kind of double-talk a reflection of a split-level ethic, or merely a subtle ploy to persuade by catch words rather than by honest argument?

Out of their deep concern for building a better world the contributors to religious journals and drafters of church pronouncements, particularly in the Protestant community, have increasingly fallen into the prose of protest and the rhetoric of revolt without supporting empirical evidence. The emotive symbols are not limited to angry clerics like Father Daniel Berrigan, William S. Coffin, Jr., and Robert McAfee Brown, but have found their way into wider church circles. Ever since the Detroit Conference on Church and Society in October 1967, for example, the vague and ill-defined term "systemic violence" has been used to indict the "system" rather than to identify specific faults in American society. The term, and its several variants, implies that poverty or functional illiteracy are manifestations of violence imposed by "the system." This debases the language and makes serious moral discourse almost impossible. There are important moral differences between poverty and violence. Where is the evidence that poverty is "caused" by the system? What about the great variations in individual ability, initiative, and responsibility? And what is meant by "the system"—the U.S. Government, local government, the market, labor unions, local prejudices?

The militant civil rights leaders, who are increasingly attempting to internationalize their concern for people of color, have been the heaviest users of unsubstantiated accusatory code words and slogans. As early as 1963, the then relatively moderate Martin Luther King asserted that Birmingham's "white power structure" left the "Negro community with no alternative" but to violate the court injunction against a planned demonstration. He seemed to overlook the obvious alternative of awaiting the verdict of a higher court. The very term "white power structure" suggests a collective racial indictment that ignores compassion among the whites and callousness among the blacks. Does it mean all whites in the "structure" are equally guilty? What does it mean?

In addition to the code words designed to incite by appealing to the confused, frustrated, and guilt-ridden, there is the more refined but equally dishonest device of pretending to present facts, but actually distorting or falsifying them. Both forms of reckless rhetoric found ample play in a remarkable speech of Martin Luther King in Riverside Church on April 4, 1967. In this strange and somewhat uncharacteristic lecture, King sought to weld the civil rights and peace movements into a single crusade. Apparently ghost written by Clergy and Concerned Laymen Concerned About Vietnam, King said the moral "burden" of the Nobel Peace Prize and the "burnings" of his "heart" compelled him to speak out against the U.S. military involvement in Vietnam.

Bowing at the outset to "the ambiguity of the total situation and the need for a collective solution," King quickly leaves ambiguity behind and accuses the United States of the primary if not exclusive responsibility for the Vietnam conflict and its termination. From then on, the speech is a simple devil-theory indictment, with Washington and Wall Street the arch villains, supported by the pervasive white "racism, materialism, and militarism" in an American "society gone mad on war."

King makes no positive references to the U.S. Government, but makes numerous attacks upon the motives of American leaders. Let him speak for himself. The Vietnam war devastates "the hopes of the poor at home" and exacts an "extraordinarily high" proportion of deaths upon the American poor in battle. We are sending "young black men . . . crippled by our society" to fight for a "freedom" in Vietnam they have been denied at home. America has used "massive doses of violence to solve" its problems and "my own government" has become "the greatest purveyor of violence in the world today."

Our "madness" in Vietnam, King continues, where "we may have killed a million [presumably civilians] mostly children," must stop. We "test out our latest weapons on them, just as the Germans tested out new medicine and new tortures in the concentration camps of Europe." We herd Vietnamese into American-made "concentration camps." They wander into the hospitals, with "at least twenty casualties from American firepower for each Viet Cong–inflicted injury." We, not the Communists, have become the "real enemy." We justify our brutality and inhumanity because of alleged "aggression from the North." How dare we "charge them with violence while we pour new weapons of death into their land?" On all vital issues, King is vague or ambiguous, except in his condemnation of the United States.

The outrageous charge that the U.S. forces killed one million civilians was a nugget of Communist disinformation and was picked up by American peace groups without verification. (In a private conversation with a Protestant clergyman, he told me and several others that he was the author of the civilian casualty section of the King speech. When asked where he got the figure of one million, he replied, "We in the Movement make up facts" to suit our needs. Perhaps he didn't mean this literally, but those who heard him were appalled by his apparent nonchalance toward relevant facts.) Unfortunately, many civilians have been killed by air strikes against military targets in spite of extensive U.S. efforts to evacuate the population beforehand—perhaps as many as one-tenth the number King mentioned—but each death has been unintentional and regrettable. And every proved case of rape or murder by a U.S. soldier—the number has been small—is punishable under our strict code of military justice. The enemy, in contrast, from the beginning has deliberately killed civilians, including the throwing of grenades into schools and hospitals. The Hanoi and National Liberation Front forces have murdered, tortured, and kidnapped tens of thousands of civilians. In 1960–61 alone, the Viet Cong murdered 6,130 and abducted 6,213 important persons. If America were under similar subversive assault, 72,000 prominent U.S. citizens would be murdered or kidnapped annually. King was silent about this massive atrocity.

America's soul, says King, is in danger of becoming "totally poisoned" as long as we continue to destroy "the deepest hopes of men the world over." In Vietnam, we "have no honorable intentions." Our minimum objective is to make it "an American colony" and "our maximum hope is to goad China into a war so that we may bomb her nuclear installations." How can he say this when successive presidents have made it crystal clear that our fundamental intention is to make Southeast Asia safe for self-determination and peaceful change? There is ample room for debate on whether our government has chosen the best available means for achieving these objectives. But certainly they are honorable, though their fulfillment may be beyond our capacity to ensure.

Vietnam, says King, is "but a symptom of a far deeper malady within the American spirit." We "are on the wrong side of a world revolution. During the past ten years we have seen emerge a pattern of suppression" by Washington that uses "U.S. military 'advisers'" in Latin America to protect "the privileges and the pleasures that come from the immense profits for American investors who have no concern for the social betterment of the countries." To get on "the right side of the world revolution, we as a nation must undergo a radical revolution" against "racism, materialism, and militarism." We "must support" revolutions "all over the globe." Because of our "morbid fear of Communism" we have become "anti-revolutionaries."

This remarkable speech—its blunt, lopsided, unfactual, and unfair attack upon the United States; its more subtle praise for the Communist and revolutionary forces of "liberation"; and its frequent use of Communist clichés and slogans (in contrast to King's customary biblical allusions) could have been drafted in Moscow, Peking, Hanoi, or Havana, except for one thing—no seasoned Communist propagandist would have dared to be so utterly one-sided in his condemnation of America in addressing a Western audience for fear of a credibility gap, even among the guilt-ridden and näive itching to hear the worst about America.

It is difficult to determine the extent King was being used by Clergy and Laymen, but his name appears with that of John C. Bennett, Edwin T. Dahlberg, Harvey G. Cox, John Wesley Lord, Paul Moore, and other clerical signers of a statement introducing a book, *In the Name of America*, published by the organization in 1968. This statement, like the King speech, is a highly distorted, one-sided, unfactual, and inflammatory critique of U.S. policy in Vietnam, which vaguely condones or excuses the murder, torture, kidnapping, and other forms of brutality by the Communist forces while charging the United States with the "indiscriminate killing of civilians" and other "war crimes."

The *In the Name of America* statement asserts that the "persistent" U.S. "violation of the rules of war . . . must inevitably induce the enemy to feel a compulsion to commit similar acts of moral lawlessness." Certainly the signers were not unaware that the Communists used torture, murder, and kidnapping as acceptable instruments of "wars of national liberation" long before U.S. combat troops ever arrived in Vietnam. Further, the so-called "documentary" section of the book fails to provide convincing evidence that U.S. forces persistently or even frequently violated the rules of war.

Whatever his motives, King's speech gave aid and comfort to the enemies of peaceful change in Southeast Asia as well as to their allies in Moscow and Peking. It directed anger against the U.S. Government—perhaps the major temporal force for peace in the world. It pronounced an indirect benediction upon the revolutionary and nihilistic agencies seeking to destroy the foundations of Western justice and freedom.

There is, of course, some injustice in our society and some justice in Communist states, but in the West, and particularly in the United States, the political institutions and practices of fair play and freedom have seldom found fuller expression. In the endless quest for dignity and justice, we Americans are sustained by a long tradition of humane law and the Anglo-Saxon conscience against all forms of human exploitation.

Whatever one might think about the necessity or wisdom of America's involvement in Vietnam, it should be clear that there are morally permissible limits to support or dissent of the Government's policy. *The same rules apply to both sides.* Every president needs constructive criticism, but none deserves irresponsible attacks that imply that he is less concerned about peace and justice than Clergy Concerned or the leaders in Hanoi and Peking.

King's speech seriously violated the moral limits of public debate and advocacy. His unrelenting attack on American society and government, his distortions and falsehoods, all presented in the garb of self-righteousness, was a disservice to the American people and a service to forces of revolutionary violence. It is difficult to escape the conclusion that this speech and other equally extremist and ill-informed statements by well-intentioned "children of light" have harmed the prospects for a responsible exercise of U.S. power abroad.

King's attempt to join the causes of "freedom" and "peace" appears to have had the effect of sowing confusion in both camps, thereby making more difficult the achievement of equality under law at home and a sound policy toward the Third World.

Since there is a close psychological and moral connection between incendiary rhetoric, anger, and overt violence, it would be fair to assume that King's speech contributed to the very violence he so frequently deplored. While he cannot be held responsible for the orgy of black terror that followed his death in 1968, it is true that he anticipated some of the angry slogans of the Black Panthers and the Students for a Democratic Society (SDS), both of whom have supported their violent words with bombing and other brutal acts of terrorism against innocent persons, all in the name of revolutionary justice.

The most serious verbal and political assault on reason, civility, the rules of evidence, the rule of law, and majority government comes mainly from spokesmen of America's extreme Left. In sharp contrast, the extreme Right poses little danger to the survival of our fundamental democratic institutions. Never strong in the United States, a radical Right that advocates or apologizes for violence finds virtually no support in the church, the university, or the mass media, and has no connection with foreign-based groups seeking to undermine U.S. foreign policy.

In its attempt to destroy the university, the SDS during the 1969–70 academic year was directly involved in 247 arson cases, 462 personal injury incidents, and 300 other violent acts on American campuses. Both extremes are morally repugnant and socially destructive in any democratic country where the channels of political organization and peaceful change are open and responsive to the majority will, where minority rights are guaranteed under law, and where the right of peaceful dissent is protected by the government.

Reckless rhetoric, especially from U.S. senators and other influential leaders, has diminished the capacity of the president to act wisely. It comforts our enemies and confuses our allies. The damage is increased by major sectors of the press and electronic media which over-report the absurd, magnify America's shortcomings, and exaggerate the popular support of extremists. Has the time not come for religious leaders dedicated to truth, for academics dedicated to reason, and for humane citizens dedicated to justice to insist, at least for themselves, on a quality of dissent and support equal to the seriousness of the problems we confront?

PART FOUR

The Evil Empire

In 1983, President Ronald Reagan called the Soviet Union an "evil empire." It was courageous for a Western leader to say this out loud, though his blunt words hardly came as a surprise to the long-suffering peoples of the USSR and the captive states of Eastern Europe. Since childhood, I had known that the Soviet government was evil because my parents often spoke of the "godless Russian regime" that killed Christians and destroyed churches. Even before Alexander Solzhenitsyn revealed the magnitude of Stalin's genocidal paranoia, I regarded Soviet totalitarianism as an implacable enemy of religious and political freedom. The confrontation between Communist tyranny and the West was, at root, a religious struggle between those who acknowledged God and those who denied God, those who honored freedom and those who distrusted it.

My European experience intensified my determination to fight Soviet and, later, Chinese Communism. My public support for firm U.S. policies to contain the Soviet Union and China and my critique of apologists for Stalin or Mao earned the reproach of the anti-anti-Communists.

16 *New Gods for Old*

After three years in postwar Europe, I resumed my studies in Christian ethics at Yale Graduate School. I compared the Marxist dream of a classless society to what I had seen in Soviet-controlled Hungary, Czechoslovakia, and East Berlin. It became clear to me that Communism was a seductive secular faith that challenged Christianity and Judaism at every level. In the essay that follows, I said that "American Communists are strangers in their own land." Appearing in a Methodist student magazine, Motive *(March 1951), this piece contrasts Christianity and Communism and assesses the role of the churches behind the Iron Curtain.*

*   *   *

In the story of Aladdin and His Wonderful Lamp there is an odd incident in which the Moorish magician walks through the streets shouting, "New lamps for old! Give me your old lamps and I will give you new!" The Moor's strange offer sounds like the fairy tale it is. Yet today in real life there is a Great Magician, far more powerful than Aladdin's pretended uncle, who is offering not to some small village but to the entire world new gods for old. "Give me your worn-out, useless gods and I will give you new ones, gods who march where men are marching and who speak the language of the modern world." Millions have already forsaken their old gods and are faithfully doing the bidding of the new.

Marshal Stalin is the new Great Magician and the shibboleths of world Communism are the new articles of faith. Nearly 800 million people have voluntarily or by force turned to Communism for salvation. To those who have done this for idealistic reasons, Communism has become their new religion. Like any other religion it demands of them complete loyalty. The former gods must be done away with. Dostoevsky's Grand Inquisitor said, "Put away your gods and come worship ours, or we will kill you and your gods."

One cannot fully understand Soviet Communism without recognizing it as a living religion in active competition with other faiths for the loyalties of men. It is an inverted form of Christianity, a secularized faith with a counterpart to every element in the Judeo-Christian tradition. Communism has established a full-fledged church complete with a theology, a mythology, a symbolism, and an obedient membership. Responding to its Great Commission, the Communist Manifesto of 1848, it has sent missionaries throughout the world. Moscow's envoys equal the thorough training and discipline usually associated with the Jesuits. The Soviet faith proclaims the Communist state as its god and Josef Stalin as its messiah.

The prophetic writings of Marx and Lenin have become the sacred scriptures, the infallible rule of faith and practice. Deviation from the orthodox dogma of dialectical materialism is authoritatively defined by the high priests in the Politburo. Just as the proclaimed orthodoxy of some Christians often bears little resemblance to the teachings of Jesus Christ, so contemporary Communist dogma is frequently the antithesis of original Marxism. Heresy, however defined, is dealt with speedily and without mercy. The forced confessions, torture, and execution of heretics behind the Iron Curtain today are tragically reminiscent of the persecution of heretics by zealous Christians in earlier times.

Communist theology has transformed the Kingdom of God into the future classless society where all men will live as brothers and war will be no more. Even though the Kingdom has not yet come, the Soviet Union is already the promised land to which the faithful everywhere must give uncompromising loyalty. By their very confession of faith American Communists are strangers in their own land. The Kingdom will be ushered in by the Messianic wars, culminating in the final struggle between Communism and decadent capitalism. The devil is variously portrayed by the Kremlin as Trotsky, Churchill, Tito, Chiang Kai-shek, Truman, and "the Wall Street imperialists and warmongers," the last being the favorite incarnation of the moment.

The Deification of Stalin

The dogma of Stalinism is buttressed by a colorful symbolism and a growing mythology. The cross of Christianity has become the hammer and sickle in the Communist revolution. The star of Bethlehem has become the red star of Moscow. The blood red of the class struggle flows through the drama, pageantry, and ritual of party functions and public demonstrations. The dove of peace has become Picasso's dove of psychological warfare and military aggression. Stalin has already been immortalized and deified.

As messiah, Marshal Stalin must be accorded continual adoration. On page one of a recent issue of *Pravda*, for example, his name appeared 101 times. In addition to Josef V. Stalin and Comrade Stalin sixty-eight times, "dear and beloved Stalin" appears seven times and "great Stalin" six times. Other variations were "great leader of entire mankind," "Stalin the genius," "protagonist of our victories," and "faithful fighter for the cause of peace."

Very rarely appearing in public, Stalin is kept before his subject millions from Berlin to Shanghai by the ubiquitous portraits of his smiling countenance. Showing him as he looked two decades ago, this official picture gives credence to the myth of his immortality. Musing benevolently beneath his noncommittal mustache, Big Brother looks down upon every man, woman, and child from billboards, public buildings, schoolrooms, offices, factories, and homes from Moscow to the remotest hamlets of Manchuria. Despite Communism's pretension of building the classless society, the gulf between Big Brother and his several hundred million little brothers is vastly greater than that between president and worker in the United States. In terms of political control, however, the Fuehrer of world Communism is closer to his subjects than Truman's picture on a television screen is to us.

Communists offer salvation to all who accept their dogma and promise to be faithful to their holy Catholic Church, the Communist Party. Rigorous catechetical instruction and a probationary period precede full party membership. Demanding duties, plus excommunication for backsliding and lukewarm members, keep the ranks of the faithful small and well-disciplined. Even in a Communist state many are called, but few are chosen. Stalin's first commandment is: "Thou shalt have no other gods before me." The second is like unto it: "Love thy Party above thyself." This total dedication to something beyond one's self is the essence of religious faith. Hence, firm Communists are more religious than those Christians whose allegiance to God is diluted by secular loyalties.

What then has happened to Christianity behind the Iron and Bamboo Curtains where the state has become god and the Communist Party the only true church? The answer is obvious. The church like any other social force must be made subservient to the state, neutralized, or liquidated. The political, social, and educational influence of the Orthodox, Roman Catholic, and Protestant churches has been effectively emasculated through a series of "church laws." When churchmen were considered actual or potential opponents to the regime they were sent to concentration camps or liquidated.

Christians Have Five Choices

While freedom of religious worship is constitutionally guaranteed in the USSR and its satellites, genuine religious liberty exists only to the extent that it is not exercised. No individual or group is permitted to express the implications of the Christian faith for the political order unless such expression conforms to the established policy of the regime. In these severely limited circumstances of the deified state, Christians have taken five different courses of action that can be identified as five kinds of churches:

1. *The political church* clings to certain outward symbols of Christianity while actually embracing the state as its god and preaching dialectical materialism as its gospel. When this occurs Communism has become its religion.
2. *The state church* solves the problem of living in a totalitarian state by making the regime sovereign over secular life and the church over the spiritual. It does not deify the ruling elite, but it is difficult for the state church to maintain its spiritual independence because it is under constant pressure from the Party to become a full-fledged political church.
3. *The otherworldly church* includes those who accommodate themselves to Communism by insisting that religion is exclusively a matter for the next world. While the Party favors politically innocuous faith of this sort over a hostile religion, it naturally prefers unqualified support.
4. *The underground church* consists of those who feel they must make an absolute witness against an absolute state. Its members, like pre-Constantine Christians, live in the catacombs and cooperate with resistance forces seeking to overthrow the evil regime.
5. *The silent church* refuses to bless the regime or to consign religion to the next world. Its members do not join the underground resistance movements. Recognizing their tragic limitations, they chart a middle course, living for the day when a more complete expression of their faith will be possible. By prayer, charity, and holy living they make a silent witness against the totalitarian state.

None of these five courses for Christians in Communist lands permits them to express fully their faith. In the non-Communist world, especially in Southeast Asia and Africa, the struggle between Christianity and Communism for men's loyalty is deepening. The old gods have failed. The tired, confused, and hungry people are reaching out for new ones. Some of them will hear the Christian message. Many more will be exposed to the incessant cry of the Great Magician, "New gods for old! Give me your old gods and I will give you new!" Millions have heeded this cry, some haltingly, some with enthusiasm.

17 *Religious Repression in Russia*

After the 1917 Russian Revolution, Lenin was determined to root out every vestige of Christianity, which he regarded as feudal superstition blocking the path to "scientific socialism." He ordered the destruction of 70,000 churches and the execution of thousands of Russian Orthodox priests. These drastic measures were later relaxed by Stalin to enlist the clergy during the Great Patriotic War against Hitler, but persecution, discrimination, and anti-God propaganda continued. The following selection appeared in the Christian Century, *September 6, 1950.*

*   *   *

Forty miles north of Moscow stands the imposing Truitski monastery founded by St. Sergius. Inside the massive walls of this 14th century landmark three great Easter services were held in April of this year with all the traditional splendor of the Russian Orthodox Church. The main ceremony was conducted in the Cathedral of the Assumption, whose high walls gleamed with lavishly painted gold and silver icons illuminated by the white and pink candles of worshipping believers. The air of the massive edifice was heavy with incense and fragrant with the scent of freshly cut pine. Thousands came to celebrate the miracle of Christ's resurrection. What happened there took place throughout the Soviet Union whenever there were churches. Today, as a thousand years ago, Easter is the greatest religious festival of the year in Russia.

In June 1949, Cyril F. Garbett, archbishop of York, who had visited postwar Russia, said that the Orthodox Church is "probably more vigorous today than it has been for centuries. The churches of Russia are crowded, and persecution there has ceased." There have been other optimistic reports about the "new liberal policy" toward organized religion adopted by the USSR in the early days of World War II. But the facts paint a different picture.

"Freedom of religious worship and freedom of antireligious propaganda" are guaranteed in Article 124 of the Soviet Constitution. This "freedom," like all other civil liberties in a monolithic totalitarian state, is granted not in principle, but under the condition that it will not be "used" against the regime or party. An individual has civil rights as long as he chooses not to exercise them! Further, Communism, combined with intense Russian nationalism and imperialism, has itself become a demanding religion which will tolerate no other gods before it. Within this context the apparent contradiction between the avowed atheism of the state and toleration of religious worship can be readily understood.

The basic policy of the USSR toward organized religion can be divided into two stages—the direct attack against the church (1917–38) and the flank attack against the church (1939–50). The earlier period was characterized by severe movements against organized religion, including three waves of antireligious campaigns with varying degrees of persuasion. The confiscation of church property and the work of the League of Militant Atheists are well-known.

Hitler's Attack Prompts a New Policy

In January 1939, the USSR inaugurated a new policy toward organized religion, and particularly the Orthodox Church. All forms of "direct action" against religion were abolished and antireligious propaganda was toned down. Shortly after Hitler's invasion of Russia, the two chief atheist periodicals, *Bezbozhnik* ("Atheist") and *Anti-religioznik*, suspended publication. Stalin's relations with church leaders became more cordial. In November 1942, Nikolai, metropolitan of Kiev and Galicia, was appointed a member of the Extraordinary State Commission for the investigation of German war crimes.

Stalin permitted the appointment of Sergius as acting patriarch of Moscow and head of the Orthodox Church on September 8, 1943. A week later the *Journal of the Moscow Patriarchate* began to appear, and a month later the Holy Synod announced plans for starting an Orthodox theological seminary in Moscow. The Orthodox Church was accorded a preferential position when a State Council on Affairs of the Orthodox Church was created in 1943. In June 1944, a similar council was set up for the non-Orthodox faiths—Roman Catholic, Moslem, Jewish, and Protestant sects. In 1945, two state decrees were issued; one returned half the church property confiscated in 1932, and the second restored certain ancient religious shrines.

Some Western churchmen hailed the Soviet concessions to the church as the dawn of a new day, the sign of a change of heart in the Kremlin. Those who knew of the close ties of the pre-Soviet Orthodox Church to the state remained critical. If the church permitted itself to be used as a political instrument of the czarist regime, might it not conceivably play the same kind of role under a new master? Ten years have passed and the answer is clear: the men of the Kremlin are as anti-religious as ever, and the "liberal" policy is only a different and perhaps more effective attack against virile religion.

Flank Attack Against the Church

That religion is being attacked today under the guise of church-state cooperation can be documented from Soviet sources. The recent concessions do no more than implement the existing constitutional guarantee of "freedom of religious worship," which officially prohibits churches from engaging in "any kind of propagandizing, moralizing, and educational activity." Such "freedom" falls far short of the World Council of Churches' definition of religious liberty, which includes the right to express one's "religious beliefs in worship, teaching, and practice, and to proclaim the implications of his beliefs for relationships in a social or political community."

The attitude of the Kremlin toward religion itself has not changed. Official statements continue to affirm the antireligious character of the Soviet regime and its leaders. In 1948, the *Young Bolshevik* warned against the "chains of religious superstitions" and said that some Communist youth were "slipping into the path of a conciliatory un-Marxist and unparty attitude toward religion." The activities of the former League of Militant Atheists have been taken over into a broader program of "political and scientific propaganda" that ridicules all religion. On June 28, 1948, *Pravda* complained that "the insufficiently aggressive character of scientific propaganda is manifested from time to time in the failure to emphasize the struggle against religious prejudices."

If the basic antireligious position remains, why was the new policy introduced in 1939? There were four major reasons. *First,* the church was no longer considered a potential locus of organized opposition to the regime. The political power of the Orthodox Church had been effectively emasculated in the first two decades of the direct attack. If the church had not been entirely converted to Communism by Stalin, it had at least been neutralized. *Second,* Orthodox and other religious leaders showed an increasing disposition to cooperate with the regime. This trend was greatly accentuated by World War II. Churches became centers of war bond campaigns and large sums were contributed to buy fighting planes. At least two tank columns were financed by the faithful and named after Orthodox saints.

Third, world public opinion, sharpened by the USSR's participation in the United Nations, pressed for a more liberal policy toward religion. Moreover, Stalin was forced to answer Hitler, who, for propaganda reasons, restored the Orthodox Church in Berlin at his own expense and in nineteen other German cities at the expense of the Nazi state.

Fourth, Stalin came to recognize that organized religion, especially the Orthodox Church, could be forged into an effective instrument of Soviet domestic and foreign policy. The church could be more than a morale-building factor in war. It could be made to serve the Soviet Union's expansionist policy in the Balkans, where "Holy Russia," symbolized by the revival of Orthodoxy, would have far greater appeal than "Red Russia."

Mouthpiece of Soviet Policy

The tragic record of the Russian Orthodox hierarchy during and since the war bears eloquent testimony to the acuteness of Stalin's calculation. For all practical purposes the Orthodox Church is the "spiritual" mouthpiece of Soviet policy, while the other churches give varying degrees of sanction ranging from parroting the Kremlin's propaganda to being politically innocuous. A few quotations will illustrate the extent to which the Orthodox Church has become a tool of the regime. The first full-scale general assembly of the Russian Church in January 1945, sent this message to Stalin: "We send our first greetings to the government and to the highly honored Josef Stalin and our thanks to the government for its aid to the church. . . . The church prays for the speediest victory of the USSR . . . over the enemy and for the successes of the Red army which is led and inspired by the great leader, Marshal Stalin."

Three years later, the Soviet army was blessed by the Orthodox Church as being "just" and entirely different from the armies of capitalist countries, "which are bent on aggression." The *Journal of Moscow Patriarchate* continued, stating that the Red Army is "a real force to resist the evil of imperialists and neofascists. . . . The church is praying for victory for the Soviet army, defender of peace throughout the world for many years to come." In his 1950 Easter message Patriarch Alexis said: "Beyond the boundaries of our homeland, which heads the movement for peace, extensive preparations for war are being conducted. . . . However, alongside the actions and utterances hostile to peace, the international struggle for peace is growing . . . and more and more millions of people are joining this holy struggle which, we believe, will end in victory."

The complete identity of these pronouncements with those of the Kremlin is appalling. But even more tragic is the Orthodox Church's conception of its own status. In hailing Stalin on his seventieth birthday, the Orthodox hierarchy thanked him for the "unrestricted freedom of worship and preaching" and for his "favorable consideration and cooperation" toward the church. Here is the pathetic spectacle of a Christian church, which has completely surrendered its independence to an atheistic and tyrannical dictatorship, looking up into the face of its fuehrer and thanking him for "freedom"!

How much religious liberty is there in Russia today? If you mean freedom to attend worship services, this does exist (and since 1917 has existed) for adult nonparty members who live close enough to a functioning church. The number of churches has been severely reduced since the Communists came to power. If you mean freedom to teach one's faith and to express it ethically in a meaningful social context, religious freedom does not exist in the USSR. In short, the Soviet policy toward organized religion has been and continues to be guided by this threefold formula: The church like all other social forces must be liquidated, neutralized, or made subservient to the totalitarian state.

18 Détente, the KGB, and Solzhenitsyn

In the mid-1970s, Soviet leader Leonid Brezhnev stepped up subversive activity in the Third World simultaneously with his efforts to reach détente—or peaceful coexistence—with the United States and the West. A primary instrument for achieving these contradictory objectives was the KGB, the "sword and shield" of the Communist Party. In his KGB: The Secret Work of Secret Soviet Agents *(1974), John Barron revealed many of the little-known facets of Soviet domestic and foreign policy, details verified by recently opened Kremlin archives. This review of Barron's book focuses on the Soviet Union's arrogant assault on intellectual dissent and religious faith. Published in the* Washington Star-News *(February 24, 1974), it anticipates the Soviet duplicity and cynicism that helped prompt Mikhail Gorbachev's reforms.*

* * *

Détente is a many-splintered thing. With one hand Moscow reaches out for American wheat and trade concessions. With the other it exiles Alexander Solzhenitsyn for telling the truth about Soviet repression. In one gesture it sends its artists and performers to the United States. In another it threatens to strip Valery Panov, former star of Leningrad's Kirov Ballet, of his citizenship because he wanted to migrate to Israel.

It may still be fashionable in some circles to overlook or downplay unpleasant realities that do not fit the illusion of détente. But after a great Soviet writer has been declared a nonperson and with almost daily reports of repression against other Soviet dissidents, it is increasingly difficult to turn a blind eye to the moral and political schizophrenia of the Soviet regime.

Or perhaps it is not the Soviets who are afflicted with a split-level ethic, but we who are confused by split-level perception. Many of us want to believe that the era depicted in Solzhenitsyn's *The Gulag Archipelago* is in the distant past and that the post-Stalin leaders have moved toward a new and less repressive political order. We want to think of the Soviet Union as an ordinary state operating by ordinary rules. When the rules are dramatically broken we are shocked and disappointed.

What kind of a political system does Moscow have today? Is it significantly different from that of the Stalin era? Important light is thrown on this question by John Barron's impressive book about the KGB—the massive clandestine agency created by Lenin to be the "sword and shield" of the Communist party, the instrument of the Politburo to enforce its will and confound its opponents. The KGB is the current manifestation of the state security apparatus originally established in 1917 as Cheka. Today, says Barron, "the KGB has the same relationship to the Politburo under Brezhnev that the Cheka had with the Council of People's Commissars under Lenin."

Solzhenitsyn, Valery Panov, and millions of other Soviet citizens have felt the brutal, often lethal, force of the KGB and its predecessors. The vast concentration camp system portrayed in *The Gulag Archipelago* and the present system of exile are their handiwork. At least 20 million Soviet citizens have died in the ruthless pogroms of the secret police. But silencing or neutralizing troublemakers is only a small part of the KGB's far-flung assignments.

A State Within a State

As an instrument of totalitarian control, the KGB has no peer, past or present. If the Soviet Communist Party is a state within a state, the KGB is in fact the "sword and shield" of the party. It penetrates every nook and cranny of Soviet life to control the words, actions, tastes, loyalties, and even thoughts of Soviet citizens.

As the obedient agent of the party, the KGB operates a border guard, an elite military force of 300,000 equipped with tanks, artillery, and armed ships. In 1965, KGB patrols captured more than 2,000 Soviet citizens attempting to escape. The KGB oversees the entire military establishment and has agents and informers assigned to the Ministry of Defense and in every military headquarters and unit down to the company level. "The slightest evidence of ideological deviation among the military can provoke swift KGB retribution." It was only in the late 1960s when "the military finally persuaded the leadership that it would be impractical to use atomic weapons in a future internal struggle" that the KGB relinquished custody of nuclear warheads.

Through its complex of directorates, the KGB penetrates the entire state bureaucracy, starting with the Politburo. "The KGB today probably has more officers and alumni in positions of power than at any other time in Soviet history."

Of the seventeen Politburo members in 1973, three have spent "significant portions of their careers in the apparatus." While the full-time staff of the KGB may be as small as 100,000, its influence is vastly expanded by a network of informers—from a concierge in Kiev to the U.S. ambassador's chauffeur in Moscow—at home and abroad that may run into the millions.

The KGB controls job and housing permits, internal and external travel, and all forms of police activity. Former KGB chairman Alexander Shelepin runs the Soviet trade union organization. The KGB monitors industry and the economy to detect and bring to justice perpetrators of crimes such as "incorrect planning," unauthorized private enterprise, and blackmarketeering.

It keeps watch on education from kindergarten through the university and on all academic and research institutes. In 1970, the KGB launched a large new division, the Fifth Chief Directorate, "to annihilate intellectual dissent, stop the upsurge in religious faith, suppress nationalism among ethnic minorities, and silence the *Chronicle of Current Events*, an underground journal."

The following year it established a special Jewish Department to intensify infiltration into Jewish circles to curtail emigration of educated Jews and to silence protest. The KGB oversees 70,000 full-time censors who control the printed word. It works through the criminal justice system and operates special KGB "mental hospitals" where prominent citizens who do not conform to "official doctrine" are taken for forcible treatment, including the use of brain-washing drugs.

All foreigners in the USSR, including tourists, are placed under the surveillance of the KGB. In 1963, an American visitor, Professor Frederick C. Barghoon, who was on open academic business in Moscow, was drugged, falsely accused of espionage, arrested, and held hostage by the KGB for the release of a real Soviet spy, KGB agent Igor Ivanov, who was caught red-handed by the FBI in New York. Professor Barghoon was released only after the public intervention of President Kennedy.

The long tentacles of the KGB reach out in support of Soviet objectives around the world. The clandestine service penetrates and uses the Foreign Ministry and all other official Soviet agencies overseas. KGB agents accompany all Soviet scientific and cultural groups abroad. As a rule, its harshest and most brutal coercion is directed against Soviet citizens at home. These tough professionals, says Barron, have a kind of respect for Americans and Northern Europeans, a respect not accorded Asians, Arabs, Latins, or Southern Europeans, though this did not prevent the abuse of Professor Barghoon or shooting with nitrogen mustard gas a German technician in Moscow who had just cleared his embassy of KGB microphones.

Foreign Operations

While there are superficial resemblances between the operations of the KGB abroad and those of the CIA and other Western clandestine services, there is one profound difference. The KGB is in the service of a totalitarian regime ideologically committed to the neutralization or destruction of non-Communist governments. Soviet objectives are different from Western objectives, and the KGB often operates by different means. In dramatic detail, Barron relates several KGB operations, some successes and some failures.

"Officers of the KGB and its military subsidiary, the GRU (Chief Intelligence Directorate of the Soviet General Staff), ordinarily occupy a majority of embassy posts," as much as 80 percent in some Third World countries. In Washington, the FBI estimates that over 50 percent of Soviet representatives, including trade officials and *Tass* correspondents, work for the KGB. In addition, many agents use the UN headquarters in New York and the Soviet Embassy in Mexico City for operations against the United States. For several years Secretary General U Thant had as a personal assistant, Viktor Lesiovsky, a KGB agent. Probably half of the 207 Soviet citizens employed by the UN Secretariat are KGB agents, and at least one was from the division responsible for assassination and sabotage.

In 1971, there were 108 official Americans in Moscow and 189 Soviet citizens with diplomatic immunity in Washington. "In Moscow the total number of accredited diplomats from 87 non-Communist countries was 809, while the Soviet Union had 1,769 accredited diplomats in the same countries." A revealing, top-secret KGB textbook obtained by Western intelligence, *The Practice of Recruiting Americans in the U.S.A. and Third Countries*, is reproduced almost in its entirety in the book's appendix.

KGB operatives abroad have made their share of mistakes and many of them have been caught and expelled. In September 1971, the British government publicly expelled 105 KGB and GRU officers, but only after Moscow had "contemptuously ignored" London's quiet request to desist from a campaign to "suborn politicians, scientists, businessmen, and civil servants." "Between 1970 and July 1973, twenty governments found it necessary to expel a total of the 164 Soviet officials because of their illegal, clandestine actions." A list of some 1,400 "Soviet Citizens Engaged in Clandestine Operations" is carried in the book's appendix. It includes only names of persons "positively identified by two or more responsible sources."

In earlier years, the Soviet Union followed a policy of supporting only those terrorist groups abroad that its agents controlled or thought they controlled. Today, the KGB trains and materially supports many more terrorist organizations, including some operating against black and white regimes in Africa, several in Latin America, the Quebec Liberation Front, Palestinian groups, and terrorists in Northern Ireland.

Many terrorist leaders are trained in the Soviet Union, but assistance to their organizations is frequently assigned to the clandestine services of Cuba, Czechoslovakia, East Germany, Poland, and Hungary. At the KGB's behest, the Cubans have trained both Palestinian and Irish terrorists. KGB operatives are also active in encouraging, supporting, and organizing "peace demonstrations," riots, and other disturbances to discredit regimes whose character or policies Moscow opposes.

Soviet Disinformation

One of the lesser known KGB activities is the "disinformation" program designed to discredit individuals, institutions, and governments by disseminating forgeries, literary hoaxes, and false information and by committing acts such as murder for psychological-political effects. The operations of a master disinformation specialist, known as Victor Louis, make interesting reading. "Twice Louis has been received at the White House: by Vice President Humphrey on October 17, 1966, and by Presidential Adviser Henry A. Kissinger on November 13, 1971."

The book is filled with demonstrably true stories that will fascinate the spy enthusiast. But precisely because it is interesting and well-written, some people may be tempted to dismiss it as a romanticized thriller. That would be a mistake. John Barron has produced a harmonious blend of journalism and scholarship to the credit of both professions.

This serious book is fully documented. For four years it has been painstakingly researched. Most of the facts came from former KGB agents, but in virtually all instances information was corroborated by independent sources cited in the chapter notes. "We believe we have interviewed or had access to reports from all postwar KGB defectors except two," says the author. Western intelligence services were consulted to verify data.

Barron had substantial research support from the *Reader's Digest*, of which he is a senior editor, including the monitoring of publications in thirteen languages by various *Digest* offices abroad. From beginning to end, the book rings true.

Coming at this time of intensified KGB efforts to suppress dissent, the book makes a singular contribution to understanding the limits of cooperation between the two superpowers. It lends valuable perspective to what appears to be current contradictions in the Soviet system.

The root problem is not the KGB, but the totalitarian character of the Soviet regime. And the evil in totalitarianism is its arrogance, its insistence that the party has the whole truth in all spheres of man's existence, the answer to all problems. Unlike Western political leaders, the men in the Kremlin are not constrained by a transcendent ethic, a law beyond the party and independent of it. The Communist party is not only the state, but God. Soviet leaders invoke terms like "the rule of law" and "human rights," but they tend to be code words used to manipulate their own people and confuse adherents to Western values.

This arrogance crushes the aspirations of the people who live in a totalitarian state. The KGB seeks to create spiritual isolation among Soviet citizens by making every person fear his neighbor or member of his family. This is why Pavlik Morozov, a fourteen-year-old boy who denounced his father in 1932 for giving refuge to fleeing peasants, was made a Hero of the Soviet Union. The father was summarily shot and enraged peasants lynched the boy. In 1965, a statue of Pavlik was erected in his honor. The house where he betrayed his father is a Communist shrine, and today he is held up as an ideal for every worthy citizen to emulate.

Barron insists there can be no full "détente until there is an end to this massive KGB aggression" against the Soviet people and against persons, institutions, and governments around the world. The "deferential silence about KGB oppressions and depredations," he says, must be shattered. Governments, he adds, should refuse to accept known KGB agents in the guise of diplomats and should "summarily expel the legions of KGB officers entrenched in foreign capitals."

Barron acknowledges that some of the brutality of the Stalin era has passed. In earlier days, Solzhenitsyn would not simply have been stripped of his citizenship and expelled. He would have been shot. But the basic moral (or immoral) foundation of the Soviet system has not changed. The spiritual pretension and political arrogance are still there. If this recognition means that anti-Communism is becoming respectable again, all to the good.

It is precisely because the Soviet Union is a tyranny that we Americans should seek intellectual and cultural dialogue with Soviet citizens. "Our society," says Barron, "can survive the clandestine activities of the KGB, but their society cannot ultimately withstand the free flow of ideas."

19 Hobnailed Boots Have No Ideology

In 1984, the year depicted in George Orwell's Nineteen Eighty-Four, *some Western intellectuals suggested that America was rapidly becoming Orwell's grim portrait of "Big Brother." They were wrong. Actually, when Orwell wrote his novel in 1948, he was courageously unmasking Soviet totalitarianism in an era when liberal political illusions dominated the literary landscape. (This piece appeared in the* Washington Times, *February 22, 1984.)*

*   *   *

Were George Orwell alive today he would be perplexed and dismayed by the persistent misreading of his *Nineteen Eighty-Four*. His "dark vision" written in 1948 is less an ominous forecast of a totalitarian West than it is a valid picture of the Soviet Union then and now.

Both *Animal Farm* and *Nineteen Eighty-Four* are exquisite extrapolations of his personal and distinctly unpleasant encounter with Stalin's political tactics and ruthlessness during the Spanish Civil War. In sharp contrast, most Western intellectuals were thoroughly confused over the morality and politics of that strange conflict. Mr. Orwell's chief contribution to political understanding is not a prophetic portrayal of a grisly future but a steely-eyed picture of a brutal present.

Mr. Orwell was a British socialist, but he was not a Marxist, much less a revolutionary. This he made plain in the words of O'Brien, the party torturer-programmer assigned to brainwash Everyman, Winston Smith: "One does not establish the dictatorship in order to safeguard a revolution; one makes a revolution in order to establish the dictatorship. The object of persecution is persecution. The object of torture is torture. *The object of power is power.* [Emphasis added.] Now do you understand me?" Winston was beginning to understand; O'Brien added, "We are the priests of power."

Mr. Orwell understood the essence of pure and uncluttered totalitarianism. Left or right made little difference. Totalitarianism is the achievement of absolute power by a self-anointed ruling elite and the total submission of each subject to this elite. Revolutionary rhetoric and ideological slogans are merely tactics to gain and maintain power. The party uses them to confuse, frighten, and control "their" people, not to enlighten, ennoble, or serve the people. The Soviet rape of Afghanistan is devoid of doctrine. A hobnailed boot smashing a human face has no ideology.

Since power must be absolute, the party has to be god—omnipotent, omniscient, and omnipresent. Big Brother must be all-powerful, all-knowing, and everywhere present. There can be no other gods, no other loyalties, no other centers of devotion, beauty, respect, or love. "God is Power," and power is god. True religion must be abolished, neutralized, or made subservient to the party's god.

On January 30, 1951, while I was a graduate student at Yale Divinity School, I wrote on the last page of *Nineteen Eighty-Four*: "Finished reading this amazing book with its tremendous psychological and political insight into totalitarianism, especially the Soviet variety. How shall we fight this monstrous evil, this demonic incarnation?"

Three years (1945–1948) in post-war Europe working among German prisoners of war had given me a first-hand look at the unspeakable evil wrought by Nazi tyranny. I visited Dachau, Bergen-Belsen, and other Nazi concentration camp sites. I also had a close-up view of the then only partially disclosed cruelty of the Soviet regime. I talked with the living skeletons of German POWs arriving from Russia and saw the anxious faces of displaced persons and refugees streaming from the East.

Though the enormity of Stalin's Gulag was not yet known, I vividly recall seeing the gripping truth painted on a wall in Brussels: "Hammer and Sickle = Swastika." I had gone to Europe in September 1945 with few illusions about the apostasy and ruthlessness of the 20th-century political religions, but I was shocked by what I saw and was forced to imagine.

The Nazi empire lay in smoldering ruins along with its monstrous pretentions. But the Soviet Union, aided inadvertently—and tragically—by our alliance with Moscow to defeat Hitler, had already devoured its war-ravished neighbors in Eastern Europe. And it was on the prowl to subvert and conquer Western Europe, China, and the Third World. I knew then what Mr. Orwell knew: Soviet messianic power was a grave and unrelenting threat to Western civilization and the precious values we derive from the Judeo-Christian moral tradition.

Mr. Orwell's real message to the West today is: Recognize the massive and multifaceted threat to human freedom and dignity for what it is, and be prepared to pay the price in moral, political, and military terms to prevent the "evil empire" from extending its domain.

PART FIVE

The Apocalyptic Premise

Since Hiroshima, guilt-ridden atomic scientists and other neopacifists have warned of a nuclear apocalypse. Manhattan Project director J. Robert Oppenheimer quoted the Hindu Living Gita, *"Now I am become Death, the destroyer of worlds." Doomsday statements were also made by historian-diplomat George F. Kennan, writer Jonathan Schell, and many mainline church leaders. Perhaps the most absurd formulation of the apocalyptic premise appeared in Schell's* The Fate of the Earth *(1982). He asserted that atomic bombs threaten planetary doom, and he called for a new man, a new politics, and the abolition of the state itself. "The task is nothing less than to reinvent politics: to reinvent the world."*

Underlying the views of these apocalyptic pacifists was the premise that nuclear weapons had introduced a radically new and evil force in history. They were half right. The force is new, but it is not evil. Nuclear energy, like all technology—and science itself—is morally and politically neutral. It can be used for good or ill, to liberate or enslave. And like fire, nuclear energy will be with us until the end of time.

Like most nuclear pacifists, Schell exaggerated the destructive potential of atomic weapons. By calling for one-sided restraint by the United States, he and others played into the hands of the Soviet disinformation campaign to persuade Washington to reduce unilaterally its nuclear arms stockpile. On no other issue has the irony and arrogance of misplaced virtue been more flagrant.

Nuclear hysteria reached a high of sorts in the mid-1950s debate over America's nuclear testing program and in the early 1980s debate over a nuclear freeze. In both cases, the issues were confused by a breast-beating moral equivalence among Western intellectuals and liberal religious leaders who failed to distinguish between the egregious evils of Soviet tyranny and the imperfections of American democracy.

20 Ethics, Calculation, and Nuclear Arms

In an article, "Foreign Policy and Christian Conscience" (The Atlantic, 1959), former ambassador to Moscow George F. Kennan, ignoring reliable scientific data, exaggerated the long-term risks of radioactive fallout and opposed American testing. "Who gave us the right, as Christians, to take even one innocent life?" he asked rhetorically. My response (Worldview, October 1959) insisted that a careful assessment of technical realities was an essential element in ethical decisions. Experts at the time estimated that a full-scale nuclear war could kill as many as 80 million people, a thousand times more than the most extreme estimates of long-term genetic damage from American and Soviet tests. As it turned out, U.S. testing enabled us to build smaller tactical weapons with less fallout and strengthened NATO's deterrent capacity, thus helping to prevent a nuclear war.

*　　*　　*

Writing in *The Atlantic* last May, George F. Kennan had some advice for moralists concerned with nuclear weapons and international politics. Much of his advice is good. He warns against "pouring Christian enthusiasm into unsuitable vessels . . . designed to contain the earthly calculations of practical politicians." His lucid statement on the limits of the United Nations and foreign economic aid and his comments on the moral ambiguities of decolonization are wise.

But when Mr. Kennan deals with nuclear weapons and bomb tests, he falls into the very legalism and moral absolutism he denounces so effectively when he analyses the UN, foreign aid, and colonialism. Perhaps the chief reason for this contradiction is his ambiguous attitude toward calculation in world politics. Pointing to "the irony that seems to rest on the relationship between the intentions of statesmen and the results they achieve," Mr. Kennan concludes that the statesman "is best off when he is guided by firm and sound principles instead of depending exclusively on his own farsightedness and powers of calculation." If it is difficult for the statesman to calculate with assurance, how much more difficult is it for the "Christian onlooker"?

He understands the limits of human calculation in politics, but he fails to recognize that calculation is both a political and moral necessity. Calculation is the rational process by which men relate human and material resources to their goals. Calculation is the life blood of politics and the heart of ethics. Calculation is the bridge between the given and the desired, between facts and dreams.

Some moralists have attempted to bridge the gulf between political necessity and high moral principle by "middle axioms" or practical rules which can guide the citizen or statesman in relating the *is* to the *ought*. But who really believes there are laws or axioms for every occasion? And if there were, who would know which one to apply?

Even "simple" human problems such as rearing a four-year-old child are too complex to be handled by a legal sliderule. A mother must take many calculated risks every day as she attempts to anticipate the probable effect of alternative lines of action on the character of her child and on the serenity of her household.

If calculation is a necessity in child rearing, it is an even greater necessity in the incredibly more complex business of world politics. Yet, Mr. Kennan advises the government, apparently as a political and moral alternative to calculation, to use "good methods" rather than "bad ones." He says we can be "as sure that the good methods will be in some way useful as that bad ones will be in some way pernicious." A government should be guided by "firm and sound principles instead of depending exclusively" on its "powers of calculation." "A government can pursue its purpose in a patient and conciliatory and understanding way, respecting the interests of others and infusing its behavior with a high standard of decency and honesty and humanity . . . sheer good manners will bring some measure of redemption to even the most disastrous undertaking." What help are Mr. Kennan's manners and principles to a statesman wrestling with the present Berlin crisis? How could they have helped the South Koreans when their country was attacked in 1950?

If Mr. Kennan has not confused manners and morals, it seems clear that he has confused manners with policy—a dangerous error for a person in a position of responsibility. In politics the substance of the response counts most. The manner of the response may be important, but it is not a substitute for policy.

Principles, goals, and values are inescapably involved in all decisions. The principles may be good or bad, the goals worthy or unworthy, the values enduring or ephemeral. These intangible ingredients are present in every political act whether the actor is a Hitler, a Khrushchev, or an Eisenhower. No statesman can make policy from principles alone. He must relate goals and ideals to the political facts of life. This means calculation.

Incidentally, Jesus of Nazareth apparently assumed that statesmen had a moral obligation to calculate, to analyze the balance of power between two hostile camps. "Or what king, going to encounter another king in war, will not sit down first and take counsel whether he is able with ten thousand to meet him who comes against him with twenty thousand? And if not, while the other is yet a great way off, he sends an embassy and asks terms of peace." (Luke 14: 32, 33.)

Mr. Kennan does not follow his own advice. He makes particular policy proposals for particular problems and he bases his proposals on calculation. His controversial "disengagement" proposals for easing tension in Europe and his more recent implied proposals for ending nuclear tests are not based on moral maxims alone. They emerged from a rational attempt to relate facts to values, which certainly included a calculation of the probable consequences of competing policies.

The larger fact is that everyone instinctively makes moral-political calculations. The real issue is not: shall we calculate or shall we not, but: what factors shall we take into account when we calculate and what weight shall we give them?

Neither statesman nor citizen can make politically wise and morally responsible judgments by consulting only his goals. He must consult the facts—the universal facts about man and history, and the particular facts about a political situation. The dream without the fact leads to this-worldly nightmares or to otherworldly escape. The fact without the dream leads to boredom and despair.

Mr. Kennan's nonchalant attitude toward facts and calculation in the area of nuclear weapons leads to less than adequate moral and political judgments. After quoting a "random sampling" of press reports on the dangers of nuclear fallout, Mr. Kennan concludes: "But whoever gave us the right, as Christians, to take even one innocent life?" His implied judgment that all bomb tests under all circumstances are morally wrong seems to be based in part upon a picture of fallout danger that bears little resemblance to the findings of leading research institutions in this country and abroad.

Expecting the Worst

Earlier contributors to this debate in the pages of *Worldview* have also made rather unqualified generalizations about the destructiveness of nuclear weapons. John Cogley says: "Modern war means that the defended will die as surely as the defenders; it means that nothing will remain for the aggressors to grab." Walter Millis seems to share the same view: "We are faced with a situation in which *any* war seems likely to escape entirely from the control of man . . . so far as we know now, *resort* to [nuclear weapons] can never promote defense." Stephen G. Cary says: "To talk of limited war in the atomic age is to try to turn back the clock. When survival is at stake . . . it appears the height of folly to talk of applying reason to the situation. War's necessity is terrible and, once released, its course lies almost wholly beyond the compass of those who seek to make it a servant of their ends." He adds: "To suggest that it is possible to control it requires a rosier view of human nature than I am able to support."

Apparently Mr. Cary overlooks the fact that control and restraint in international politics, and human relations generally, do not depend mainly on the "goodness of men" but rather in a balance of forces and interests among sinful men. Both the Communists and the United States showed great restraint in the Korean War. Neither side used atomic weapons. The Communists did not use submarines and we did not bomb beyond the Yalu River. It was in the interest of both sides to exercise restraint. Is it too much to suggest that in a future conflict, even in the nuclear age, there may be important factors on both sides which in the name of prudence, even expediency, make for restraint? To suggest that this is a possibility does not imply a "rosy" view of man. Rather it acknowledges that God can make the self-interest of hostile nations to praise Him.

Many other morally concerned persons tend to expect the worst in the event of serious hostilities and to exaggerate the worst. According to the best projections available, the *maximum* loss of life from a general nuclear war involving the full present capacities of the Soviet Union and the United States would be 20 percent of the earth's population. The number killed might well be considerably less. There would be practically no casualties of any kind south of the equator. If the United States had a comprehensive fallout shelter program in operation, millions of additional American lives probably would be saved. These estimates include persons killed by blast and radioactivity.

Among the eighty percent who would survive such a war, the natural genetic damage to the human race might be doubled in areas of heavy fallout. Any injury is always an individual tragedy. But genetic damage resulting from tests or general war or both, like the number of automobile deaths in the United States, is well within the range of what a civilized society is prepared to tolerate. Every human life is precious in the eyes of God, and even one innocent death or crippling disease is one too many. Any decent human being recoils from the horror of a lynching or a nuclear war.

What national security policy should the United States pursue? Faced with the possibility of a catastrophic nuclear holocaust on the one hand, and a dynamic and expansionist Sino-Soviet bloc on the other, shall we make a radical change in our present policy, as many pacifists and neo-pacifists advocate?

Not a Radically New Situation

My comments are directed primarily to the neo-pacifists who insist that we are confronted by an entirely new situation as a result of the techno-logical revolution. Mr. Cogley says: "We must begin to think of living in a world without war. With the development of modern weapons, war has lost its last semblance of logic." Mr. Kennan says: "I am skeptical of the meaning of 'victory' and 'defeat' in their relation to modern war between great countries." Today, says Mr. Cary, "the old rules and the old assump-tions no longer apply."

The assumption that we are in a radically new situation, upon which these appraisals are made, is itself subject to question. The basic realities of politics among sovereign states have more in common with previous eras than they have differences. The main elements then and now are the visions, interests, and demands of morally ambiguous men projected from the vantage point of national power. The new element is technolog-ical, but even the drastic discontinuity in this realm does not mean that there has been a corresponding discontinuity in the history of man, much less in human pride and passion.

If calculations of those in the best position to know are reasonably ac-curate, the worst nuclear war possible now would leave 80 percent of the earth's population alive and healthy. Such a war is probably the least likely contingency, but it seems to be the only one that the neo-pacifists talk about. It is possible, perhaps probable, that World War III will be less destructive than World War II, or even than World War I. Many students of military strategy believe that it is militarily redundant and politically unwise to knock out population centers, and that a future war may well be more concentrated on military targets, such as air and missile bases, than was World War II.

And there is nothing in history or in Judeo-Christian ethics that makes a general nuclear war inevitable. We may have limited wars, limited by political objectives, and therefore limited by the weapons employed. Ko-rea was limited. So was every violent conflict since the end of World War II. We can have limited conventional wars like Korea. We could have a limited atomic war. Limited wars are dangerous because they contain the seeds of a general conflict, but the possibility of prudential restraint should neither be overlooked nor counted upon. In short, there are many possible forms of military conflict. None of them is attractive, but cer-tainly a limited engagement is far less unattractive than an unlimited holocaust.

What does this mean for moralists and statesmen who are wrestling with the nuclear weapons question? Does it mean we should destroy our stockpile of atomic weapons regardless of what the USSR does? Does it mean that we should unilaterally stop U.S. nuclear tests? Without dealing with specific policy questions, I am gratified that the United States has extended a self-imposed nuclear test ban until the end of 1959 to give our negotiators at Geneva more time to reach a viable ban agreement with Moscow. I hope that an effective test-ban agreement with adequate international inspection provisions can be hammered out.

One final point. In addition to emphasizing the moral necessity of calculation based upon the most significant relevant facts, one is obligated to examine with equal thoroughness the probable consequences of the policy he advocates and the policy he rejects. A policy designed to save ten thousand persons from possible future death by radioactivity which had the actual effect of inviting the death of ten million persons or the enslavement of a hundred million persons today could hardly be called morally responsible or politically wise.

21 Can Nuclear War Be Just?

A full-scale nuclear exchange between the Soviet Union and the United States would have been a catastrophe for both superpowers and for the world. And a limited nuclear war would have been very dangerous. But neither happened. The bombing of Hiroshima and Nagasaki, which killed far fewer civilians than the fire-bombing of Tokyo and other Japanese cities, may have saved a million or more Japanese and American lives.

During the Cold War, theologians passionately debated whether a "just nuclear war" was possible. Opposing the nuclear apocalyptics, I argued that building an American nuclear arsenal, threatening to use it, and actually firing nuclear weapons could, under certain circumstances, meet the requirements of the Christian just war doctrine. (My views appeared in Christian Ethics and Nuclear Warfare, *edited by Ulrich S. Allers and William V. O'Brien and published in 1961.)*

* * *

I believe the traditional just war theory is relevant in principle to the nuclear-missile age; that morally sound and politically wise judgments must be based upon an adequate understanding of technical, military, and political facts; and that the nature of the world struggle rules out either capitulation to Communist demands or preventive war—i.e., a preemptive strike—as morally viable responses for the United States.

Every political decision is a moral decision because it affects for good or ill human beings whose essential dignity is rooted in God. Foreign policy decisions are incredibly complex, but their complexity does not excuse the statesman or citizen from his responsibility. Every decision involves at least six interrelated elements.

First, moral decision must have a point of reference that transcends the arena of action. For the Christian this point of reference is God and God's will for men. Although finite man can never know fully the will of the Infinite, he must attempt to ascertain it and act accordingly. This reference provides the basis for a moral standard above the conflicting purposes and interests of men and nations. Morality cannot emerge from the context of action, but it must be relevant to it.

Second, God's will for men must be translated into specific social and political terms. The unachievable ideal of love must be translated into achievable or almost achievable goals of order, justice, and freedom. Goals somewhat beyond present attainments give statesmen and citizens a sense of perspective; they evoke humility without despair and hope without illusion. This is what is meant by "the relevance of the impossible ideal."

Third, moral decision requires an understanding of the essential facts of the situation which calls for action. It is at this point that contemporary moralists often fail. To analyze helpfully the problems of national security in a nuclear age, one must understand the limits and possibilities of nuclear weapons systems; the relative nuclear capabilities of the two chief adversaries; and the probable military, political, psychological, and biological consequences of nuclear weapons under a variety of potential uses. One should be aware of the likelihood of different kinds of nuclear and conventional war. All these possible military contingencies must be seen in their basic political context. One must also understand the military and political developments that tend to strengthen stability and to deter nuclear war.

Fortunately, there is a growing body of literature on military doctrine and political theory that throws light on the problems of arms, arms control, and mutual deterrence. Many moralists who presume to speak on nuclear weapons are only vaguely aware of this serious writing by specialists who represent different disciplines, and who are as morally sensitive as the moralists. This is not to suggest that the specialist, statesman, or citizen has nothing to learn from the moralist.

An Understanding of History

Fourth, moral decision is instructed by the actor's understanding of history. Sound decisions must be based upon the concrete facts found in the *New York Times*, the insights developed in the serious literature, and the larger "facts" about the nature of man and history.

Christianity takes history seriously because it holds that man has a measure of genuine freedom. And because it takes history seriously, it takes politics seriously. World politics can be defined as the inevitable struggle of human egos projected from the vantage point of sovereign political power. The persistent conflict of purpose, will, and interest among nation states is an extension of human nature with its opposing elements of "original sin" and "original righteousness." History is ambiguous because its chief actor, man, is morally ambiguous. The outcome of history is open. Its deepest meaning and its fulfillment lie beyond history. This understanding of history enables one to be concerned without being strident, serene without being nonchalant.

Many moralists today are tempted to embrace an apocalyptic ethic based on an apocalyptic view of history. We are living in an era of galloping technology, the argument runs, and man must match the quantum jump of science with a quantum jump in moral stature and political behavior. This is wishful thinking. The raw stuff of history is human nature, and man has amply demonstrated through the millennia that he stubbornly resists reform, to say nothing of drastic reconstruction. History is characterized by continuity, not by radical discontinuity. The political decisions and institutions of tomorrow will closely resemble those of today. Human nature precludes a giant step. Technology has advanced by giant strides, but the essential moral capacity of human beings remains the same. Science has added a new urgency, if not a new dimension, to the old problem of conflict among sovereign powers; but the old wisdom is as relevant to the problems of today as it was when it was first recorded. The strident call for a radical change in man or in politics is an escape from responsibility.

Fifth, moral decision must look both to the present and the future. Moralists can indulge in the luxury of focusing exclusively on the future with impunity, but statesmen must come to grips with the present. A wise politician will have one eye cocked to tomorrow, but he is morally obligated to be preoccupied with the urgent requirements of today. A sensitive statesman cannot escape the inevitable conflict between short-term demands and long-term hopes. But he would be derelict in his duty if he sold out the present for the future, if he sacrificed the security and welfare of the people from whom he draws his power in the name of a more distant (and uncertain) world of peace and justice. His first duty is to the present generation, not to generations yet unborn. Yet, he must seek to reconcile the demands of the present and future so that neither constituency is wholly sacrificed for the other. As a general guide the political certainties or near certainties of the present have a prior claim over the uncertainties of the future.

When a man dies in a just cause, he dies to help the present generation. Hopefully his death will also benefit future generations, but this is by no means certain because the generation he helps to save may betray his sacrifice. There are also many other unforeseen developments which can dash the hopes of a person who sacrifices a present good for a future good.

As this is being written, President Kennedy is facing a perplexing decision—should he order nuclear tests in the atmosphere because the Russians have resumed such testing? He must balance the advantages of such testing to the present security position of the United States against the disadvantages of raising the level of fallout. According to generally accepted estimates, the fallout from all nuclear tests (prior to the recent Russian series) has increased up to five percent the total biological damage now resulting from the natural level of radiation. This is unevenly spread, and some areas may for a brief time have a radiation count 40 percent greater than normal. But, at some future time if accumulated fallout reaches the critical level and constitutes an actual hazard to a great number of human beings, the decision to resume atmosphere-poisoning tests would be much more difficult to justify than it would be today.

Sixth, moral decision requires calculation. No responsible decision, however simple, can be made without calculation. There are always conflicting values and demands that must be resolved in the light of one's transcendent reference, one's knowledge of the relevant facts, the resources available to the actor, one's understanding of what is possible, and one's assessment of the competing claims between the present and the future. Most day-by-day decisions of citizens are relatively simple. They are made largely on the basis of habit and custom. Statesmen confronting the novel and complex problem of nuclear weapons in the face of Communist power, pretension, and fanaticism must engage in complex calculations. There is no moral slide rule, code, or set of maxims that can lift the burden of this painstaking calculation.

To assert the moral necessity of calculation is not to espouse an ethic of calculation. Nor is it a contextual ethic which, incidentally, is a contradiction in terms. Calculation has its limits. After engaging in all the analysis that is humanly possible the citizen or statesman must act, recognizing that many of the elements of decision are not subject to precise measurement and that prediction in politics is tricky at best.

A Responsible Just War Theory

The recognition of the dynamic interrelationship of these six elements in moral decision points to an ethic of responsibility as opposed to a code ethic, a single factor ethic, or a perfectionist ethic. An ethic of responsibility is always a multi-consideration ethic in which the actor responds to the will of God, to the needs of his neighbor, and to his own conscience in the light of the existential situation and the human and material resources available.

An ethic of responsibility so defined is compatible with a just war doctrine and is relevant to the contemporary security dilemma. Versions of the just war theory that are legalistic or make quantitative applications seem to me irrelevant because they simply cannot take into account all the essential factors in moral decision. Consider several examples of the legalistic approach.

Item: If self-defense is a requirement of a just war, how does one decide which side struck first? In the total struggle we call the Cold War, this is often a legal impossibility. What about provocation? What about client wars, unconventional war, and subversion?

Item: If the waging of war by an entity having legitimate authority is a condition of a just war, how is legitimacy determined? Was the United States military action in Korea, prior to endorsement by the United Nations, legal? Suppose our Government intervenes in a direct military way in Laos? In Cuba? What about indirect intervention? Any government possessing the capacity to act effectively against injustice thereby has the responsibility to act.

Item: If only minimal and incidental harm to civilians is permissible in a just war, how can one draw a meaningful line between civilian and military in an era of total war? Suppose the killing of 100 soldiers and 1,000 civilians had the intended and actual result of saving 10,000 or a million lives? Is this just? The incidental evil should not, of course, outweigh the intended and actual good made possible by military action—here is where complex calculation enters in. But the traditional legal distinction between combatants and noncombatants would be more difficult to observe in a nuclear war.

Rejecting these legalistic and cultural-bound applications of the just war theory, I would like to suggest three fundamental standards for the just use of coercion that I believe are relevant to nuclear war, conventional war, and unconventional conflict.

First, the cause must be just. The maintenance of order, justice, and freedom is worth fighting for. Their preservation is not always guaranteed by the physical survival of the state. For the Christian, the sheer physical survival of one's nation is not itself a just objective. Some states may have become so corrupt that they are not worthy of defense—Nazi Germany, for example. The national interest narrowly defined leads to smugness, national self-righteousness, or fanaticism. The national interest, when defined in terms broad enough to take into account the legitimate interests and rights of other nations, is a morally acceptable guide for statesmen. The physical security of the United States is worth defending because justice and freedom are guaranteed by that security.

The destruction of tyranny and the curbing of injustice are also worthy causes for the use of coercion, as long as the evil consequences of such coercion do not outweigh the benefits. This does not mean that military action, to be justified, must immediately usher in a new era. It does mean that it must create conditions conducive to greater order, justice, and freedom.

Second, the means must be just. Appropriate means must be found to achieve the just objective. Politically or morally inappropriate means may betray the just intention. Can nuclear weapons ever be placed in the category of just means? Unless one is a pacifist who believes that the use of all military coercion is morally inadmissible, there is no categorical answer. It depends on many factors, some of which stubbornly resist calculation. If one could be sure, for example, that a nuclear attack on a military target would result in the death of one thousand Russians, but without further destruction, and would prevent the Soviet conquest of West Germany, would such an attack be just?

The point here is not to get into quantitative analysis (which can never be wholly ignored), but rather to show the irrelevance of the absolutist or legalistic approach to the question of means. Some people accept the possible just use of small nuclear weapons, but rule out 20-megaton weapons and above. Such a "mass destruction" weapon, they argue, could under no conceivable circumstances be justified. Yet some exclusively military targets, such as industrial regions, cover many square miles. Ironically, the use of such a weapon on such a target would respect civilians more than an old-fashioned, World War II blockbuster on industry located in a residential area. (I am not justifying, much less advocating, the use of 20-megaton weapons!)

In short, the means must be as precise as possible to achieve the desired objective and should result in minimal collateral destruction. The degree of restraint exercised should be determined by the moral and political requirements of the just cause, by respect for the innocent (an exceedingly difficult category to define), by the specific military objective to be gained, by calculations of probable error, and by the requirements of effectiveness.

Third, the coercion should be effective. A statesman with a just cause should choose means of coercion that have a reasonable chance of success. He should plan to win and expect to win. If he lacks the will or the resources to succeed, he should not undertake the action. This is simple prudence. In a situation where the power of one nation may be hopelessly outmatched by an adversary bent on conquest, the statesmen of the weaker nation may take up the sword in the name of honor—"Give me liberty or give me death." This type of sacrifice is usually more appropriate for an individual patriot than for the responsible government of a state.

If the statesman has moral reservations about the justice of his cause or serious inhibitions against the use of coercion, his acknowledged or unacknowledged feeling of guilt may restrict the effective use of force and thus invite failure. Perhaps misgivings on the part of some of Mr. Kennedy's advisers about the use of force against Cuba were responsible for the Bay of Pigs fiasco in April 1961. A half-hearted use of coercion is often more destructive than abstention on the one hand or a marginal over-use of force on the other. If the cause is just, it has a moral right to succeed.

It can be argued that these three requirements for the just use of force give little precise guidance either to the statesman or the moralist. My comments are not intended to provide answers to specific policy questions, but rather to counter the moralists who think that precise answers can be given in advance or that certain concrete acts of coercion are categorically and unconditionally wrong in all circumstances.

In the real world the dilemma is faced most poignantly by the statesman who must reconcile political necessity with ethics. If he is morally sensitive, politically wise, and well-informed, his decisions are more likely to be just than if he is insensitive, stupid, and ignorant. High-ranking American political leaders for the most part are intelligent, well-informed, and morally concerned; but moral concern is not an adequate substitute for moral wisdom. It is at this point that theologians and moral philosophers should be of assistance. But I fear that we, who in some sense can be called "religious leaders," will have to put our intellectual house in order before we can contribute to the political wisdom demanded by these days of unprecedented peril.

22 *Arms Control vs. Disarmament*

As the debate over nuclear arms intensified, the neopacifists and others insisted that the best way to avoid war between the superpowers was to disarm—to reduce drastically the level of missiles and warheads—preferably by formal international treaties. But as scientists and statesmen wrestled with the political and technical complexities of the Cold War, a new arms control approach emerged, one that emphasized the balance—rather than the level—of nuclear weapons between the United States and the USSR. My introduction to a symposium I edited, Arms and Arms Control *(1961), advocated this "new arms control consensus." The symposium included the diverse views of John Kennedy, Nikita Khrushchev, Hubert Humphrey, Herman Kahn, Henry Kissinger, Bertrand Russell, Hans Bethe, Edward Teller, Fred Iklé, Morton Halperin, and others.*

*　　*　　*

The current upsurge of interest in arms control and disarmament in the United States is a remarkable phenomenon. The growing stream of articles, pamphlets, and books, both scholarly and popular, threatens to overwhelm the concerned citizen whose desire to understand the complexities of world politics is sometimes pre-empted by his eagerness to do something now to prevent nuclear war. This new concern coincides with the most serious and comprehensive disarmament effort the United States Government has yet undertaken.

It is ironic that this new interest in arms control should be gaining momentum at a seemingly inauspicious time. It follows a decade and a half of fruitless negotiations to control or eliminate weapons by international agreement, and it coincides with the collapse of an intense and protracted effort to achieve a limited measure to mitigate danger—an agreement for an inspected ban on nuclear-weapons tests. And it comes at a time of increased intransigence and hostility in Soviet foreign policy.

This widespread concern is a fresh recognition that something more feasible than drastic disarmament should be undertaken now to reduce the risk of a nuclear holocaust. Three major approaches to making nuclear war less likely or less destructive, or both, are found in the current literature. Two minority views cluster around incompatible poles. A third middle position represents an emerging consensus on what should be done to enhance international security.

At one end of the spectrum are nuclear pacifists who are convinced that the destructive power of nuclear weapons has made war politically obsolete and morally indefensible. No national interest or purpose, they hold, can justify the use of nuclear weapons. Some also oppose limited war fought with conventional weapons because it might spiral into a nuclear war. If war is no longer a rational or morally acceptable instrument of national policy, they argue, the weapons of mass destruction should be eliminated by mutual agreement if possible, and by unilateral action if necessary.

At the opposite end of the spectrum are those who focus almost exclusively on the Soviet military threat and on military means to deal with it. Power is what our adversaries understand, they say. Power is what deters them from attack, and the more military power we have the more effectively we can frustrate their expansionist ambitions. To restrict our military strength unilaterally or reciprocally is to weaken ourselves dangerously. Such a course, they argue, would permit our adversary the luxury of using with impunity his weapons of subversion and terror.

These two polar approaches have the appeal of simplicity and internal consistency. But they obscure the depth and complexity of the challenge. Each in its own way is too preoccupied with the military aspects of the struggle. The bomb banners, hypnotized by the bomb, tend to overlook the dangers of aggression and tyranny. The bomb builders, in their preoccupation with aggression and tyranny, tend to overlook the political and moral dangers of nuclear war. Since the American people sense the dangers of both war and tyranny, neither of these two simple approaches is likely to attract broad support.

A New Arms Control Consensus

Between these two views lies an emerging consensus among students of national security. Participants in this consensus are concerned both about the threat of war and the dangers of an externally imposed tyranny. They attempt to take into account all facets of the Cold War. Persons who share this perspective prefer the term *arms control* to *disarmament*, because the latter suggests only one way of lessening the risk of war—drastic reductions in the level of arms—the least feasible path. Even if drastic arms cuts were politically possible it would not necessarily make war less likely, although it might make it less destructive.

The new consensus focuses on military stability and its contribution to national security and international peace. In a stable military situation, by definition, there is no general war and the likelihood of such a war is small. A policy directed toward enhancing stability seeks to create a military environment of mutual deterrence in which both the Soviet Union and the United States would have the capacity to deter the other from initiating a strategic attack. Accordingly, both we and the Soviets should attempt to develop and maintain sufficient retaliatory capacity to make certain that the punishment for a first strike would be unacceptable to the aggressor.

The new strategic and arms-control consensus is concerned not only with premeditated attack, but also with the danger of unintended war. Students of this approach have grappled with proposals to reduce the probability of a general war by accident (human error or technical failure), by the "escalation" of a local conflict, by the catalytic action of a smaller power, or by the miscalculation of one or both sides. Implicit in this concern with efforts to prevent inadvertent war is the belief that a nuclear catastrophe is more likely to result from escalation or miscalculation than from deliberate design.

Our immediate strategic objective is to achieve stability, even if it must be based upon a balance of terror. The long-range objective is to maintain stability at decreasing levels of destructive capacity. A viable arms control measure should maintain, restore, or enhance strategic military stability. If it does not pass this first and crucial test it should be rejected. A lopsided control agreement conferring a significant advantage on one side might tempt it to exploit the advantage by threat, blackmail, or outright attack. If a proposal passes this first test, it is then appropriate to ask whether it will reduce destruction should war occur. A measure that passes both tests is, of course, preferable.

Three Paths to Security

The new consensus recognizes three major paths to greater security. *First*, significant measures can be taken unilaterally by the United States or the Soviet Union to develop a less menacing military posture and thus reduce the danger of war. Much can also be done by either side to erect safeguards against war by accident or escalation. If the Soviet Union develops a less menacing stance, we can then afford to do the same. If we emphasize defensive and second-strike weapons, the Soviets can safely follow suit. There are numerous possibilities in unilateral action that, if acted upon, would make a safer world.

The *second* path is closely related to the first—tacit agreements between the nuclear powers. By self-restraint, one side can sometimes induce restraint by the other. This mutual restraint can lead to tacit understandings that are in many ways as effective as formal agreements. The reciprocal moratorium on nuclear tests, in effect for almost three years, is an illustration of a tacit agreement, but it was broken by the resumption of Soviet atmospheric tests in September 1961.

The *third* path is the traditional disarmament approach—the formal negotiated agreement. Explicit agreements appeal to many people because they provide for specific and tangible constraints. But it is precisely in this area that no progress has been made since the end of World War II. Although the prospects for successful arms negotiations appear dim, the participants in the new consensus insist on exploring every possibility for a viable treaty, with adequate safeguards and controls.

Whether a government seeks to mitigate the danger of war by unilateral measures, by tacit agreements, or by formally negotiated treaties, collaboration with the adversary is always involved. Such collaboration tends to encourage mutual restraint, which is the essence of arms control.

The emerging consensus is the prevailing approach today among independent scholars and researchers and has been gaining increasing acceptance within the U.S. Government. President Kennedy is a spokesman for the new approach. And it appears to be more acceptable to the American people than either the views of those who call for drastic arms cuts with little regard for the requirements of mutual deterrence or of those who seek to solve international problems almost exclusively by military might.

23 *ABM Is a Shield, Not a Sword*

In the late 1960s, America became increasingly concerned about a possible So-
viet missile attack, and President Nixon proposed an anti-ballistic missile
(ABM) system called Safeguard. Since it was vigorously opposed by National
Council of Churches leaders, I requested and received a chance to rebut their po-
sition in the council's magazine, Tempo *(August 15, 1969). I argued that Safe-*
guard was a shield and not a sword, an argument later used to defend President
Reagan's Strategic Defense Initiative. I assumed that Safeguard was feasible, but
technical questions aside, the concept of missile defense was and is morally and
militarily sound.

*   *   *

In our dangerous world where nuclear war is possible, though not probable, any humane citizen wants his government to pursue policies to prevent a nuclear holocaust. Will President Nixon's proposed Safeguard
ABM system make nuclear war more or less likely than alternative ways
of dealing with the strategic threat of the mid-1970s?

The President and most strategic experts believe we will confront a new
and serious nuclear threat within five years if present trends in the United
States and the Soviet Union continue. In the past decade Soviet spending
for strategic nuclear weapons has increased about 70 percent, while ours
has declined about 50 percent. For several years Russia has been spending
substantially more on its strategic forces than we have on ours.

By the mid-1970s Russia's massive SS-9 intercontinental missiles will
be sufficiently accurate to wipe out our land-based Minuteman missiles
in their reinforced concrete silos in one devastating blow—unless we develop an active defense for them before that time. This widely accepted
judgment is based on Russian military capability, not on Russian political
intentions. We have no way of knowing what Soviet leaders intend to do.
But we do know from history that political leaders sometimes are prepared to use maximum military power to achieve their objectives.

To put it another way, the strategic stability that now prevails between U.S. and Soviet forces, and which thus far has prevented nuclear war, is now being seriously challenged by the dramatic upsurge of Soviet missile might. The situation is further complicated by the capacity of both sides to develop multiple warheads on one missile—MIRVs, multiple independently targetable reentry vehicles—though neither we nor they have completed a testing program.

Doctrine of Mutual Deterrence

The major strategic problem is to prevent a first nuclear attack from either side. If we succeed in this prime objective there will never be a deliberate nuclear exchange. This is where the doctrine of mutual deterrence comes in. Each side must have the capacity to deter a first strike by the other. This means a second-strike force sufficient to deliver an unacceptable blow to the homeland of the other—thus deterring any rational and responsible government from launching an attack in the first place.

There are two principal ways of maintaining a credible deterrent force. One is to deploy more offensive missiles than the adversary can destroy. The other is to deploy a smaller number of offensive weapons, but have them better protected.

It is this second alternative that Safeguard is designed to make possible. Since hardening Minuteman sites will not provide adequate protection for them in the mid-seventies, an active defense is required. As such a system, Safeguard will provide an effective deterrent without a significant increase in U.S. offensive weapons.

Safeguard is an ABM system designed to destroy attacking missiles before they reach their targets and without detonating the nuclear warhead of the attack missile. Its long-range Spartan missile intercepts the attack missile 200 to 400 miles above the earth. The smaller Sprint missile destroys warheads missed by Spartan within 40 miles of the target. No one claims perfection for this complex system which involves radar and computers, but most informed scientists believe it would be about 80 percent effective.

Five Arguments for Missile Defense

I reject as immoral and dangerous the argument that a substantial increase in U.S. strategic missiles is the best way to counter the new Soviet threat. There are five reasons why President Nixon's Safeguard system is preferable to the alternative of deploying additional offensive weapons.

First: Safeguard will more effectively protect our deterrent than the multiplication of new offensive missiles. It is better to protect the weapons we have than to build and deploy additional offensive weapons.

Second: Safeguard is not as provocative to the Soviet Union as the multiplication of offensive weapons. *A shield is less menacing than a sword.* Recognizing this, the Russians have deployed ABM weapons at some 60 sites and have repeatedly asserted the desirability of defensive weapons. We have deployed no ABM weapons. The fact that Moscow has made no official protests against our ABM plans suggests that the Soviet leaders accept the mutual need for a limited ABM system, at least against the common threat from Red China.

Third: Safeguard would have a stabilizing effect on strategic arms expenditures on both sides, while a new round of offensive weapons could launch a strategic arms race. The mutually provocative character of offensive missiles has been demonstrated in the past. After declining 50 percent in the past ten years, U.S. strategic expenditures have leveled off substantially below current Soviet strategic spending. It is important to note that U.S. strategic expenditures (including research, development, hardware, maintenance, and manpower) constitute about 15 percent of the defense budget, the remaining 85 percent going for general purpose forces.

Fourth: Safeguard is less expensive than a significant increase in offensive weapons. The requested ABM appropriation for 1970 is $893 million. The total cost of the projected ABM program from 1968 (the year Congress authorized it) through its completion in 1976 is estimated at $10.2 billion, or about eight percent of U.S. strategic expenditures, less than two percent of each defense budget, and about one-fifth of one percent of the GNP. By any measure this is a tiny fraction of our total resources, and in any event, defense "savings" are not transferable to any other program in the federal budget.

Fifth: Perhaps most significant of all, Safeguard increases the military, diplomatic, and moral options of the President in any serious confrontation with a nuclear adversary or in the event of a nuclear accident. If a nuclear event should occur now, the President has two options—he can do nothing militarily or he can unleash nuclear retaliation against Russian cities. We hope that no president will ever be faced with a deliberate nuclear attack or even a nuclear accident, but what humane and rational man would deny him a third option in that fateful moment?

A Third Option

Safeguard provides that third option between capitulation and retaliation. If a nuclear event occurs after we have a deployed ABM system, the President will not be limited to doing nothing or pushing a button that may kill millions of Russians. He will have an ABM button, a damage-limiting option, which may save millions of American lives without killing a single Russian. Who would deny the President this chance to save lives, to reflect, to plan? Furthermore, Safeguard strengthens mutual deterrence and thus reduces the probability of an attack in the first place.

Our world is becoming more dangerous and uncertain because of China's growing nuclear might. By 1975, Peking will be able to launch a nuclear attack against the United States. Both Communist giants have serious internal stresses, and a leadership crisis at the top could erupt at any time. In the ensuing power struggle there could be a breakdown of restraint and a nuclear event, by design, miscalculation, or accident, could occur. If the United States were the target, we want to be in a position to limit damage to ourselves and to avoid a full-scale nuclear exchange. Only an ABM system can make this possible. Offensive missiles can retaliate and cause damage, but they cannot prevent and limit damage. Safeguard can prevent and limit damage, but it cannot cause it. Safeguard is a shield, not a sword.

24 *The Elite Press and the Present Danger*

Has the flood of words and images in our media-saturated culture made us better informed on the crucial issues facing America as a humane superpower? Has the liberal elite media made it easier or more difficult for our leaders to make responsible decisions? In an article in ORBIS *(spring 1976), I addressed these questions and drew upon a two-year study conducted by the Institute for American Strategy that resulted in a book I wrote in 1974,* TV and National Defense: An Analysis of CBS News, 1972–1973. *Since writing this article two decades ago, the near-monopoly of the "big three" TV networks has been shattered by the advent of cable channels, particularly CNN and C-Span. This has introduced greater perspective and coherence in foreign policy reporting.*

*   *   *

The recent dramatic TV series, *The Adams Chronicles,* apart from being a superb portrayal of the impact of a gifted family on the birth and early development of the United States, was vivid reminder of how relatively easy it was for the early presidents and their secretaries of state to make and execute difficult foreign policy decisions. The new republic was imperiled from abroad, as it is today, but the internal obstacles to prudent policies then were not as great as they are now. Washington, John Adams, Jefferson, Madison, and their successors for over a century were largely spared the pressures and harassments of present-day participatory democracy. They were not required to spend much of their time massaging Congress, pacifying pressure groups, or mollifying the predatory press. *The Adams Chronicles* also reminded us that there is no necessary connection between the wisdom of a national decision and the breadth of debate that preceded it or the intensity of acrimony that followed.

The Founding Fathers lived in a simpler world. They drew their strength and wisdom largely from a view of the nature and destiny of man—nurtured by the Judeo-Christian faith, Greek culture, and Roman law, and refined by the English insistence on the dignity and worth of every person. The rulers and the ruled were united by these common values that were enshrined in the Declaration of Independence and the Preamble to the Constitution.

Through all men were "endowed by their Creator with certain unalienable Rights" including "Life, Liberty, and the pursuit of Happiness," the Founders provided for a restricted franchise. The right to vote was considered a solemn duty to be exercised by free, male citizens who had the responsibility of owning real property.

Because of this limited franchise, the Founders were later criticized as autocratic elitists who made arbitrary decisions in the interests of the privileged at the expense of ordinary people, a charge hardly sustained by the record. Those distinguished men were endowed with a sense of the general good which was amply demonstrated by their major domestic and foreign policy decisions and in the Constitution which permitted, indeed implied, the broadening of the franchise and the extension of basic rights to all Americans, including slaves.

The Western ethic provided the moral cement of the new nation, but it did not answer the practical problems of how to organize it nor dictate the modes of intercourse between the governor and the governed. To insure a responsible relation between the political authorities and the public will, the Constitution established a government based on a separation of powers and called for a free press to facilitate communication between the people and their leaders. Both the structure of government and the need for a free press were based on the assumption that men were not angels, that no man was above the law, and that public policy was subject to error and, therefore, in need of public criticism and review. The press was to act as a watchdog over government.

The American Press Is Unique

The role of the press in America is unique. The vital responsibility of keeping a democratic electorate informed lies largely in the hands of private entrepreneurs who are neither directly nor formally accountable to the political process or the general will. The U.S. Government does not publish a newspaper or own a broadcasting station, much less operate a TV network.

Throughout our history, the political influence of the press has been significant and controversial. The thesis of this essay is that recent developments in the mass press, which both reflect and exacerbate certain flaws in American society, jeopardize the future of the United States as a great and humane power.

The mass press is taken to mean the major channels for transmitting the day's intelligence, particularly the events at home and abroad that bear upon the central decisions of the Federal Government. The press reports news about events and developments, views of political and other leaders about these events, and opinions of the editors and readers. So defined, the mass press excludes journals of opinion. We are concerned with the elite press: *New York Times, Washington Post, Time,* and *Newsweek,* and the three TV networks—ABC, CBS, and NBC.

The problems of the press and politics have persisted with little fundamental change from the earliest days. The most notable is the inevitable, and to some extent desirable, tension between the demands of secrecy by the government and the demands of disclosure by the press, which often acts as though its First Amendment rights were absolute. In recent years press demands for the disclosure of secret national security information have greatly increased along with actual disclosures. One need only mention the publication of the Pentagon Papers, accounts of sensitive CIA and FBI activities, and other secret documents stolen or otherwise procured from the government and given to the press by government employees, members of Congress, or congressional staff.

Throughout our history journalists have been torn between the material and status rewards associated with sensational exposures and a patriotic sense of responsibility that calls for restraint. There are numerous cases of commendable voluntary restraint, especially in wartime. But far too often zealous newsmen and their media insist that the disclosure of sensitive and compromising foreign policy secrets, regardless of the consequences, will somehow serve their country's interests.

In giving vent to this particularly American "mania for disclosure," as one British paper put it, the zealots of the press have found a responsive echo in Congress in the form of the Freedom of Information Act. As amended in 1974 over President Gerald Ford's veto, this law requires any Federal agency to release any data requested by any citizen within ten working days or give him an explanation of why it cannot. If the agency refuses on national security or any other grounds to provide highly classified information, the requester can take his complaint to a Federal District Court, which "shall determine the matter *de novo*" and decide whether the requested material is "in fact properly classified." This gives the Court the final authority to determine what information will or will not injure national security or foreign relations, a responsibility hitherto vested in the Executive Branch.

Since the Freedom of Information Act came into effect in February 1975, it has been extensively used by the critics of U.S. foreign policy, notably Morton Halperin of the ACLU, to pry secrets from the CIA, the National Security Council, and the State Department. Considerable information so secured, along with secrets leaked from congressional sources, has already been headlined by the press.

Our post-Vietnam passion for disclosure has given the American people, our allies, and our adversaries more secrets about recent U.S. foreign policy than in any earlier period. No government in history has had to operate so fully in the glare of critical publicity. The untimely publication of state secrets has embarrassed the United States and its allies, paralyzed our capacity to act in certain crises abroad, and given aid and comfort to our adversaries.

Catering to Radical Chic Voices

With the technical capacity for obtaining instant and vivid news stories from anywhere on the globe, the American public might expect to have a more coherent picture of the threats and opportunities facing us than when it took weeks, and even months, to get occasional and sparse reports of foreign developments. We live in a media-saturated society, but the information explosion has hardly increased the historical perspective or understanding of our international role.

We are assailed by too many words, images, and sounds—a barrage of information without a framework of understanding. As in the past, media coverage is episodic, partial, sporadic, though TV has made it more dramatic, immediate, and emotional. "TV news," said one critic, "is like getting socked in the belly by a ghost. You look to see what hit you, and it's gone." This has often meant impact without perspective, sensation without understanding.

In the past we learned the details of battles months after they were fought, but during the Vietnam War gory episodes—usually one-sided stories that reflected unfavorably on the United States or our ally—were portrayed daily on the three TV network evening news shows. This had a profound impact on U.S. policy. *New York Times* columnist James Reston said: "Maybe the historians will agree that the reporters and the cameras were decisive in the end. They brought the war to the people . . . and forced the withdrawal of American power from Vietnam." Roger Mudd of CBS looked into the future and wondered whether any "democracy which has uncensored TV in every home will ever be able to fight a war, however moral or just."

The public schools and later the radio were credited with achieving the American miracle of E Pluribus Unum, and television was expected to advance the cause, to further homogenize and enlighten the mass public which was now enfranchised without regard to race, creed, color, or state of literacy. This has not happened. Television has had a leveling and politicizing effect, but paradoxically it has also encouraged cultural diversity, ethnic particularism, and political divisiveness, all of which affected, and not necessarily for the better, perceptions of ourselves and our role in the world.

The divisive political impact of television can be traced largely to the medium's inordinate attention to the unusual, violent, freakish, and dramatic events, often at the expense of more significant but less sensational stories. This weakness for the off-beat, bizarre, and unorthodox has been especially evident since the mid-1960s when assorted protesters, radicals, militants, and malcontents—the ones who tore up the place, shouted the loudest, or were most obscene—tended to push off the screen the more moderate and thoughtful spokesmen, who represented the views of a great majority of Americans. The fulsome coverage of radical chic favorites like Jane Fonda, Angela Davis, Daniel Ellsberg, Ramsey Clark, Daniel Berrigan, and William Kunstler tended to generate anger and alienation, and hence divisiveness, among millions of middle Americans who felt their values were not being fully or fairly reported. Millions of confused young people were thus "taught" to distrust the establishment and the democratic process. This peculiar mix of confusion and polarization reflected deeper changes in the American elite.

Far more consequential than the hopefully temporary political alienation of millions of Americans from their government is the creeping spiritual alienation of a significant segment of American intellectuals from Western values, including allegiance to free institutions and the rule of law. Important elements in the prestige press—the three television networks and papers like the *New York Times* and *Washington Post*—have both reflected and encouraged this development by selective reporting and editorial advocacy. (Much of their reporting, to be sure, has been responsible.)

The political manifestations of this alienation are seen in the questioning, and even rejection, of fundamental democratic premises and in the attack on the institutions of American government, particularly on the instruments of security—the military, the CIA, the FBI, and the agencies of civil law enforcement.

The hard-core attack has gone beyond the bounds of necessary and constructive criticism. Some of it springs from a belief in economic determinism or an addiction to the revolutionary rhetoric of the new or old Left. Some critics reflect a strange amalgam of nihilism, guilt, and breast-beating which exaggerates the small sins of liberal democracy and excuses the big sins of messianic dictatorships. Whatever the psycho-political sources, these people sanction violent demonstrations, bombing, and even murder in the name of ending American "repression." Reparations are demanded to compensate for past sins.

A protracted though slackening crusade against the armed forces has been carried on by an anti-military complex of intellectuals, idealists, and radical critics. Washington is advised to withdraw its aid to authoritarian, anti-Communist regimes that are no threat to the peace, and simultaneously to extend the hand of friendship to militant totalitarian regimes (e.g., Cuba) that have no inhibition against imposing their will on other countries by force. Such critics were more concerned about the presence of a few South African troops in Angola than about the 12,000 Cuban mercenaries there. The South Africans came in with the support of Zaire and Zambia to assist the moderate forces against the Soviet-sponsored forces and to guard a South African–built dam a few miles inside the border. They evacuated thousands of war refugees to safety. In sharp contrast, the heavily armed Cuban expeditionary army under Soviet control came to impose its will on Angola by massive force.

Alienated from Middle America

To many of these alienated people, Ho, Che Guevara, and Mao are the real liberators. America, not the totalitarians, is the real oppressor in the world. The radical chic set is very small, but the media—some of whose practitioners have radical chic credentials—have greatly magnified their influence by overreporting their views and actions, often in a sympathetic vein, and underreporting the activities of attitudes of traditional democratic groups.

Major media spokesmen have made it clear that their mission goes beyond communication and embraces advocacy. In their eyes, they have a duty to not only report history, but a duty to make history. Some of the more zealous ones have become partisans in the stories they report. Tom Wicker of the *New York Times* became an open advocate of the rioting prisoners at Attica. Daniel Schorr of CBS gave a secret House report on intelligence to the press. Charles Collingwood, also of CBS, visited North Vietnam during the war and asked Hanoi's leaders if there was any specific message he could convey from them to the American people through the medium of CBS.

In each case, the reporter became a partisan in a highly controversial issue, and in each he identified himself with or unwittingly served an interest opposed to constituted democratic authority. Mr. Wicker, though not a lawyer, represented convicted criminals against the State of New York. Mr. Schorr, though not an elected official, transmitted a stolen, secret document which the House of Representatives had voted to keep confidential. Mr. Collingwood, though not a diplomat, dealt with a dictatorial regime at war with the United States, and thus advanced its propaganda objectives.

Ironically, some of these same people and their publications have moral scruples against providing vital information to their own government. The *New York Times* published the top secret Pentagon Papers, but refused to give Congress or the government the names of CIA employees who violated their secrecy oath by giving classified information to investigative reporter Seymour Hersh. The *Times* justified its refusal by saying it received the information on a confidential basis. Some journalists, moreover, who found it appropriate to write laudatory reports about life in North Vietnam or Cuba, find it immoral for men of the Fourth Estate to cooperate with the CIA. This dual ethic of the press which insists on disclosing state secrets and refuses to provide information to the government in criminal and national security cases, cannot be justified by the First Amendment or any other canon of democratic responsibility. The press is not above the law. Freedom of the press is not absolute.

Sectors of the media, particularly in New York and Washington, have either joined or become sympathetic to what Daniel Patrick Moynihan has called an "adversary culture" that is often hostile to democratic values and institutions. Columnist Robert Novak says the national prestige media weld journalists into "a homogenous ideological mold, joined to the liberal establishment, and alienated from the masses of the country." Theodore H. White advances the same theme. He speaks of an adversary "press-television complex" hostile to middle Americans and the presidents they elect. According to Mr. White, this concentrated communications elite in New York and Washington is the result of technology, not conspiracy, but it has created a "change in American journalism as profound" as the advent of "the muckrakers seventy years before" and with even more unpredictable results.

The media are jealous of their power to sway public opinion, a power that has increased considerably since Abraham Lincoln acknowledged the significance of those who wield it: "With public sentiment, nothing can fail; without it, nothing can succeed. Consequently, he who molds public sentiment goes deeper than he who enacts statutes or pronounces decisions." In Ben Franklin's day, only a few thousand citizens read the *Pennsylvania Gazette*, but today more than 50 million Americans view the evening news shows, a bully pulpit by any measure. Most citizens of all educational levels now say they rely more on TV for current news than on any other source.

TV and National Defense

The three commercial TV networks—ABC, CBS, and NBC—bear an enormous responsibility because they constitute a virtual monopoly on vivid current intelligence. Their responsibility is all the greater because they reach an audience of millions who do not or cannot read the printed press, but whose votes count as much as those of well-informed citizens.

The airwaves are finite and belong to the public, so the Federal Communications Commission has promulgated the Fairness Doctrine. It requires all broadcasters to serve the public interest by providing news and public affairs programs and "a reasonable opportunity" for the expression of opposing views on all controversial issues. The Fairness Doctrine, which has the force of law, should not be confused with the "equal time" provisions for political candidates. Under the doctrine, the networks have an "affirmative duty" to seek out opposing views to assure "robust debate" on the "vital issues of the day."

Network spokesmen have sought to nullify or eliminate the Fairness Doctrine, insisting that radio and television should have the same freedom provided newspapers under the First Amendment. At the same time, they each claim their network is presenting fair and unbiased news. Walter Cronkite said the FCC "imposes artificial and arbitrary standards of balance and objectivity," and the only way to free broadcasting "from the constant danger of Government censorship is to free it from any form of Government control," except for technical channel allocation; he added: "We're big. And we're powerful enough to thumb our nose at threats and intimidation from Government. I hope it stays that way."

Whatever one may think of the Fairness Doctrine, it is difficult to fault its objectives which, incidentally, are largely embraced in the two major broadcast codes. In reporting national defense and foreign policy stories, the networks have a responsibility to give their 50 million viewer-citizens a reasonably fair picture of the day's events that bear on the security of the United States and its allies, including major developments that increase or diminish external threats and facts about Soviet military intentions and capabilities.

Taking these common sense standards into account, it may be useful to summarize the performance of America's most widely viewed TV news program—CBS Evening News with Walter Cronkite. The findings noted here are drawn from an intensive content analysis of two full years (1972 and 1973) of the half-hour Cronkite show, a total of 321 weekday programs or 196 broadcast hours, exclusive of commercials. They are analyzed in my book, *TV and National Defense: An Analysis of CBS News* (1974).

An attentive American viewer relying wholly on the Cronkite show for 1972 and 1973 would have received a partial and highly distorted picture of the dangers confronting his country, his government's response, and opposing views on national defense. The show carried almost no news on growing Soviet military might in missiles, aircraft, warships, or manpower. The ceremonial aspects of the SALT I agreement in 1972 were well-covered, but there was no direct reference to a new long-range Soviet submarine missile, the annual production of five to nine Soviet nuclear submarines, a new generation of Soviet ICBMs capable of destroying U.S. Minuteman missiles, or a new Soviet system that could shoot down our reconnaissance satellites. There was no mention that Soviet military expenditures exceeded U.S. defense spending and that their spending was rising while ours was falling. In the two-year period, only one minute was devoted to direct comparison of Soviet and American military power, but one minute and fifty seconds were devoted to missing tableware in Pentagon cafeterias.

The Cronkite show painted an overwhelming negative picture of our military establishment: 69 percent of the stories cast the military in an unfavorable light, 18 percent were favorable, and 13 percent were neutral. The composite impression was a military that fought a bloody, unjust, racist war in Vietnam where mutinous and drug-ridden U.S. forces engaged in widespread atrocities and illegal bombing. The war was prosecuted by a profit-hungry, military-industrial complex that drained the taxpayer by waste, cost overruns, and design faults. Among the few positive stories were: Air Force doctors devised a new kidney operation, the Navy taught a whale to retrieve objects in deep water, and a Marine camp in California was interested in the environment. Much in the military deserved criticism, but this steady attack, virtually unrelieved by the reporting of perspective-lending facts or opinions, threatened to undermine the legitimacy of the armed forces.

The Cronkite show's 1972 reporting of events and views on Vietnam was massively lopsided. Dividing opinion into three categories—the government's view, those who urged Washington to increase defense spending (hawks), and those who urged a military cutback (doves)—CBS reported on the dovish position forty-eight times more often than on the hawkish view, even though there were numerous thoughtful spokesmen for the latter.

The 1972 show carried more stories critical of the United States and South Vietnam than of North Vietnam. According to a theme analysis, 19.03 percent of the stories were supportive of Washington's policy and 80.97 percent critical. For Saigon, 16.67 percent were supportive and 83.33 percent critical, and for Hanoi, 57.32 percent were supportive and 42.68 percent critical. Hanoi was presented in far more favorable light than Saigon. This was done by reporting laudatory or apologetic comments about North Vietnam from persons like Jane Fonda, Ramsey Clark, and CBS newsmen themselves, and omitting supportive statements of the U.S. effort by Bob Hope, American officials, and others.

The biased reporting on the Cronkite show was reinforced, not corrected, by other CBS-TV news and public affairs programs. It is fair to conclude that in its national defense programming, CBS violated the Fairness Doctrine, the industry codes, and its own standards. It failed to provide many of the readily available vital facts or to give a "reasonable opportunity" for the expression of widely shared opposing views. Further, it engaged in advocating one particular view in the guise of straight news reporting.

CBS has a right to advocate, but it is obligated, even by its own code, to label advocacy as such. The 1972 Cronkite show gave more time to CBS newsmen's Vietnam views (299 sentences) than to the views of the president and all other administration spokesmen combined (250 sentences), or to those of all members of Congress (134 sentences). The only non-Vietnam foreign spokesmen reported were those critical of U.S. policy (18 sentences). In fairness, it should be noted that on at least one defense issue CBS provided balanced coverage—the draft vs. the volunteer army.

When confronted with the findings in *TV and National Defense* in 1974, Walter Cronkite denied the allegations of CBS bias and then confirmed them: "There are always groups in Washington expressing views of alarm over the state of our defense. *We don't carry those stories.* The story is that there are those who want to cut defense spending." Also in fairness, there is some firm evidence that CBS defense reporting has improved as a result of the study.

Defense reporting in 1972–1973 by NBC and ABC fell short of presenting a full and fair picture, though the refreshing exception of ABC's Howard K. Smith should be noted.

The *New York Times, Washington Post, Time,* and *Newsweek* did a better job than the networks, not necessarily because they were more objective, but because they had more space for news. To different degrees they all advocated in their news columns, earlier on Vietnam, and more recently on reporting the attack on the CIA and FBI. The *Times* in particular lent its prestige to the sensational and sometimes unsubstantiated charges of Seymour Hersh against the CIA. Mr. Hersh acknowledged that he had a "very strong bias" against the agency and was committed to making an "impact" which, he said "is my heroin." By May 1975, Hersh had won the Sidney Hillman and George Polk awards for his writing. The *Times*, nevertheless, embraced diversity on the CIA issue. Its defense correspondent, Hanson W. Baldwin, called Hersh's stories "exaggerated inaccurate or irresponsible." And C. L. Sulzberger warned the efforts to "cripple our intelligence service" will let "the Soviet KGB move into the vacuum." But the fact remains—Hersh got the screaming headlines.

Decline of the West?

If the West has already begun its final decline, as Henry Kissinger is alleged to believe, or is on the verge of collapse as Alexander Solzhenitsyn fears, the press will facilitate the process unless some recent ominous developments within it are corrected. Whatever happens to the United States at home or in the exercise of its power abroad will be greatly influenced by the press, particularly network television, because of its unmatched capacity to mold "public sentiment." The three networks constitute a triopoly which is not effectively controlled by law or the political process and is not directly accountable to the general will or public values. Television programming is more sensitive to the economic marketplace than to the marketplace of ideas—the free exchange of values and attitudes that make up the richness of America. This is likely to continue until the monopoly of the big three is broken up by cable television, a development ABC, CBS, and NBC have vigorously opposed.

The American people in their bicentennial year may be entering the nation's period of greatest peril. The totalitarian challenge is stronger, more persistent, more brazen, and more confident than ever before. The United States, relative to the Soviet Union, is weaker, more divided, and less confident than ever before.

Our capacity to respond effectively to the unconventional mix of brazen and subtle challenges has been greatly weakened by the profound division and confusion among American leaders, including the media elite. The broad foreign policy consensus which sustained the largely wise and humane exercise of American power from 1945 to 1965 has been shattered by the combined impact of Vietnam, revisionist ideology, disillusionment with détente, and weariness with the burdens of global responsibility. The earlier "illusion of American omnipotence" has given way to the paralysis of power.

What role will the press play in the agonizing reappraisal of America's purpose and resolve in the face of external pressures and internal confusion? The answer depends on what parts of the press one is talking about. Certain prestige periodicals like the *Wall Street Journal, Fortune, National Review, Commentary,* and *U.S. News and World Report,* and specialized journals as various as *ORBIS* and *Reader's Digest* have unambiguously reaffirmed traditional Western values and interests and have warned of the peril from "the new barbarians."

Unfortunately, the same cannot be said of influential segments of the elite press that have lost their faith in the democratic approach to freedom and justice, or give more attention to the views of the alienated intellectuals than to Americans who affirm traditional values. The flaws of the press are rooted in the flaws of American liberal intellectuals in the academy, churches, and Hollywood.

It is ironic that network TV, and to lesser extent the prestige papers, did not report the full dimensions of the Soviet challenge until they belatedly started to cover the Solzhenitsyn story. Largely ignoring quiet, thoughtful, and persistent prophetic voices within our own country, they latched onto an eloquent and dramatic spokesman of freedom who had long suffered the whiplash of Soviet tyranny.

One final caveat and hint of hope. The failure of some liberals to grasp the dimensions of the moral struggle between freedom and tyranny is indeed profound. Another Angola, a Middle Eastern war, or a new Pearl Harbor, hopefully non-nuclear, may destroy their illusions and restore their faith in Western values. Short of this, the illusions of the coercive utopians, the nihilism of the cynics, or the moral emptiness of the alienated—all of which play into the hands of the confident totalitarians—will not easily surrender to a realistic and hopeful understanding of America's heavy responsibility for the survival of the West.

25 *Moral Symmetry and Nuclear Arms*

Advocates of a "nuclear freeze" of both Soviet and American arms in the early 1980s avoided the stigma attached to unilateral U.S. disarmament. But the Soviet-sponsored idea was deceptive because it would have frozen the existing asymmetry in superpower forces that strongly favored Moscow, especially in Europe where the USSR had a monopoly in medium-range missiles and a significant advantage in conventional arms. I supported President Reagan's deployment of U.S. Pershing II missiles to counter the Soviet SS-20s, which forced Moscow to abandon them. This was the single most significant arms reduction of the twentieth century. My rather simply stated views were expressed at a Washington, D.C., seminar sponsored by the Saint Joan Peace Institute on March 7, 1983, and were published by the institute in Our Moral Duty to Defend Freedom.

*   *   *

The present nuclear arms debate in the United States and Western Europe is poisoned by an appalling ignorance of easily ascertainable facts and by an inordinate fear of nuclear war. Prudential fear is essential for survival and contributes to ethical and politically wise behavior. But inordinate fear leads to hysteria, bad ethics, and bad politics. There is a difference between a man-eating tiger and pussy cat. Soviet disinformation efforts have played a significant role in sponsoring inordinate fear.

Both facts and faith can dispel inordinate fear and instill prudential fear. The basic problems in ethics can be stated in the form of two simple questions. The first is: "What is going on here?" and the second is: "What ought we to do about it?"

The first question points to the major flaw in the debate—a failure to understand the nature of the threat. The issue is not simply one of war versus peace. The issue is also one of tyranny versus freedom. Freedom is under siege everywhere around the world. The new barbarians also have the bomb, and they lack an ethic of restraint. The USSR would like to take over Western Europe intact. Its ambitions and appetites are not confined to Europe, as we can see with the rape of Afghanistan, the sway of the Soviet Union in Southeast Asia, and its penetration into Ethiopia, Angola, Cuba, and Nicaragua.

The threat today is greater and more subtle than the threat forty years ago when the face of Nazi evil was easy to discern. Then we confronted an evil man who said he hated democracy, he hated Jews, he hated peace; he told us what he believed and he followed through. We are now facing an adversary adept at doubletalk and disinformation. He has snatched and distorted our slogans about peace and freedom.

There are many people in the nuclear freeze movement who look upon the bomb as the enemy, but this is not the case. Nuclear weapons can be used to deter war and defend freedom. They can also be used to launch war and to destroy freedom. The weapon itself is neutral. The will of man projected from the vantage point of national power is where the problem lies. In our time the problem is a messianic totalitarianism and a Soviet leadership that did not shrink from an attempt to assassinate Pope John Paul II. These barbarians are aided by people in the West who are beguiled by noble phrases and assailed by self-doubt.

One such is Jonathan Schell who declared that nuclear arms make war inevitable, and to avoid it we must reinvent the world. The first step in reinventing the world, he says, is to impose a nuclear freeze.

Such a freeze now is profoundly wrong on practical, political, and moral grounds. The USSR naturally wants a freeze in the European theater where some 340 SS-20s, with more than 1,000 warheads, are targeted against cities from Oslo to Istanbul. NATO has no countervailing weapons—no intermediate range missiles in place in Europe. On the conventional side, Moscow has at least a 3-to-1 tank advantage on the ground. Soviet doctrine is offensively oriented and its forces are offensively deployed.

NATO forces, in sharp contrast, are defensively deployed. Nobody who is not twisted by ideology can seriously believe that NATO contemplates an attack on Eastern Europe or the Soviet Union. We want to defend what we have, to hold the line. In our view, security means holding what we have. In their view, security means holding what they have and getting what they want.

A nuclear freeze in Europe would ratify Moscow's significant superiority, thus encouraging two very dangerous developments.

First, it would encourage a first-strike by Moscow. This would be particularly true if our freeze—even a bilateral freeze—were accompanied by a no-first-nuclear-use pledge on our side. Such a pledge would be a form of nuclear unilateral disarmament.

Second, a freeze in Europe would enable the Soviet Union to use nuclear blackmail against us, that is, threaten to get what it wants without paying the price of either a nuclear or conventional war. A freeze also presents a verification problem because it is virtually impossible to verify without on-site inspection. Since the late 1940s, the United States in arms control negotiations with the Soviet Union has sought adequate verification measures, and the Soviet Union has always resisted on-site inspection. As Senator Hubert Humphrey once said, "Verification is a substitute for trust."

Finally, what should our response be to the Soviet threat? First, all peace-loving people should support President Reagan's zero-zero option in Europe. This proposal is the most radical, far-reaching arms reduction proposal ever advanced by a head of state in recent memory. The president proposes to banish from the face of the earth a highly destabilizing category of weapons—intermediate-range nuclear weapons. They are destabilizing because of their short warning time.

Mr. Reagan's proposal would require the Soviet Union to destroy its SS-20s. I doubt whether Mr. Andropov will take this proposal seriously, but perhaps it will enable us to force Moscow to decrease the number of SS-20s in its arsenal. To negotiate seriously, we must arm to defend and we must arm to deter. We should deploy our Pershing II and cruise missiles on schedule this year. This will show our determination to restore the balance and to negotiate seriously.

Our failure to deploy in the absence of a Soviet willingness to cut back on its intermediate missiles would be an act of appeasement. Our choice today is not unlike that faced by the British people over forty years ago. The choice is between the moral wisdom of a Winston Churchill or the moral cowardice of a Neville Chamberlain.

PART SIX

Third World Battleground

The shorthand term Third World *is an imprecise designation for the cluster of diverse states in Africa, Asia, and Latin America that became a battleground in the Cold War, which President Harry Truman in 1947 called a struggle between "alternative ways of life." Most leaders of the newly independent states declared themselves nonaligned, but many played up to both sides to gain maximum advantage in the East-West conflict. Prime Minister Nehru of India, for example, declared himself politically neutral: "The only camp we should like to be in is the camp of peace and goodwill." In contrast, the Shah of Iran openly sided with the West.*

Not an imperial power in the traditional sense, America nevertheless assumed imperial responsibilities when confronting the chaos, poverty, and rising expectations in the Third World. Washington's diplomatic, economic, and military efforts were calculated to supplement the stabilizing influence of the departing European powers in Asia and Africa while countering the expansionist activities of the Soviet Union and later the People's Republic of China.

In the global contest between tyranny and freedom, the United States faced severe dilemmas in certain Third World countries where authoritarian right-wing regimes were under siege from left-wing totalitarian forces.

The selections in Part Six reflect insights drawn from my visits to more than fifty Third World countries between 1949 and 1988.

26 *Five Myths About the Third World*

With their primary focus on the Soviet threat in Europe and the risk of nuclear war, most Americans knew little about the Third World, and what they thought they knew was often wrong. The following address, given at Iowa State University, was published in Vital Speeches of the Day, *February 15, 1988, two years before the collapse of the Soviet empire.*

*   *   *

In addressing controversial, confusing, and sometimes emotional issues of U.S. policy toward the Third World, we must use our words carefully. I am reminded of the enthusiastic lady who said, "I'd give my right arm to be ambidextrous!" Or the lady in Madrid who received the order of chastity, "second class."

The *Third World* is a delightfully ambiguous but useful phrase. It embraces a wide diversity of countries and regimes that do not fall easily into the First World (largely Western countries that have democratic political systems, market economies, and a developed industrial system, e.g., the United States, Britain, West Germany, and Japan).

The *Second World*: The Communist world including the USSR and the People's Republic of China and their "colonies." They all have totalitarian political systems with centrally run economies and severely limited human rights. Eastern Europe, Cuba, Angola, Ethiopia, and Vietnam are controlled by Moscow, and Nicaragua may not be far behind.

The *Third World*: Most countries in Asia, Africa, and Latin America. Many have authoritarian regimes; a few are fledgling democracies. They tend to be underdeveloped economically; poverty and disease are widespread. Political rights are often limited. Though most have democratic constitutions, their governments are frequently changed by bloody or bloodless coups.

During the past twenty-five years, I have visited some fifty Third World countries in Africa, Asia, and Latin America, many of them several times. My views toward them are instructed by my political philosophy made more vivid by actual observation.

As a citizen of a democratic superpower—and leader of the First World—I speak as a humane realist, concerned about security, peace, prosperity, and human rights. With this brief introduction, permit me to refute five myths about U.S. policy toward the Third World.

Myth 1: Third World poverty is the result of First World wealth. This myth asserts that the United States and other "capitalist" powers, in their quest for raw materials and political power, have exploited the underdeveloped areas for private profit. The chief culprit in this exploitation is the multinational corporation.

Facts: Poverty never needs to be explained. It has existed since man's earliest days. Only the absence of poverty requires an explanation. The real question is: Why and how have some societies worked their way out of scarcity and want?

Until they were colonized by the European powers, most areas in Asia, Africa, and Latin America were traditional societies based on kinship authority structures and barter economies. During the colonial period and since, many traditional ways have persisted. Feudal structures have characterized South and Central America. But now most Third World countries have mixed economic systems.

Their poverty is a result of their tradition—feudalism, primitive technology, and the absence of modern ways of thought and the work ethic. In virtually every case, the colonial power increased productivity and developed some infrastructure for communication and commerce. Britain, for example, made a great contribution to the modernization of India. In the post-colonial period, foreign investment and multinational corporations have further developed the economies. The multinational corporations have been engines of productivity.

Third World regimes should welcome foreign corporations. At the same time, they should control them. Foreign businesses do not fight their way into El Salvador, Ecuador, or Nigeria. They go where they are invited and believe they can make a reasonable profit, enough to compensate for the risk of expropriation and war. A recent study found that these so-called profit-hungry corporations have made about 12 percent profit in foreign investments compared to approximately 11 percent in the United States.

Perhaps the best way for a Third World country to develop economically is to create an environment that attracts foreign investment and multinational operations.

Myth 2: Socialism is the best path to political liberation, prosperity, and economic justice. By socialism I mean the doctrine and practice of the Soviet Union, Cuba, or Communist China, or some mixture of Marxist doctrine and Leninist practice applied to Third World conditions.

Facts: The application of socialist or Marxist practices by any Third World country has always led to economic stagnation and political repression. In some cases like Cuba, the political structure has moved from authoritarian to totalitarian; most human rights have been snuffed out. Grim examples of the "socialist model" include North Korea, Vietnam, Ethiopia, and Angola. Unless the West responds vigorously, Nicaragua and Afghanistan will fall into this tragic category.

Conversely, the rejection of the Marxist model and the adoption of a market economy, i.e., democratic capitalism, has led both to economic prosperity and to greater political freedom and respect for human rights. The most dramatic though less-than-perfect examples are South Korea, the Republic of China on Taiwan, and Singapore.

The clear message for those with eyes to see is that socialism leads to disaster while democratic capitalism can lead to greater abundance and respect for human dignity. There is a profound difference in the quality of life possible under totalitarian North Korea, on one hand, and South Korea on the other.

Myth 3: Third World regimes can be reformed by U.S. preaching or economic sanctions. According to this view, the United States should attempt to overthrow or modify "undemocratic" or otherwise flawed regimes by withholding economic aid or imposing economic sanctions. These actions should be accompanied by public condemnation of the unacceptable practices of the target regimes.

Facts: Economic sanctions (boycotts, forced disinvestment, export controls, etc.) have never succeeded in their proclaimed objectives. In most cases they have been counterproductive. The best that even the mighty United States can do in the vast external realm is to nudge history in the right direction. Our most powerful weapon is our example of a democratic and humane society. As secretary of state, John Quincy Adams expressed this approach to American responsibility in 1821: "Wherever the standard of freedom and independence has been or shall be unfurled, there will be America's heart, her benedictions, and her prayers. But she goes not abroad in search of monsters to destroy. She is the well-wisher to the freedom and independence of all. She is the champion and vindicator only of her own."

We must avoid the danger of reform intervention, conscious of our own shortcomings and recognizing that each society must earn its own human rights and pay the price of self-determination and independence. Mao Zedong once said that revolution cannot be exported. He is right. Likewise, democracy and human rights cannot be exported. They must be won by hard work and sacrifice. In contrast, revolution and tyranny can be imposed. Democracy by definition cannot be imposed. But we must acknowledge that the United States under the legitimacy of an occupation statute did a good job in Japan after World War II.

In dealing with less-than-perfect regimes, we can combine our example with quiet (not silent) diplomacy and appropriate policies. We must, however, speak out against gross evils like terrorism, aggression, and genocide. Totalitarian brutality by the Soviet Union against its own people and in Afghanistan deserves public outcry.

In the Third World, where repressive regimes have been sponsored, imposed, or supported by Moscow, we have an obligation to help the forces of freedom, specifically in Afghanistan, Angola, and Nicaragua.

Myth 4: The United States always supports right-wing dictatorships. The flip side of this myth is that Washington fails to support liberation movements and just revolutions in the Third World. This myth assumes that Third World countries can be liberated only by revolution, and usually revolution is defined in Marxist or socialist terms.

Facts: The United States has no preference for right-wing, authoritarian regimes. It has a strong preference for democratic governments that respect human rights and encourage economic development.

But Washington has to deal with the existing regime, good, bad, or in between. Or, it can choose to wash its hands and have no contact. Rarely do we take this drastic step.

In dealing with the regimes as they are, we are limited by history, custom, and circumstance. At best we can nudge things in a humane direction. We can, as the diplomats say, "keep in touch with the next government," as indeed we were during the recent transition of power in the Philippines.

There are profound differences between right-wing authoritarian regimes and left-wing totalitarian regimes. No totalitarian regime of the left or right has ever made a peaceful transition to a more democratic government. In contrast, many right-wing authoritarian regimes have evolved into more democratic ones. This movement is clearly visible in South Korea and Taiwan.

President Carter was too hasty in discrediting the Shah of Iran as corrupt and repressive and in welcoming the "revolutionaries," who in short order became more corrupt and repressive. He helped to cast out one devil and seven new devils swooped in to take his place. Politics and ethics are concerned with the lesser of two evils, not with a simple choice between light and darkness.

The United States wisely has not enlisted in "revolutions" supported by those liberation theologians who insist that revolutionary violence alone will bring earthly salvation to the repressed. Some even say that a combination of Marx and Christ is essential to merit eternal salvation. As far as I can ascertain, no violent revolution in our century has created greater justice or freedom than the "old order" it replaced.

By all measures, including millions voting with their feet and millions of boat people, human beings have stated emphatically their repugnance of revolutionary regimes. During the darkest days of the Vietnam War, when the United States was being castigated by the blame-America-first chorus, there were no boat people fleeing the cruel war there. Only after they were "liberated" did millions of Vietnamese risk their lives for freedom. And the Berlin Wall was not built to keep West Germans from fleeing into "liberated" East Germany.

Myth 5: U.S. military power, military assistance, foreign bases, and military action reinforce repression and block reform. Or, as the World Council of Churches put it, U.S. militarism and capitalism go hand in hand in stifling progress toward justice and liberation.

Facts: Of the five myths, this comes closest to being the celebrated big lie. Every major use of U.S. military power since Pearl Harbor has increased the chances of security, freedom, and human rights. This does not mean that every specific action, or every bit of military aid, or every expenditure was wisely used. But consider the record:

1. If it were not for U.S. military power, Hitler and the Japanese may have prevailed and be running the world today.
2. U.S. military occupation of Japan and Germany has advanced the cause of freedom and democracy.
3. In Vietnam our cause was just—to prevent the Communist North from conquering the South. When we left, the revolutionaries took over. Now Hanoi, with the support of Moscow, has brutalized its people and millions have fled to sea in leaky boats.
4. U.S. military action liberated tiny Grenada.
5. U.S. military action diminished Libyan support for international terrorism.
6. U.S. military assistance (including a quarter of a million troops in Germany and the nuclear deterrent) has protected Western Europe from a Soviet attack.
7. The U.S. military response to North Korea's attack against the South in 1952 has enabled the Republic of Korea to be free and independent. Our continued presence there with some 35,000 troops has defended South Korea against the expansionist North, and provided the security that enabled the country to develop economically and politically toward greater democracy.
8. U.S. military assistance to more than fifty countries in the Third World has helped these regimes withstand external and internal revolutionary pressures that are encouraged, supported, or sponsored by the USSR.

In short, with rare exceptions, U.S. military assets have been employed to make a more peaceful and secure world, thus enabling Third World countries to go about the peaceful pursuit of building viable economies and more open political systems. Security is a prerequisite for the development of institutions to guarantee human rights.

Let me close on a note of caution and humility. We live in a very dangerous world. Freedom and security are gravely threatened by the predatory utopianism of the Soviet Union. Third World chaos and instability exacerbate the problems of economic and political development.

The United States has a responsibility commensurate with its capacity to affect external developments. I fear that we are not fully prepared to use our moral, economic, and military assets to deal with the threats that confront us. We have not yet shaken off the shroud of self-doubt that our defeat in Vietnam has draped over our shoulders. I worry far more about the paralysis of American power than I do about the alleged arrogance of American power.

America is a great society, but we are not without flaws. The democratic experiment is never complete. Yet we cannot wait until we reach perfection to act. Abraham Lincoln once said: "No man is good enough or wise enough to be president, but someone has to be." Similarly, no country is good enough nor wise enough to be the leader of the Free World, but we have no choice.

27 Hypocrisy of Neutralism

In 1962, I examined the public statements of three leading Third World neutralist leaders—Prime Minister Jawaharlal Nehru of India, President Gamal Abdel Nasser of the United Arab Republic (Egypt), and President Kwame Nkrumah of Ghana. All clothed their nonaligned stance in the garments of virtue, though none went as far as Premier Saeb Salaam of Lebanon, who said in 1960, "We, the small, uncommitted nations . . . represent the unbiased conscience of humanity."

Lacking the moral courage to take a firm stand between totalitarianism and democracy, the neutralists cynically played Washington and Moscow off against each other, giving the lie to a self-serving African proverb invoked by Kenya's former president Jomo Kenyatta: "When two elephants fight, the grass gets hurt." Hypocritical nonalignment was the bastard offspring of the Cold War.

The following conclusions drawn from my chapter in Neutralism and Nonalignment, *edited by Laurence W. Martin (1962), are equally applicable to Nehru, Nasser, and Nkrumah and reflect the views of other Asian and African leaders.*

*   *   *

This study of the views of Nehru, Nasser, and Nkrumah on neutralism yields nine general observations that apply equally to other nonaligned states of Asia and Africa:

1. The primary concern of all neutralist states is *not* neutralism. Their first task is to build a viable nation-state, to consolidate their newly gained political independence, and to develop economically. For them, the chief struggle is the conflict between nationalism and colonialism, not the conflict between the Communist world and the Free World, or between the Soviet Union and the United States, or between Communism as a political system and Western democracy. The main threat to their interests and aspirations, as they see it, is colonialism, not Communism, although we can expect a gradual lessening of the colonial issue during the decade ahead.

2. Neutralism, or nonalignment, as the neutrals prefer to call it, is primarily a response to the Cold War, and only in part a product of rising nationalism. It takes three to make a neutral. Afro-Asian neutralism is a function of bipolarity. The foreign policies of the new states are influenced by both the colonial past and the Cold War, but there is no necessary or consistent relation between the two. Some new states clearly lean toward the Communist bloc, and others toward the West; Pakistan and the Philippines, for example, are aligned militarily with Washington.

3. The leaders of the new states who have chosen nonalignment believe that this position best serves their national interests. Though they admit that prudence and necessity dictate a neutralist stance, the three leaders often interpret and justify their nonalignment at home and abroad in terms of high moral principles. Sometimes they say their policy stems from their tradition, and sometimes they claim that it is the best way for their country to advance world peace. Of the three men, Nehru is the most inclined to interpret his policies in moral terms, and Nasser the least. In justifying their foreign policy, the neutralists are little different from the leaders of aligned states that interpret their policies in the most acceptable terms. Under the pressure of serving the national interest, their attachment to neutralism is pragmatic rather than doctrinaire; instrumental rather than absolute; and transitory rather than permanent.

4. Because they represent countries that are small and relatively uninvolved in Cold War conflicts, Afro-Asian neutralist leaders tend to feel morally superior to the leaders of aligned states. They sometimes feel that they are uncorrupted by power and that they possess an innocence and detachment that qualifies them to speak for reason and humanity—a role denied to powerful and "guilty" nations.

Nehru reflects this mood more fully than either Nasser or Nkrumah, and he has attempted to serve as a mediator between the Cold War adversaries. With this conception of his mission, Nehru must have been shocked when Nepal, in 1960, pointedly included India, along with America, the USSR, and China, among the countries that should not interfere in its affairs.

All three men have supported efforts for the elimination or reduction of nuclear weapons using humanitarian arguments, but they have shown little concern for the merits of alternative proposals for dealing with the problem.

5. The neutralist nations both suffer and profit from the existence of the Cold War, but they probably profit more. By playing one side against the other, consciously or unconsciously, Nehru, Nasser, and Nkrumah have each received economic aid from both. The great bulk of India's aid has come from the United States, the preponderance of Egypt's aid from the Communist bloc. If there were no Cold War, these and other Afro-Asian neutrals would be getting less outside help. They enjoy an additional

economic advantage because of their military uninvolvement in either camp—by remaining unaligned, their defense budget may be smaller than it otherwise would be. As a result, they can devote a larger portion of their national resources to economic development.

To put it another way, the relative balance of power between the chief Cold War antagonists has produced a degree of military stability in the world. Both the United States and the USSR tend to deter each other from attacking independent states. This "extended deterrence" provides a measure of security for the uncommitted states, security they would otherwise have to gain by membership in an alliance, a bigger defense establishment, or both. In short, neutrals are more protected than endangered by the Cold War. In the long run, the Cold War may, of course, erupt into a hot nuclear war in which the whole world, including the neutrals would suffer.

6. The contribution of the neutrals to the preservation of international peace and stability is severely limited. Their efforts to mediate big-power disputes are effective only when the big powers are willing to compromise their differences. If that willingness is present, an agreement can probably be reached through normal diplomatic channels without mediation. When the big powers do agree, neutrals can often make an instrumental contribution by providing personnel or armed forces for an impartial observation team or a UN police force.

Theoretically, one neutral state, or a bloc of neutrals, could play a role as a balancer, but in the present situation of nuclear bipolarity, with the great disparity between nuclear and nonnuclear powers, this role is not feasible. Further, the neutrals do not possess enough unity to form a coherent and viable bloc.

The Times of India, in 1960, pointed out that "the Afro-Asian bloc has tended to overestimate its capacity for peacemaking largely as a result of the misplaced enthusiasm" of certain Western and Soviet spokesmen for "the so-called third bloc," and added: "It is necessary to reject such fulsome flattery in favor of a less idealized version of what the Asian-African powers can do to promote world peace."

7. Since neutralism is not rooted in an absolute principle, but rather is an outgrowth of circumstances, we may expect constant adaptation in the foreign policies of neutralist states in response to changing conditions. There have been small but significant modifications in India's policies as a result of Communist China's expansion into Tibet and her penetration of India's northern frontier. Nasser has also modified his policies in response to Communist pressures in the Middle East. Neutralism as a policy will be discarded when it no longer serves the national purpose.

8. While it is relatively easy for an Afro-Asian state to pursue a neutralist policy, it is difficult, if not impossible, for it to be objectively neutral in a world torn by a profound struggle between the West and the Commu-

nist bloc. Secretary of State Dean Rusk, in March 1961, after he had talked with Nehru, was asked what the United States meant by a neutral government in Laos. He replied: "A country which is not committed in any military sense to any side, that is not a base of penetrational operations for anyone, that is, a country not under the domination of outsiders, a country whose own leaders can order its affairs, including its own foreign policy."

By this definition, few Afro-Asian nations qualify for memberships in the neutral club. Moreover, even an objectively neutral nation will cease to be so if its vital interests demand temporary alignment in a time of crisis. In short, neutrality tends to be an ephemeral luxury enjoyed by certain states blessed by a favorable combination of geographic, economic, military, and political factors. In a bipolar world, neutrality is a viable posture only when the nation's vital interests are not threatened by either side.

9. The degree of foreign policy unity among Afro-Asian neutralists depends upon the issue in question. At the United Nations, these states usually voted as a bloc because they were responding either to the "colonial problem" or to general resolutions on peace. This unity based on either anticolonialism or a vague desire for world peace tends to give way to differences when local interests and conflicts are involved. One American official observed: "They may all vote together for the big generalities of peace and disarmament, but when it comes to dividing up aid, they're at each other's throats."

This is to be expected, because these countries are by no means identical in history, culture, or economic development, and they are divided by many rival political interests. In spite of this diversity, the African heads of government at the twenty-nation conference in Monrovia in May 1961 passed a resolution declaring that they will, in the future, vote as a single bloc at the United Nations. This declaratory statement really means that on general issues of peace, disarmament, and colonialism, they will probably vote as a unit. It hardly means they will vote as a bloc on an issue involving a dispute between two or more of their own members. At the 1961 Belgrade Conference on nonaligned states, Nehru sounded a more realistic note. He warned his fellow neutrals to weigh correctly "both our actual and potential strength and lack of strength," pointing out that the unaligned nations possess neither the prerequisite unity for a consensus on specific world issues nor the power to impose such a consensus if they could reach it.

28 America's Uncertain Military Burden

Chafing under our heavy and ambiguous military involvement in Vietnam, President Richard Nixon sought to reduce our burden there by helping the South Vietnamese to defend themselves. In 1970, he enunciated conditions for determining when the United States should not engage in "a direct combat role" anywhere abroad. His statement, which pointed to the dangers of indiscriminate involvement, emphasized the need for a clear definition of our vital national interests. It became known as the Nixon Doctrine. This article appeared in Worldview, *June 1970. The wisdom of the Nixon Doctrine was vindicated by the U.S. decision to throw back Iraq's forces in the Persian Gulf War.*

*   *   *

Most Americans agree that our protracted involvement in the defense of South Vietnam has become a watershed in our security commitment to the Third World, but there is less agreement on what the central "lesson of Vietnam" is. For a few persons, "no more Vietnams" means the virtual renunciation of our non-nuclear military commitments, but for most of us, including the President, the ambiguities and frustrations of Vietnam mean that we should be even more selective about our active military participation in the future than in the past.

The evolving Nixon Doctrine, enunciated first at Guam and elaborated in the State of the World message, calls for selective involvement in the defense of friendly states in the Third World and non-involvement in the internal affairs of any state, friendly or otherwise. The Nixon formulation is new, but an underlying principle of selective military commitment and involvement has instructed our foreign policy decisions since 1945. After all, the United States became seriously involved in only two of some fifty local conflicts since Hiroshima. What Mr. Nixon has done is to codify and further clarify the principles of selectivity implicit in the behavior of his predecessors. Like them, he has repeatedly declared that he will honor our commitments to protect our allies who are seriously threatened by external aggression, direct or indirect.

In spelling out the conditions for active U.S. military support of an endangered state, Mr. Nixon properly gives the highest priority to America's national interest: The crisis in question must present a threat to the vital interests of the United States. This is really a restatement of the problem, because in diplomatic parlance a *vital* interest is one we are prepared to fight for. There have been certain clear and present dangers around which the American people have quickly united. One such challenge was Pearl Harbor and another was the Cuban missile crisis.

Most Third World crises have been less clear and hence more debatable. Vietnam is a case in point. As the burden of our involvement became heavier in blood and treasure, many supporters of U.S. policy began to question whether the defense of South Vietnam was vital to our interests. Certainly a Hanoi victory over Saigon was no immediate threat to the United States, but was it a serious threat to the stability and independence of the states of Southeast Asia? And would a Communist-dominated Southeast Asia significantly alter the power balance in that part of the world to the detriment of the global balance of forces which, since 1945, has prevented both nuclear war and capitulation to the more dangerous designs of Moscow and Peking?

Without explicitly answering these questions about Vietnam, Mr. Nixon suggests more specific criteria for active U.S. military involvement in Third World conflicts, criteria that help determine the importance of a particular conflict to the United States and to world peace. The criteria can be stated in the form of three negative propositions. The United States should *not* become a military combatant in any conflict: (1) that is largely internal and does not threaten the political or territorial integrity of neighboring states; (2) that is confined to a less-than-vital region and does not threaten the balance of forces in that region; and (3) that does not involve significant combat troops of a major adversary power. In sum, to quote from the State of the World message: "a direct combat role for U.S. general purpose forces arises primarily when insurgency has shaded into external aggression or when there is an overt conventional attack. In such cases, we shall weigh our interests and our commitments, and we shall consider the efforts of our allies in determining our response."

The invocation of the Nixon Doctrine would not rule out non-combatant military assistance to Vietnam, nor automatically preclude a combatant role if Hanoi's aggression is regarded a serious challenge to the security of a region judged vital to the U.S. position in the world. These crucial judgments are still being hotly debated.

The three criteria, however, provide helpful guidance in assessing many less complex challenges. Several examples will illustrate the point.

Though the conditions may not have been explicitly stated, Washington did *not* become involved, even as an arms supplier, in the recent Nigerian tribal-civil war, in spite of the provision of Soviet war planes for Lagos and indirect French support for Biafra. By the same standards, the United States should not have become involved militarily (albeit by proxy through a United Nations expeditionary force) in the Congo crisis of 1960–1963 that was also essentially a civil war that threatened no neighboring state.

The Israel-Arab confrontation presents perhaps the most agonizing test of the Nixon Doctrine. In an attempt to maintain a balance in the area, U.S. arms have been selectively provided to both sides. The Soviet Union has armed Egypt. In spite of Israel's territorial conquest in the Six-Day War, the basic power balance of the region has been maintained and the conflict has not yet threatened global equilibrium. And no major power has become a combatant in the Mid-East conflict. As long as these conditions prevail, the Nixon Doctrine would preclude active American military involvement in behalf of either side. The situation would radically alter if Israel employed a nuclear weapon against Egypt, if the Soviet Union became a belligerent, or if some other turn of events threatened the U.S. position in the Mediterranean and thus weakened the southern flank of NATO.

The Nixon Doctrine is also being tested by our present involvement in Laos, which in an ancillary way is replete with most of the ambiguities that have dogged us in Vietnam. It would appear that the President will continue to provide logistical support and air cover for Laotian troops in their effort to hold back the Hanoi invaders, not only to defend Laos but also to protect South Vietnam during the transfer of combat responsibility from U.S. to Vietnamese units.

Non-Combat Military Aid

A rigorous reading of the Nixon Doctrine and a backward glance at recent history suggest that the Third World in the near future will present few crises that require direct U.S. combat involvement. In sharp contrast, the need for American non-combat security assistance is likely to persist for a long time. Since 1945, Washington has provided such assistance to more than eighty-five governments. In fiscal year 1967, for example, some eighteen thousand men from sixty Third World countries requested and received some form of U.S. military training. Approximately the same number received military hardware from the United States and many of them received public safety assistance to enhance the capability of their police services. These programs are continuing on a slightly reduced scale. Washington also has military alliances with no fewer than forty governments. The widespread and voluntary security reliance of many small states upon one great state is unique in history.

Why have so many governments turned to Washington rather than to Moscow for protection? The obvious answer is that they trust us and our purposes more than those of the Soviet Union. And with good cause. Moscow has hardly demonstrated a consistent interest in the peace and integrity of the states of Asia, Africa, and Latin America. On the contrary, it has engaged in active and widespread subversion in these areas. As Mr. Nixon noted in his State of the World message: "We cannot entrust our future entirely to the self-restraint of countries [read USSR] that have not hesitated to use their power against their allies [read Hungary and Czechoslovakia]."

In certain isolated instances the Soviet Union has joined with us in calming troubled waters, but usually only when strategic considerations were involved and when prompted by an implicit threat from Washington. On the strategic level Moscow has entered into a limited partnership with Washington to curb the spread of nuclear weapons and to maintain mutual deterrence. The 1970 SALT talks will be a test of the Soviet interest in arms control.

Because we are the preponderant Western power and the only truly global power, and because both the Soviet Union and Red China appear to have a short-term stake in selective turbulence in the Third World, we cannot expect the heavy burden of peacekeeping to shift to other shoulders in the near future. Nor can we expect a great deal of help from Britain and France, who have largely withdrawn from their responsibilities in Asia and Africa. Mr. Nixon speaks about partnership, but it takes two to tango. We seek partners in the heavy task of keeping the peace, but a realistic appraisal suggests that in many future crises, large and small, we will bear the major burden. This burden we cannot escape with honor because we have a political and moral responsibility commensurate with our capacity to act.

The role of the peacekeeper is always hard and rarely appreciated, especially when the peacekeeper is powerful and wealthy. It requires a courage born of responsibility and self-confidence chastened by humility. The perils and obligations of power were perfectly understood by Edmund Burke 175 years ago when he commented on the situation of imperial Britain: "I must fairly say, I dread our *own* power and our *own* ambition; I dread our being too much dreaded . . . we may say that we shall not abuse this astonishing and hitherto unheard-of power. But every other nation will think we shall abuse it."

29 State-Building in Tropical Africa

A Nigerian president once called Africa "the Third World of the Third World." Certainly, tropical Africa, which lies between the Sahara and the Zambezi River, is far less developed than either Asia or Latin America. My research trips to the former Belgian Congo (now the Democratic Republic of the Congo), Nigeria, Ghana, Ethiopia, and a dozen other new states focused on the role of the military and resulted in three academic books. The following selection is excerpted from Spear and Scepter: Army, Police, and Politics in Tropical Africa *(1970).*

*   *   *

The peaceful dissolution of the European colonial order in most of tropical Africa in the early 1960s inaugurated a turbulent and unpredictable era of political conflict, change, and adaptation in a vast underdeveloped region three times the size of the United States. The hundred million indigenous people living between the Tropic of Cancer and the Tropic of Capricorn belong to more than two thousand tribes and speak twice that many languages and dialects. The great majority of these people are illiterate and live in small villages. Their primary identity is the traditional tribe, which severely limits their social loyalties and their view of the larger world.

The political responsibility for these villagers and their kinfolk living in or near the European-built cities was transferred in a massive and precipitous shift of sovereignty from mature, metropolitan governments in Europe to fledgling African leaders with little experience in the art of state politics. These partially Westernized politicians, varying widely in education, political sophistication, and patriotism, have declared their determination to maintain and develop the thirty states bequeathed them. Each of them has repeatedly declared his intention to develop a modern welfare state along general Western lines, supported by an expanding economy based on foreign trade and investment, and secured by statewide military and police services.

It has been argued that most new African states are not economically and politically viable and that therefore their boundaries should be redrawn to create larger or smaller units corresponding to tribal lines or economic realities. This abstract argument flies in the face of the determined view of the great majority of Africa's leaders who insist on maintaining present frontiers and oppose any territorial changes by force or subversion, or even by "peaceful" annexation or secession. The new rulers understandably show no disposition to merge their recently attained autonomy into a more inclusive sovereign entity, much less to have their territory emasculated by secession. Even when it looked as though Biafra had a good chance, only four of the forty members of the Organization of African Unity (OAU) recognized the secessionist state. As President Julius Nyerere of Tanzania observed at the founding OAU conference in 1963, we all could agree that "our boundaries are so absurd that they must be regarded as sacrosanct."

To maintain and develop any new state is a formidable task. In tropical Africa this task has been exacerbated by the character of the pre-colonial societies as well as the ambiguous colonial heritage and the abrupt and premature transfer of sovereignty. Precolonial Africa south of the Sahara was largely an iron-age culture. Unlike the Mediterranean world, it developed no literature, no science, and only the most primitive forms of architecture and artifacts. The wheel and mathematical calculation were unknown. Animism was the dominant religion. The primary social unit was the extended family, the primary source of identity the tribe. The imagination and historical memory of the traditional African were wholly circumscribed by his tribal identity.

The tribe was also the primary political unit. The tribal chief wielded final political authority, though larger kingdoms were established by conquest by the stronger warrior tribes. Tribal wars were frequent and savage by modern Western standards. Ritual cannibalism and indigenous slavery were widespread. The Atlantic trade in slaves was stimulated by Africa, and the African leadership of the day fought fiercely against abolition of the slave traffic.

The conquest of Africa by the European powers in the nineteenth century had a unifying, not balkanizing, effect upon the continent. The tribes fell under a political system of some fifty administrative territories and six European language zones. The colonial administrators, along with Christian missionaries, brought education, medical care, and better living standards. Law and order were imposed. Slavery was abolished. The rudiments of Western justice were made available to a large portion of the population.

Most consequential of all, the imperial presence in Africa fostered among a partially Westernized elite a sense of supratribal identity and a desire for political authority and autonomy coextensive with the territorial state. But neither the elite nor the larger population was prepared for wider political responsibility. The ambiguous legacy of the colonial period was a desire for self-determination without the capacity for self-government.

From Colony to State—Tribe to Nation

Political independence came too abruptly and too soon to tropical Africa. States were established by fiat, not by conflict. Statehood was essentially a gift, made in response to an indigenous "demand" generated by the Western conscience and the desire of an increasing number of Africans to enjoy the fruits of industrial society. Authority was handed over with little struggle, thus delaying the reaction to the "trauma of independence." A people who must fight to control a territory learn more about the exacting requirements of exercising political power than those who simply observe a colonial administration or participate in the civil service of an alien authority. This element of struggle helps to explain President Jomo Kenyatta's strength in Kenya.

The delayed shock of the birth trauma can also be attributed to the apparently smooth and successful early transitions of authority in Ghana and the Sudan. The illusion was shattered within a few years by a spate of mutinies, assassinations, coups, counter-coups, and civil-tribal wars in a dozen countries. The severity of the conflict in the Congo, Nigeria, and the Sudan has bred a more sober and realistic recognition of the shock and burdens of independence. The catastrophic effects of both colonization and decolonization have been recognized, along with the probability that the effects of the latter will continue "for generations to come," to quote Alan Paton.

Decolonization in Africa can be described as the fragmentation of sovereignty at the periphery of empire. Under political pressures, large pieces of territory were cut loose, not to fend wholly for themselves, but to become independent and self-determined states that would be sustained in a large measure by continuing cultural, economic, and security ties with the former colonial power. These new states, seriously deficient in the disciplines, habits, and institutions essential to modern economies and political development, have been correctly described as weak, fledgling, embryonic, makeshift, and soft.

A major reason for this weakness is the fact that the former transfer of legal authority is not accompanied by a transfer of power. The shift of sovereignty, symbolized ceremoniously by the lowering of an old flag and the raising of a new one, is a relatively simple transaction involving a commitment by the old government to cease exercising authority and by the new to accept the responsibilities of government. Political power and capacity, in contrast, can only be drawn from the human and material resources within the new state. It is impossible to predict whether a newly installed government possesses that capacity even though it has a firm promise of help from its former metropolitan power or other friendly states.

A small state may be in a perpetually precarious position, but it is not an anachronism. A small, poor, and tribally diverse state with an overwhelming illiterate population can survive indefinitely if it is surrounded by friendly neighbours and is sustained by a propitious balance among the great powers. If it also receives trade, investment, and other forms of support from industrial states, it can even prosper.

The most serious barrier to national identity and the most serious internal obstacle to effective statewide government is the persistence of tribal identity, thought, habits, and social structures. Increased attention is being given to the problem of bridging the gulf between the intimate tribe and the remote nation. Tom Mboya of Kenya, who understood this problem and decried "negative tribalism," was ironically the victim of a tribal assassination in 1969.

Colonial rule has been criticized for showing too much respect for indigenous institutions. African societies might now be in a better position for "take-off" if colonial exploitation had been harder on them—if the colonial powers had destroyed traditional structures and had prepared Africans socially and psychologically to build a new nation. Since the colonial authorities were not tough enough, the new leaders are in the awkward position of being "nationalists without nations."

A cohesive national identity is an asset in state-building, but its absence is not an insurmountable obstacle. Though a multiplicity of tribes tends to retard national unification, it need not be a barrier to the state's survival. Indeed, the larger their number and the smaller their size, the better are the chances of effective amalgamation. Rivalry between large tribal communities for leadership and the fruits of power was the primary cause of the bloody civil war between Biafra and the Nigerian government.

Contemporary African leaders, as former Secretary of State Dean Rusk put it, operate from the "premise that the various ethnic groups . . . can and should reconcile their differences within present national boundaries and in the process build national identities reflecting African values and African necessities." But there is no assurance that a larger identity will be realized in all areas of tropical Africa in the foreseeable future.

Paucity of Western Norms

The supratribal territorial state in tropical Africa is a European import, alien in concept, function, and external manifestation. Nevertheless, the great majority of African leaders have declared their intention to develop a modern state based upon a money economy and a universal franchise.

The most immediate and urgent political task is that of "state-preserving," as distinct from the longer range task of state-building. Political development embraces the disciplines of state-preserving and state-building, including all changes that enhance the government's capacity to maintain the security of its people and to enforce the law throughout its territory. The movement toward a more just, responsible, and democratic exercise of power may be defined as democratic political development. The first task of government is to govern. In terms of Western values, the second task is to govern justly, the third to govern democratically. As of 1970 few tropical African states had made notable progress in the second and third tasks. Only eleven out of forty countries ruled by blacks or Arabs had an opposition party, and most rulers regarded such an opposition as highly undesirable.

Overcoming Inertia and Corruption

Tribal identity—expressed in special preferences for tribal brothers—often compromises loyal service to the state. Widespread nepotism, along with the avarice that asserts itself during periods of great political change, contributes to a high level of corruption. This corruption as a system of government in tropical Africa has been dubbed "kleptocracy."

In sharp contrast to Western culture, traditional African society tends to be static, and strongly resistant to change, innovation, and adaptation. This massive inertia is destined to have a profound and largely negative effect upon political and economic development for a long time to come. "A Fool lies here who tried to hustle the East," Rudyard Kipling's epitaph in *The Naulahka*, is even more appropriate to tropical Africa.

A tiny but slowly growing indigenous elite has some understanding of the requirements of political authority and the disciplines of government, including the necessity to collect taxes. This Westernized vanguard, varying in size and competence includes many top politicians, professional people, and businessmen. More detribalized than urban dwellers or educated villagers, they are the chief bearers of rising expectations.

Between the elite and the static mass stands the semi-detribalized African—the product of European industry or Christian missions. He is a marginal man, semi-literate, confused, and often restless, both an asset and a liability. His precarious identity can be exploited by rabble-rousing politicians or be eased by gainful employment or by fuller participation in the larger nascent political community.

Role of the Army

The post-colonial rash of coups and upsurge of conflict and chaos in tropical Africa has belatedly focused attention on the army and the police as consequential and hitherto largely overlooked actors in the political drama. A principle reason for this neglect is the fact that these legal instruments of coercion were not a political problem in the colonial period; they were necessary to maintain law and order and with very few and temporary exceptions were loyal to the colonial power. No armies in tropical Africa played a "liberating" or revolutionary role and none had a discernible effect on the pace or character of decolonization. Yet, by 1970 there had been more than thirty coups or abrupt changes in government in which the new army played a major role.

On independence day the African armies were essentially non-political and non-conspiratorial. Their European and African officers fully expected to continue serving the new regime as they had the old. The African officers accepted the Western doctrines of civilian supremacy and a non-political army, learned by example from the colonial powers and by precept at Sandhurst and St. Cyr.

Virtually all African armies continued to be heavily dependent upon European officers and advisers and on material support provided by the former power. Even in such countries as Ghana and Nigeria, where the Africanization of the officer ranks was most advanced, European officers continued to predominate in top command and training positions during the first several years of independence.

During and following the transition to statehood in most African countries the army was the strongest symbol of continuity between the old and the new orders. When the frail and inexperienced regimes could not withstand the centrifugal forces unleashed by the withdrawal of externally imposed restraints, the military in a dozen states moved in to fill the vacuum. The circumstances varied widely, but in those where military intervention appeared justified to save the state from disintegration, as in the Congo, or from dictatorship, as in Ghana, the officers were obviously uncomfortable in their unexpected role.

The government of an independent state must, by definition, have reliable instruments of coercion at its disposal to protect its people against internal and external dangers. The scepter, a symbol of sovereign political authority, must be upheld by the men who wield the spear. This does not mean that governments are maintained on the points of spears, but that governments, sustained by the passive or active consent of their people, also must enjoy a monopoly of the legitimate use of violence within their territory. In any state—old or new, past or present—the military establishment by its very existence cannot avoid having a significant impact on political affairs, even when it refrains from acting.

In view of these classic political postulates, confirmed in everyday events, the neglect of the military (and police) in new states must be attributed to the modern movement away from classic political theory, prejudice against the military as an institution, and a preoccupation with the more familiar noncoercive factors.

African armies tend to be the most detribalized, Westernized, modernized, integrated, and cohesive institutions in their respective states. The army is usually the most disciplined agency in the state. It often enjoys a greater sense of national identity than other institutions. In technical skills, including the capacity to coerce and to communicate, the army is the most modernized agency in the country.

A more vivid symbol of sovereignty than the flag, the constitution, or the parliament, the army often evokes more popular sentiment than a political leader. The officer corps is an important and conspicuous component of the tiny ruling elite. In trim and colourful uniforms the army marches in independence day celebrations and its top brass stand with the head of state and prime minister on the reviewing platform. The political leaders understand only too well their dependence on the loyalty and effectiveness of the army in upholding their authority and in putting down any major challenge to the regime.

The army's capacity to play a constructive political role has been compromised by two developments. In some places the rapid Africanization of the officer corps has eroded professional skill, discipline, and loyalty to the regime. Saying this, we must acknowledge that disloyalty to a corrupt regime can be a virtue, e.g., the army-police coup that overthrew Nkrumah in Ghana.

The other problem is an army's temporary regression to earlier forms of tribal warfare. In the Congo, Nigeria, the Sudan, and elsewhere, Western rules of war—respect for civilians, fair treatment for prisoners, etc.— have given way to atavistic and brutal behavior that shows no mercy for civilians or prisoners and is more intent on ravishing the countryside for booty than achieving military objectives. The deterioration of discipline, usually associated with the breakdown of civil order, has occurred in part because of the absence of European or African officers trained in a tradition of civility. In the Western democratic world the chief function of the military is to deter and prevent war, while in the tribal tradition—particularly of the more aggressive tribes—the vocation of the warrior is to make war, to "wash his spear" in blood as it is sometimes put.

To address these problems, the former colonial powers in most African states have maintained military ties, including advice, officer training, and equipment assistance. As a newcomer to tropical Africa, except for Liberia, the United States has also provided military training and assistance, although it would be virtually impossible to assess the efficacy of such ties.

30 *The Cambodian Bloodbath*

The fall of Saigon to the Communists on April 30, 1975, led to concentration camps and thousands of Vietnamese boat people. The fall of Cambodia to the Communists two weeks before unleashed one of the bloodiest massacres in history. In both cases, American-backed regimes were overthrown and American diplomats were hurriedly evacuated by helicopter. The Saigon story saturated the media, but the grisly aftermath of Phnom Penh's fall was barely mentioned at the time. My analysis of the media's failure to report the Cambodian bloodbath appeared in TV Guide *on April 30, 1977. Later, this genocide, sometimes referred to as "the killing fields," was widely publicized.*

* * *

Let's suppose that Castro were abruptly overthrown and replaced in Cuba by a non-Communist regime determined to wipe out all vestiges of the old order—Castro's army and secret police, the Communist Party, political commissars, and the entire Soviet apparatus, along with the revolution's vaunted social achievements: child-care centers, workers' schools, student cane-cutting battalions, and the Marxist intellectual class.

Let's further suppose that Cuba's new rulers pursued their ends, not by legislation, trials, or reeducation, but by a massive program of "class" executions and forced migration from cities, a program that within twenty months would bring brutal death to one Cuban in every six or seven.

If such a bloodbath took place, the world press would scream with condemnation and the United Nations would vote sanctions.

Unfortunately, this scenario is not make-believe. The bloodbath has already happened, not in Cuba but in Cambodia. In the face of this massive atrocity, the president, the Congress, and the United Nations have remained all but mute. American newspapers and TV, with rare exception, have neither reported the facts nor condemned what the *Christian Science Monitor* has called one of the most "brutal and concentrated onslaughts in history."

The Cambodian bloodbath began on April 17, 1975, two hours after the first Communist squads started "liberating" Phnom Penh. Within days, there was enough evidence from the lips of escaping Cambodians and foreigners to rivet mankind's conscience on Cambodia.

According to numerous eyewitness accounts verified by several independent and reliable sources, this is what happened. From the start, the Communist High Command decided to eliminate all "enemies of the people," a category that expanded as the grisly drama unfolded. First executed were the officers and men of the Lon Nol army and their wives and children. Then came higher civilian officials, followed by lesser ones—hamlet chiefs, doctors, nurses, teachers, and even students. In most cases, the families were also killed in the frantic effort to obliterate every trace of the old regime by the first anniversary of the Communist takeover.

To "purify" the culture, historic buildings, shrines, schools, and even cities were targeted for oblivion. Two million citizens of Phnom Penh, considered a cesspool of corruption, were evacuated at gunpoint, as were a million more from smaller towns. The sick were driven from hospitals. Tens of thousands met death by beating, exhaustion or slow starvation. The lucky ones were shot.

According to two experienced researchers who sifted testimony from refugees in Thailand, France, and the United States (*Murder of a Gentle Land*, by John Barron and Anthony Paul, Reader's Digest Press), at least 1.2 million Cambodians died between April 17, 1975 and January 1, 1977, as a direct result of Communist policies—over 100,000 from massacres and executions, over 20,000 during escape attempts, over 400,000 during the expulsion from the cities, and 680,000 from disease and starvation. One Cambodian in six met a painful end. U.S. Government agencies and other authorities do not dispute these grim statistics.

On September 5, 1975, Ieng Sary, a Cambodian official, on arriving in New York said: "The towns have been cleaned." When he appeared at the United Nations, he was warmly applauded. He neglected to say he represented a country "without universities, commerce, art, music, literature, science, or hope," to quote Barron and Paul.

American newspapers and TV networks barely pierced what the *New York Times* called the "veil of silence."

In the 20 months following the "liberation" of Cambodia, the ABC, CBS, and NBC evening TV evening news shows spent a total of four hours and 55 minutes covering Cambodia, but only 7 percent on the bloodbath. The three shows combined gave one minute of news a month to a purge that in terms of relative population exceeded the slaughter of Hitler's and Stalin's concentration camps. The attentive viewer—able to watch only one channel at a time—received only 20 seconds a month from the medium most Americans rely on for their news.

Equally appalling was the skeptical and even apologetic tone of most of the early stories. The May 8, 1975, reporting was typical: ABC says bloodbath theory is widely believed by refugees; no confirmation. CBS says tales of executions are not confirmed; *New York Times* newsman Sydney Schanberg suggests Americans have stake in bloodbath theory. ABC and CBS report the Khmer Rouge troops are well-disciplined.

During the next eighteen months the three networks combined carried ten brief references to brutality and death, but there was not a single comprehensive report on the bloodbath. The near absence of Cambodian bloodbath news on TV was not attributable to a lack of evidence. Among the 50,000 Cambodians who escaped, there are thousands of eyewitnesses. And some enterprising newsmen did interview them.

The performance of America's serious newspapers was not as poor as that of TV news. Of the sixty-three stories examined, it appears that only one hit page one, on February 2, 1976, in the *Washington Post*. As on TV, only a few press stories carried the bloodbath story without misgivings or apology.

It took two explicit atrocity reports by Secretary of State Kissinger to get the attention of the networks. This May 13, 1975, statement appeared in several papers. His June 24 report was noted briefly by TV and the papers, but it was not followed up by either.

The bloodbath, the very essence of dramatic human-interest news—when carried at all—was treated more frequently in signed opinions and editorials than in the news columns. To their credit, the *New York Times*, the *Christian Science Monitor* and the *Wall Street Journal* reported and condemned the bloodbath. On July 9, 1975, the *Times* compared it to the "Soviet extermination of the Kulaks [and] the Gulag Archipelago." In April 1976, the *Journal* said: "The enormity of this kind of atrocity . . . is mind-numbing" and asked why the "weak outcry from the usual wellsprings of moral outrage around the world."

Why, indeed? The press is frequently outraged by small or even alleged crimes. The media reported fully and sometimes joined in the condemnation of the Spanish government in 1975 for executing five terrorists convicted of murdering policemen. But where is the condemnation of the murder of a million innocent people?

The *Wall Street Journal* suggests a partial answer—the frequent partnership of moral outrage and revolutionary zeal. The "crimes of the Khmer Rouge, even though they dwarf some other state crimes of our time . . . have attracted less attention because they are inflicted in the name of revolution."

31 *Trivializing Human Rights*

From his first days in the White House, President Jimmy Carter lectured Ameri-can allies in the Third World about their human rights abuses, while seeming to overlook the much more egregious violations of our totalitarian adversaries. I criticized Carter's stance in a New York Times *op-ed piece and later elaborated my critique in a* Policy Review *(January 1978). Excerpts of the latter were widely reprinted in the United States and in Latin America. A shortened version follows. My outspoken position eventually led President Reagan to nominate me to be assistant secretary of state for human rights. This precipitated a protracted Left-liberal attack that in invective anticipated the controversy over Robert Bork's nomination to the Supreme Court six years later. After a negative vote by the Senate Foreign Relations Committee, I withdrew my name. As a consolation prize, I was appointed a special counterterrorism consultant to Secretary of State Alexander Haig.*

*   *   *

Our Founding Fathers wrestled with the problem of creating a free and independent country ruled by a government with sufficient authority to deal with domestic and alien threats and with sufficient openness to re-spond to the will of the people. Their formula was the judicious balance between authority and freedom embraced in the Declaration of indepen-dence and elaborated in the Constitution. The former asserted that "gov-ernments are instituted among men, deriving their just powers from the consent of the governed" to secure certain fundamental rights, among them "life, liberty, and the pursuit of happiness." The Constitution was promulgated to "establish justice, insure domestic tranquillity, provide for the common defense, promote the general welfare, and secure the blessings of liberty."

This audacious experiment prospered in an inauspicious world. In the face of new challenges, the American system provided for increasingly broader political participation and other specific rights spelled out or implied in the Constitution and its amendments. Our history is not without blemish, but compared to other political communities past and present, the American record is a beacon of freedom and justice in a world bedeviled by chaos, authoritarian rule, and messianic tyranny.

The Current Human Rights Campaign

The current wave of concern for human rights around the world was foreshadowed by several developments, notably Woodrow Wilson's crusade for "self-determination" and the Universal Declaration of Human Rights adopted by the United Nations in 1948. The U.S. campaign to make the advancement of human rights abroad an objective of foreign policy is more recent, but it did not start with President Jimmy Carter. He simply built on the lively interest in Congress expressed largely in foreign aid legislation. The 1974 Foreign Assistance Act prohibited or restricted economic or military assistance to any government "which engages in a consistent pattern of gross violations of internationally recognized human rights, including torture or cruel, inhumane, or degrading treatment or punishment, prolonged detention without charges, and other flagrant denial of the right to life, liberty, and the security of person" (Section 502B). Most of the congressional human rights activists have limited their advocacy of punitive measures to Chile, South Korea, and Iran. In practice, the restrictions have had little effect on limiting aid, loans, or military sales, even to these countries.

Human rights was a natural cause for President Carter. As a born-again Baptist and a latter-day Wilsonian, he repeatedly stated his intention to restore integrity and compassion to American domestic and foreign policy. In his address at Notre Dame University on March 22, 1977, Mr. Carter deplored our "intellectual and moral poverty," illustrated by our Vietnam policy, and our "inordinate fear of Communism which once led us to embrace any dictator who joined us in that fear." He called for a "new" American foreign policy, "based on constant decency in its values and an optimism in its historical vision."

The most conspicuous manifestation of his new policy is his effort to promote human rights in other countries by means of U.S. statecraft, including private diplomacy, public preaching, and measures to deny or threaten to deny economic, military or nuclear assistance. Mr. Carter's campaign has been given bureaucratic visibility by establishing a new post, assistant secretary of state for human rights and humanitarian affairs, currently filled by Patricia Derian, who sometimes discusses her assignment in moralistic rhetoric alien to traditional diplomatic discourse.

The human rights campaign has received mixed reviews at home and abroad. Last July in a *New Yorker* article friendly to the effort, Elizabeth

Drew reported that Mr. Carter's people "are pleased, and some even a bit awestruck," at the impact that the human-rights campaign has had thus far. "I think" says one, "that the mulish world has noticed the two-by-four."

There is no doubt that the threatening plank has been noticed, and probably in isolated cases it has accomplished some good. But it should be recorded that some un-mulish elements in the world, including friendly and allied governments, have also seen the two-by-four and are not convinced that its whack, however well-intended, has always been redemptive. There is no doubt that it has harmed relations with some allies and has both irritated and comforted adversaries.

It is by no means clear that the campaign has resulted in any significant relaxation of Soviet restrictions against emigration or political dissent. There is evidence that the opposite may be the case. On December 30, 1977, a *New York Times* page-one story reported: "The small Soviet human rights movement . . . is at its lowest point in years after a campaign of arrests, threats, and forced exile."

It is clear, however, that a score of allies has been unhappy with a policy they regard as arrogant and unfairly applied. Brazil, Argentina, Uruguay, and Guatemala have been alienated to the point where they have refused military assistance from Washington. And Brazil has served notice that it wishes to withdraw from its Security Assistance Agreement of twenty-five years standing. This alienation of allies gives aid and comfort to Moscow that more than offsets the minor embarrassment it suffers from Mr. Carter's conspicuous "intervention" on behalf of Soviet dissidents.

Six Flaws in Carter's Policy

President Carter's campaign has confused our foreign policy goals and trivialized the concept of human rights. It both reflects and reinforces serious conceptual flaws in the worldview of its most articulate spokesmen. These flaws, if permitted to instruct foreign policy, or even influence it unduly, could have catastrophic consequences for the security of the United States and the cause of freedom in the world. Six interrelated flaws deserve brief mention:

1. Underestimating the Totalitarian Threat

Human dignity and freedom are under siege around the world. It has been ever so. The islands of community protected by humane law have been contracting ever since postwar decolonization began. The citizens of most of the newly independent states in Asia and Africa now experience less freedom and fewer guaranteed rights than they did under Western colonial rule.

But the greatest threat to human rights comes from messianic totalitarian regimes whose cruel grip brooks no opposition. Their self-anointed and self-perpetuating elites have become the arbiters of orthodoxy in every sphere—politics, economics, education, the arts, and family life. The ruling party even usurps the place of God. In totalitarian states like the USSR, Cuba, Cambodia, and Vietnam, there are no countervailing forces to challenge the power, will, or policies of the entrenched elite.

In spite of notable exceptions, the general political situation in the Third World is characterized by chaos and authoritarian regimes. Democratic and anti-democratic ideas and institutions are competing for acceptance. In this struggle, we should not underestimate the attraction of the totalitarian temptation to leaders who are grappling with the perplexing problems of moving traditional societies into modern welfare states.

The human rights activists tend to underestimate the totalitarian threat to the West and the totalitarian temptation in the Third World. Hence, they neglect or trivialize the fundamental political and moral struggle of our time—the protracted conflict between forces of total government based on coercion and the proponents of limited government based on popular consent and humane law. In their preoccupation with the minor abridgment of certain rights in authoritarian states, they often overlook the massive threat to the liberty of millions. They attack the limitation of civil rights in South Korea and at the same time call for the United States to withdraw its ground forces, an act that may invite aggression from North Korea. It would be a great irony if Washington in the name of human rights were to adopt a policy that would deliver 35 million largely free South Koreans into virtual slavery.

2. Confusing Totalitarianism with Authoritarianism

In terms of political rights, moral freedom, and cultural vitality, there is a profound difference between authoritarian and totalitarian regimes. Most Asian, African, and Latin American countries are ruled by small elites supported by varying degrees of popular consent. Some are run by genocidal tyrants like General Idi Amin of Uganda, others by one-party cliques, military juntas, or civilian-military committees. Almost all authoritarian regimes permit a significantly greater degree of freedom and diversity than the totalitarian ones in all spheres—political, cultural, economic, and religious. Authoritarian rulers often allow opposition parties to operate and a restrained press to publish. Foreign correspondents usually can move about freely and send out uncensored dispatches. They often permit and sometimes encourage relatively free economic activity and freedom of movement for their citizens. The quality of life possible under such rule, of course, depends not only on the character of central control, but on the cultural and economic level of the population as well.

There is, for example, far more freedom of choice, diversity of opinion and activity, and respect for human rights in authoritarian South Korea than in totalitarian North Korea. There is also far more freedom and cultural vitality in Chile—even under its present military government—than in Cuba. There have been political prisoners in Chile and there may be a handful now, but there are an estimated 15,000 to 60,000 political detainees in Cuba. These facts are noted, not to praise Chile or condemn Cuba, but to emphasize the consequential difference of human rights under the two kinds of regimes.

Another crucial difference is the capacity of authoritarian rule to evolve into democratic rule. This has happened recently in Spain, Portugal and Greece. In sharp contrast, a Communist dictatorship has never made a peaceful transition to more representative and responsive rule.

3. Overestimating America's Influence Abroad

If the human rights zealots do not indulge in what Denis Brogan once called "the illusion of American omnipotence," they tend to overestimate the capacity of our government to influence the external world, particularly domestic developments in other countries. America is powerful, but not all-powerful. Our considerable leverage of the 1950s and even our diminished leverage of the 1960s has been seriously eroded by OPEC, the great leap forward in Soviet military might, and our abandonment of Vietnam.

Quite apart from our limited capacity to influence intractable realities abroad, there is and should be a profound moral constraint on efforts designed to alter domestic practices, institutions, and policies within other states. Neo-Wilsonian attempts to make the world safe for human rights is rooted in a persistent idealistic stream in the American character. But there is another and quieter stream equally honorable, but less pushy and perhaps more persuasive—symbolized by the Biblical parable of a candle upon a candlestick or a city set upon a hill, an example to the "lesser breeds without the law," as it was put in a more candid era.

John Quincy Adams expressed this more modest understanding of America's external responsibility: "We are the friends of liberty everywhere, but the custodians only of our own." Thirty years later, Abraham Lincoln spoke of "liberty as the heritage of all men, in all lands everywhere," but he did not claim that the United States was the chosen instrument for fulfilling this heritage.

4. Confusing Domestic and Foreign Policy

Many human rights crusaders confuse the fundamental distinctions between domestic and foreign policy that are rooted in age-old practice, international law, the UN Charter, and common sense. They do not take seriously the distinctions in authority and responsibility that flow from the concept of sovereignty that underlies the modern state system. Our president and all other heads of state have authority to act only in their own states, within the territory of their legal jurisdiction. They are responsible only for the security and the welfare of their own people, including their citizens living or traveling abroad.

There are, of course, multiple modes of interaction and cooperation between states based on mutual interest, ranging from trade, investment, and cultural exchange to military assistance and alliance ties. These activities are consistent with the concept of sovereign equality and non-interference in internal affairs. But short of a victorious war, no government has a right to impose its preference on another sovereign state. The mode and quality of life, the character and structure of institutions within a state should be determined by its own people, not by outsiders, however well-intentioned. The same is true for the pace and direction of social, political, or economic change.

U.S. foreign policy toward another state should be determined largely by the foreign policy of that state. Domestic factors and forces are significant determinants only if they bear on external realities. Washington is allied with Iran, Taiwan, Thailand, and South Korea, not because their governments are authoritarian, but because they are regarded as vital in the struggle against the expansion of Soviet or Chinese power. It is appropriate to provide economic or military assistance to them, even if they do not hold regular elections. In sum, U.S. aid can properly be given to encourage a friend or ally to pursue constructive external policies, but not to force internal reforms opposed by the assisted government.

5. Ignoring the Perils of Reform Intervention

The impulse to impose our standards or practices on other societies, supported by policies of reward and punishment, leads inevitably to a kind of reform intervention. We Americans have no moral mandate to transform other societies, and we rightly resent such efforts on the part of the totalitarians. There is more than a touch of arrogance in our efforts to alter the domestic behavior of allies, or even of adversaries.

As noted above, the Foreign Assistance Act states that a principal goal of U.S. policy is to promote internationally recognized human rights abroad. Further, Title IX of the act says that U.S. aid should be used to encourage "democratic private and local government institutions" within the recipient states. The implications of this seemingly innocent phrase are disquieting. Should U.S. assistance be used to alter domestic institutions? Should we insist on an ideological or reform test before providing aid? Is this not a form of uninvited interference in domestic matters? If we take sovereign equality seriously, we will recognize that the people of every state should determine their own system of justice and how they want to defend themselves against domestic or foreign dangers.

Third World states may request assistance from friendly governments on mutually agreed terms. But outside governments, however nobly motivated, cannot impose justice, human rights, or freedom on other states without resorting to conquest. It may be possible to "export revolution"—as the phrase goes—but we cannot export human rights or respect for the rule of law. Freedom and justice are the fruit of long organic growth nurtured by religious values, personal courage, social restraint, and respect for the law. The majesty of law is little understood in traditional societies where ethnic identity tends to supersede all other claims on loyalty and obedience.

6. Distorting Foreign Policy Objectives

A consistent and single-minded invocation of a human rights standard in making U.S. foreign policy decisions would subordinate, blur, or distort other essential considerations. Our foreign policy has vital but limited goals—national security and international peace—both of which have a great impact on human rights. Aggressive war and tyranny are the two chief enemies of freedom and justice. Our efforts to deter nuclear war and nuclear blackmail are calculated to protect the culture and free institutions of Western Europe and North America. In the Third World we seek to maintain a regional stability conducive to responsible political development and mutually beneficial economic intercourse among states. Economic productivity alleviates stark poverty and thus broadens the range of cultural and political choice.

Our policies of nuclear deterrence should be determined by our understanding of the Soviet nuclear threat and our trade policies toward Moscow should be determined by our economic and security interests. Neither should be influenced, much less determined, by the extent of human rights violations in the Soviet Union. Likewise, in dealing with Third World countries, their foreign policy behavior should be the determining factor, not their domestic practices. Even though South Korea has an authoritarian government, we should continue our security support because it is a faithful ally under siege from a totalitarian neighbor and because its independence is vital to the defense of Japan and Japan's independence is vital to the U.S. position in the Western Pacific and the world.

What Is America's Responsibility?

In a formal and legal sense, the U.S. Government has no responsibility—and certainly no authority—to promote human rights in other sovereign states. But this is hardly the whole story. Because of our heritage, our dedication to humane government, our power, and our wealth, we Americans have a moral responsibility, albeit ill-defined, in the larger world consistent with our primary obligations at home and commensurate with our capacity to influence external events. We are almost universally regarded as a humane power and as the champion of freedom and decency. We should be proud of our non-vindictive occupation policies in Germany and Japan. But we enjoy no occupation authority now, and the role of our government abroad is less clear. Saying this, the American people and their government can make two major contributions to the cause of human rights in other countries.

First, in the spirit of John Quincy Adams and Lincoln, we can be worthy custodians of the freedom bequeathed us by the Founding Fathers and thus continue to encourage the aspirations of peoples everywhere. We can give hope to those in bondage by illustrating what the late Reinhold Niebuhr has called "the relevance of the impossible ideal." We can never fully realize our own ideals. And in most other cultural settings, full respect for human rights cannot be expected in the foreseeable future. A quick change in government will not enshrine liberty or justice. Serving as an example of decency is our most effective way to nudge forward the cause of human dignity.

Second, our government can advance human rights by strengthening our resolve to defend our allies who are threatened by totalitarian aggression or subversion. This requires security guarantees, military assistance, and in some cases the presence of U.S. troops on foreign soil. Our combined effort to maintain a favorable balance of power has succeeded in preserving the independence of Western Europe, Japan, and South Korea.

We have a domestic consensus for continued support of our NATO allies and Japan, but some of our commitments elsewhere have been eroded by confusion over the nature of the threat. We are being severely tested in Taiwan, South Korea, and southern Africa. In each case, the totalitarians are pressing relentlessly by military, economic, political, and subversive means to destroy and replace Western influence. The struggle in these areas is hardly one of pure freedom against totalitarianism, but human rights (as well as peace) are clearly at stake. Any regime installed or sponsored by Moscow or Peking in Seoul, Taipei, or Pretoria would certainly provide less justice and freedom than the imperfect regime it displaced.

Beyond serving as a good example and maintaining our security commitments, there is little the U.S. Government can or should do to advance human rights, other than using quiet diplomatic channels at appropriate times and places. Moscow and other governments should be reminded of their pledges in the UN Charter and the Helsinki Agreement. Public preaching to friend or foe has limited utility. It is both embarrassing and contra-productive to threaten punitive measures against friendly, but less than democratic, regimes that are attempting to achieve a reasonable balance between authority and freedom at home, often under severely trying circumstances, and are pursuing constructive policies abroad.

The Irony of Virtue

The Carter Administration is not of one mind on the significance, purpose, of effects of the human rights crusade. The administration is even less united in the implementation of the program in specific cases. During his visit to Iran last December, President Carter gave his final approval for the sale of six to eight nuclear reactors to that country whose government has been the target of human rights activists as well as of Marxist groups. Alleged rights violations by the Shah's government have apparently had little effect on U.S. arms sales there. The same appears to be true of South Korea. In fact, some observers believe that the entire campaign so far has been more rhetoric than reality, and some suggest that it was launched more to satisfy the impulses of U.S. domestic groups than to effect real changes in the external world.

In any event, there appears to be a growing recognition of the moral and political limitations of a foreign policy crusade that, to quote Mr. Carter, is based on "constant decency" and "optimism." While defending the campaign in principle, Secretary of State Cyrus Vance notes some of its reservations and flaws. In a Law Day address, April 30, 1977, he warned against a "self-righteous and strident" posture and said "we must always keep in mind the limits of our power and of our wisdom." He added that "a doctrinaire plan of action" to advance human rights "would be as damaging as indifference."

The tone of Mr. Vance's address stands in sharp contrast to President Carter's Notre Dame speech, which has been criticized as arrogant, self-righteous, and naive by Senator Daniel Patrick Moynihan, Jeane Kirkpatrick, and other foreign policy observers. The critics took exception to Mr. Carter's view that there have been "dramatic worldwide advances in the protection of the individual from the arbitrary power of the state." In his pragmatic response to political realities, however, the president is far closer to Mr. Vance's words than to his own rhetoric.

The canons of prudence, statesmanship, and accountability all suggest that Carter tone down his rhetoric. He should quietly recognize the political and moral limits of promoting particular reforms in other societies. He should recognize that a policy rooted in a presumption of American righteousness and in our capacity to sponsor virtue in other states often leads to the opposite effect. In some circumstances, the invocation of a rigid standard could undercut our security ties and invite a disaster in which millions of persons would move from partial freedom to tyranny.

Mr. Carter's policy drips with irony, precisely because his good intentions may lead to dire consequences. Irony is not the result of evil intention or malice, but rather of a hidden defect in virtue. In Mr. Carter's case, the defect is a kind of vague, romantic optimism with an excessive confidence in the power of reason and goodwill. This comforting view of human nature, the offspring of the Enlightenment, differs sharply with the more sober biblical understanding of the nature and destiny of man. Be that as it may, the president should not be judged on his philosophical consistency, but rather by the actual policies he pursues. Since there is some relation between how one thinks and feels and what one does, it is not inappropriate to recall the words of columnist Michael Novak: "One of the best ways to create an immoral foreign policy is to try too hard for a moral one."

32 Central America Under Siege

During his years in the Kremlin, Leonid Brezhnev launched adventures through-out the Third World, including Central America. The Marxist Sandinista national anthem in Nicaragua declared the United States the "enemy of humanity." In 1983, President Reagan's efforts to bolster anti-Communist forces in this vital area were widely opposed by America's media elite. William Safire phoned me asking if I would write an op-ed piece for the New York Times *supporting Reagan's Central American policies because he "couldn't find any other responsible person to do it." My response appeared on July 31, 1983. Three months later, USA Today asked me to comment on our October 25 invasion of Grenada. The piece was published the next day. Both articles are reprinted here. During Nicaragua's 1996 election campaign, the refurbished Sandinistas replaced their earlier anthem with Beethoven's* Ode to Joy. *But they were not returned to power.*

* * *

President Reagan's decision to conduct naval exercises in international waters off Central America and the Pentagon's announcement that U.S. military personnel will take part in joint exercises in Honduras have shocked some Americans. Others see in these traditional shows of force evidence that at least we may be overcoming the paralysis of power that has gripped us since the fall of Saigon.

Some Americans are reluctant to recognize that we live in a tragic and dangerous world. The frontiers of freedom are shrinking. Over the last decade or so the Kremlin has installed regimes in Afghanistan, Vietnam, Laos, Cambodia, Ethiopia, Angola, and Mozambique. Moscow continues to determine the destiny of its captive nations from the Baltic to Bulgaria. Its control always means an overwhelming denial of human rights.

Moscow subsidizes Cuba at the rate of $8 million a day and uses it as a springboard to topple Latin American governments. Nicaragua and other surrogates also provide weapons for terrorism and military conquest. There are 6,000 Cuban advisers in Nicaragua, at least 2,000 of them military. There are 55 U.S. military advisers in El Salvador.

A war is raging in Central America. One side will ultimately prevail. What should the United States do to insure that the wrong side will not win? The conflict poses a clear threat to our vital interests. Further, under the Rio Pact and the Charter of the Organization of American States, the United States has a legal and moral responsibility to uphold the security of countries in the region.

The most urgent task is to end the war in El Salvador. This can be done only by military means, not by land redistribution or elections—unless by some miracle the Marxist forces suddenly abandon their conviction that victory comes from the barrel of a gun.

Mr. Reagan's call for increased military and economic assistance to El Salvador, Honduras, and Guatemala is thus wise and necessary. Alone and unaided these fragile governments are no match for Soviet power and ambition. Their forces need greater discipline and training, but at this stage only modest U.S. aid is required. This assistance, backed by the show of strength and commitment symbolized by the planned military exercises, may provide the margin of victory.

United States military support can also lay the foundation for fruitful negotiations. Talks are not an end in themselves; diplomacy is the conduct of war by other means. The ultimate test of policy, morally and politically, is the quality of the agreement, not the process that led to it. The president seeks a peace that insures genuine self-determination, not one that merely stills the guns while external control continues.

Poverty Is Not the Problem

It is often said that poverty and repression are responsible for conflict in Central America. They are factors, but they are not the cause of the violence. Poverty does not cause Communism—on the contrary, Communism, when victorious, perpetuates poverty. The President is committed to supporting a comprehensive development effort. First, the violence must be ended. Peace must precede prosperity; order is a prerequisite for greater justice. Peace must be pursued by a judicious blend of U.S. military aid, covert action, and other manifestations of resolve.

The accusation that President Reagan is leading us into another Vietnam has little merit. We failed to contain Communist expansion in Indochina because we did not act decisively. A more valid and encouraging precedent is the Truman Doctrine, which saved Greece and Turkey from the Soviet yoke. In 1947 these two war-weakened countries were severely threatened by Soviet subversion. Harry Truman knew that only military force could save an ally threatened by military force. He acted and prevented Moscow from extending its empire to the Mediterranean.

Now Mr. Reagan has acted with the same insight. His deployment of a carrier force and his call for increased military and economic aid merit the support of Congress and the American people. This modest but timely demonstration of will may well make it unnecessary to order a blockade or send an expeditionary force later on.

The Soviet Union is on the offensive around the world, probing for soft spots. Our determination is being severely tested in Central America. If we fail to respond with a firm and restrained use of power to achieve our humane objectives, the Communists are likely to succeed in imposing their brutal order. If the President receives the support he deserves, his initiatives in Central America will help restore our credibility as a champion of freedom and will stiffen the spines of our allies in Europe and Asia. As the leader of the Free World we should do no less.

Rescuing Grenada

I breathed a sigh of relief when President Reagan announced that U.S. troops had landed on the tiny Caribbean island of Grenada and secured the two airports. This was one more bit of evidence that America was recovering from the paralyzing self-doubt that had prevented us from employing decisive force abroad since our defeat in Vietnam.

One reporter asked the President whether we have "the right to invade another country to change its government," but the President had no time to answer. Here is my response to that question.

As a general rule, the United States does not have the "right" to change other governments by military means, but in this case the action was amply justified for four reasons:

1. The U.S. landing was made at the request of and in collaboration with six Caribbean governments.
2. It was designed to ensure the safety of perhaps 1,000 Americans, some of whom wanted to leave but could not because the airports were closed.
3. It sought to restore "law and order" after—to use the president's words—"a brutal group of leftist thugs violently seized power." Such order would increase the chances of genuine self-determination for the people of Grenada.
4. Most important, the combined operation will probably rid the Caribbean of one source of Cuban and Soviet mischief in the region.

Evidence suggests that the present ruling elite in Grenada, like the recently ousted one, is subservient to Moscow's imperial ambitions. Why should the United States and its Caribbean friends tolerate an unsinkable

Soviet aircraft carrier in their midst? Moscow invaded Afghanistan uni-laterally with brutal force, including the use of chemical weapons against defenseless civilians, to impose tyranny. Washington intervened in Grenada, with minimum force and full respect for the safety of the civil-ian population, to prevent a Marxist ruling elite from subverting the frag-ile democracies in the area and providing a base for Soviet military action in the Western Hemisphere.

President Reagan acted "strongly and decisively" in the interests of se-curity, freedom, and human rights. He deserves our support.

PART SEVEN

The Neo-Wilsonians

President Woodrow Wilson was not a consistent Wilsonian, but the label clings to him like an ill-fitting garment. His frequent utterances about war, world politics, and national self-determination were sufficient to characterize him as a sometime idealist, if not a utopian. Like Lincoln, he wanted to believe in the better angels of our nature, but unlike Lincoln, he was less prepared to accept the realities of a world torn by war, tyranny, aggression—and original sin.

An idealistic internationalist who desperately wanted to keep America out of the war raging in Europe, he proclaimed his neutrality and labored in vain to negotiate an armistice. Finally, in anger and disappointment, he idealized the struggle as a "war to end all wars"—a war that would "make the world safe for democracy." He saw the Allied cause as a righteous crusade rather than an effort to restore a balance of power in Europe.

Wilson's Fourteen Points served as the basis for armistice terms and a League of Nations to guarantee peace through collective security. Many Europeans hailed Wilson as a savior who promised the millennium. But French Premier Georges Clemenceau scoffed at Wilson's Fourteen Points, noting that God managed with a mere Ten Commandments, and he said that "talking to Wilson is something like talking to Jesus Christ." Wilson personified the irony of misplaced virtue.

Despite the tragedy of World Wars I and II—and the illusory and ignoble weekend between them—and despite the inhumanity of totalitarian regimes, some Americans still harbor Wilsonian illusions. They believe we can escape or ease the burdens of world leadership by internationalizing world politics through multilateral organizations such as the United Nations. Others cling to the Wilsonian dream that we can export democracy. They are not consistent in their demands, but their idealistic appeals occasionally distract policymakers from grappling realistically and pragmatically with external challenges.

As the following selections indicate, my criticism of Wilsonian idealism has been consistent from 1952 until the present.

33 *The UN Cannot Prevent War*

During World War II, liberal Protestant leaders showed a greater interest in cre-
ating an international postwar organization to keep the peace than in the out-
come of the war itself. Even before it was established in 1945, the United Nations
was vigorously oversold by the U.S. National Council of Churches. Though then
a member of the NCC's executive staff, I openly criticized the multilateral moral-
ism of my colleagues. This piece is excerpted from Intercollegian *(November*
1952), a journal of the National Student YMCAs and YWCAs.

*   *   *

During World War II, the Federal Council of Churches, predecessor to the
National Council, strongly urged the United States to ratify the UN Charter. Since its founding in 1950, the NCC continued to support the UN as
the major instrument for maintaining peace, but it emphasized the UN's
nonpolitical activities over its security mission. This essentially nonpolitical bias is indicated in repeated expressions of support for the Universal
Declaration of Human Rights, Genocide Convention, peace observation
commissions, arms control, economic assistance to underdeveloped areas, relief measures, refugees, welfare of the non-self-governing territories, protection of holy places in Jerusalem, and provision for prayer at
the UN headquarters.

A striking exception to the churches' preoccupation with the nonpolitical matters was the response of the NCC and the World Coucil of
Churches to the Communist attack on South Korea on June 25, 1950. Both
commended the UN Security Council for its prompt decision to resist aggression in Korea; the NCC authorized a commission "to study the problem of collective security." The churches were reluctant to deal realistically with the underlying power factors, despite the 1949 Study
Conference on World Order that promulgated the concept of the "responsible use of power."

Mainline Protestant leaders heralded the UN as the last best hope of earth, as a super-gadget designed to banish forever the scourge of war. The super-gadget did not work—it didn't prevent aggression in Korea. Disillusionment with the UN today can be traced in part to the over-selling or mis-selling of the UN by well-intentioned people who had never learned the lesson of the League of Nations.

These seekers of a new world failed to realize that the UN was not God, not even a weak world government. Like the discredited League, the UN had not succeeded in doing away with national sovereignty, conflicting national interests, balance of power tactics, or "power politics," the only kind of politics there is.

What Then Is the UN?

The United Nations is a forum, a meeting place where sovereign states can come and hammer out their differences—if they are so disposed. The UN is a tool, an instrument to be used, abused, or brushed aside by its member states. It does not have the power to end the Cold War or prevent World War III. It cannot resolve the global bipolar struggle—it can only reflect it. Basic decisions affecting the Soviet–Free World conflict will not be made in the tall glass building on the East River; such decisions must be made in Washington and Moscow. Even Eleanor Roosevelt recognized this when she said: "The United Nations is not a cure-all. It is only an instrument capable of effective action when its members have a will to make it work."

34 Limits of UN Crisis Intervention

The United States may not have supported UN intervention in Somalia, Bosnia, and Haiti in the 1990s if it had learned the bitter lessons of UN intervention in the former Belgian Congo in the 1960s. (At that time, Leopoldville was the capital of the Congo; later, the name was changed to Kinshasa.) After a three-year study of that crisis, I concluded that "UN emergency intervention to shore up and rebuild a collapsing system of political and military authority in a fragmented state is almost bound to fail." A multilateral organization is singularly ill equipped to engage in state-building, to say nothing of nation-building. Indeed, most crises that threaten the integrity of a government or regional peace can be addressed far more effectively by invited help from friendly states—as demonstrated by the contrast between the 1960 Congo crisis and the Tanganyika crisis of 1964. This selection, excerpted from an article in Review of Politics *(January 1968), examines the severe limits of UN crisis intervention against the backdrop of Third World realities.*

*   *   *

The strangely unreal debate on the feasibility of United Nations intervention in Rhodesia or South Africa (to overthrow "colonialist" regimes) or in Vietnam (to stop or de-escalate a war) would benefit from a more serious examination of the largest and most daring UN experiment on record. The peacekeeping mission in the former Belgian Congo was unique, controversial, and costly. The growing body of empirical data about this four-year operation provides a solid basis for understanding the severe limits of the UN as an instrument for political reform and crisis management in the Third World, to say nothing of the more difficult tasks of state-building and nation-building.

For the first four years of its independence, the chaotic Congo was the grudging host to the most complex operation ever authorized by an inclusive international organization and managed by an internationalized secretariat. The UN Force drew upon 94,000 men from thirty-four countries who contributed 675,000 man-months of service. The cost was $411 million; the United States paid about 42 percent.

An examination of this unprecedented mission, with its sweeping and ambiguous mandate, provides some concrete answers to two questions: To what extent can action through the Security Council serve as an effective alternative to traditional ways of preventing or putting out brush fires? To what extent can the perplexing tasks of building the political and military sinews of a weak state be assisted by an internationalized mission under the executive control of the Secretary General and the political direction of the Security Council?

The limits of UN crisis intervention become even more apparent when the Congo operation is compared to the Tanganyika crisis in January 1964, and the American-Belgian rescue mission to Stanleyville in November of the same year. The fundamental constraints on UN action are political and rooted in the nature of the multistate system. The legal and financial problems in the UN system are largely reflections of the deeper pattern of conflict and accommodation among states.

The Uncertain Congo Mandate

The Security Council mandate for the peacekeeping mission in 1960 was sweeping, ambiguous, and uncertain in contrast to the clear-cut and limited mandate that established the UN Emergency Force in the Middle East in 1956. In the Gaza Strip and Sinai there was a truce to be kept, a demilitarized zone to patrol, a line to observe. The mandate was clear—the UN observers had simply to report any violations of the border by Israel or Egypt and they were authorized to use firearms only in self-defense. They performed this limited function well until the Mid-East crisis erupted in May 1967 and Secretary General U Thant withdrew the UN Force at the request of President Nasser.

In sharp contrast, the Congo in 1960 was a crucible of unresolved conflict. There was no demilitarized zones, no truce lines, and no peace for the peacekeepers to keep. In August there were four separate armed forces in the Congo—the Belgian troops, the Congolese Army, the Katanga gendarmerie, and the UN Force—with no clearly defined relationship among them. A few months later the Congo Army itself was split into three factions led by contending political groups.

There was no solid agreement among the states supporting the UN Congo effort on whether there was a threat to international peace, and if so, where the threat lay. Each government saw the crisis in terms of its own interests. Washington and the West generally wanted to arrest chaos, fearing it would be exploited by the Soviet Union. Moscow and some of the militant African states wanted to "radicalize" the Congo and help Prime Minister Patrice Lumumba to become the leader of a "socialist revolution" in Central Africa. The Communist and the Afro-Asian leaders were less interested in restoring peace and more interested in successful "decolonization," a euphemism for expelling Belgian influence and overthrowing Moise Tshombe's secessionist regime in Katanga.

In spite of these conflicting ways of looking at the Congo crisis, there was a temporary consensus in the Security Council in July 1960, sufficient to authorize the Secretary General to "provide the Government with such military assistance as may be necessary" until the Congo's "national security forces may be able, in the opinion of the Government, to meet fully their tasks." The July 14 resolution, on which Britain and France abstained, also called upon Belgium to withdraw its troops. This agreement was possible only because the United States and the Soviet Union for a brief period believed that UN intervention was the least costly way to prevent the other superpower from realizing its objectives in the Congo.

Reflecting the diversity of the supporting coalition, which throughout was led but not dominated by Washington, the UN mandate was broad and ambiguous. The several Congo resolutions identified five objectives for the UN mission. The first three were directed to the internal situation, the last two to external problems:

1. Restore and maintain law and order throughout the Congo.
2. Prevent civil war and curb tribal conflict.
3. Transform the Congolese Army into a reliable internal security force.
4. Restore and maintain the territorial integrity and political independence of the Congo.
5. Eliminate outside interference in the Congo's internal affairs.

These far-reaching goals were set forth without reference to the enforcement provisions of Chapter VII of the UN Charter which authorizes the Security Council to take military measures against a state persisting in peace-threatening behavior. At no point did the Council declare Belgium or any other state an aggressor, but there was an implicit assumption that Belgian support of Tshombe was a threat to the peace. The UN Force was essentially a "pacific settlement" mission under Chapter VI.

The internal conflict, greatly exaggerated by the press at the time, was threatening the lives of a small number of Congolese and Europeans in the Congo, but it was not endangering any neighboring state. The crisis was not as violent as the Mau Mau uprisings in Kenya (1953–1955), the Algerian war (1954–1962), the tribal slaughter in Nigeria (1966), or a score of other conflicts in the Third World in which the UN did not intervene.

Washington vs. Moscow

Given the rapidly unraveling situation and the widespread commitment to "decolonizaation" at the time, the intervention of Belgian troops and the gingerly support of some circles in Brussels for Tshombe's secession made superficially plausible the Soviet claim that Belgium was attempting to reassert colonial rule, at least in Katanga. But the facts simply do not sustain this allegation. The introduction of Belgian troops after the breakdown of order in July 1960, was almost wholly a case of humanitarian intervention designed to safeguard European lives and property. European and Congolese lives were saved and the Belgian troops were withdrawn within ten weeks, except for 231 officers and other ranks who stayed behind to direct Katanga's gendarmerie and police, and these left a year later, by September 1961.

The ambivalent support of Brussels for Tshombe was not a serious threat to the integrity of the Congo. The Belgian government never recognized an independent Katanga, though its Defense Ministry did provide modest assistance to keep the secessionist province a going concern. Throughout the crisis the Foreign Ministry wanted a united and viable Congo. Brussels was trying to cover all bets, but from the beginning it supported the UN resolutions.

Within three months after independence day the Congo was threatened by the Soviet Union which used the UN operation as a cover to intervene with planes, trucks, and KGB agents in support of the deposed Lumumba who was attempting to overthrow the Central Government.

The three internal objectives of the UN mission can be explained primarily by a prior disposition of Secretary General Dag Hammarskjold to extend nation-building assistance to the new state. After the local army mutinies, which, incidentally were directed more against Lumumba than the Belgian officers, Lumumba and President Joseph Kasavuba asked for UN aid to restore discipline in the army and to shore up the administration weakened by the Belgian exodus. Hammarskjold quickly expressed his willingness to provide UN technical military assistance to come primarily from African states. The provision of military aid through UN channels was a radical departure from anything that had been done before.

On July 12, 1960, Foreign Minister Bomboko requested 3,000 American troops to restore order. President Eisenhower turned down the request and advised the Congo to seek UN aid. That same day Kasavuba and Lumumba solicited urgent UN "military assistance" because of the "external aggression" and "colonialist machinations" of Belgium. The following day they said UN aid was "not to restore the internal situation" but "to protect the national territory against acts of aggression committed by Belgian metropolitan troops." This change in the tone and substance of their appeal reflected a fundamentally new assessment of the crisis.

Achievements and Failures of the UN Mission

Given the breadth of the mandate and the highly limited means available to the UN Force (UNF), to say nothing of the Congo's chaos, the high expectations for the mission were certain to be dashed. The UNF, severely hobbled politically, legally, and militarily, was a marginal actor in the drama. Its very existence depended upon the active cooperation of a voluntary coalition of states. Without the diplomatic, financial, and logistical support of Washington, it could neither have been mounted nor sustained.

The Congo in 1960 had no effective central government, no reliable statewide army or police force. The UN was not equipped to provide, even temporarily, these basic requirements of statehood. The UNF was not given the authority of an occupying power or a substitute government. The Congo was not a UN trust territory. The UNF was restricted largely to the use of force in self-defense, but later resolutions broadened the mandate to permit force necessary to "prevent the occurrence of civil war," and to apprehend prohibited foreigners.

The UNF operated under a forthright prohibition against interfering in internal Congolese affairs. The August 9 Security Council resolution asserted that the mission "will not be a party to or in any way intervene in or be used to influence the outcome of any internal conflict, constitutional or otherwise." This unambiguous constraint was patently impossible to observe in an arena of internal turmoil, especially since the Council itself was strongly partisan, that is, against Tshombe.

The net effect of the UN's four-year intervention, however, was to lend support to internal and external forces working for a strong central government against those seeking a loose confederation. The effort, allowing for temporary exceptions, also supported the political moderates over the militants. The mission as a whole tended to further the objectives of the United States and the West, and to frustrate the objectives of the Soviet Union and the militant Afro-Asian states.

The UNF did remarkably well under the extenuating circumstances. For four years it was the chief factor in maintaining minimal order. No major civil war erupted and tribal strife was largely contained. The Force held down the lid, but it did not significantly improve the internal security picture. (The mid-1964 crisis, discussed later, may well have been a more serious challenge to the Central Government than the 1960 crisis. In

1964 the rebels, encouraged and materially supported by Peking and Moscow, controlled or harassed one-third of the country.)

UN authorities failed to transform the fragmented , irresponsible, and virtually leaderless Congolese army into a reliable force, and temporarily blocked efforts by Brussels, Washington, and other states to assist the Leopoldville government in achieving this key objective. The major problem was the absence of an effective officer corps caused by Lumumba's summary dismissal of 1,100 Belgian officers and NCOs in July 1960. In the short run, the problem of making the army a constructive force could have been solved only by filling the great majority of these posts with Europeans, and virtually the only qualified officers acceptable to the Congolese were Belgians. Hammarskjold ruled out the most obvious and immediate source of military aid because he regarded the Belgians as morally disqualified. The disastrous effect of this UN policy was to delay, perhaps by three years, bilateral military assistance desperately needed and wanted by Leopoldville.

On the deeper psychological and political level, it should have been clear from the outset that a multistate effort serving as the instrument of a voluntary coalition of governments whose interests often clashed was a singularly inappropriate way to help a weak and divided government to deal with the highly sensitive problem of rebuilding a shattered army.

The clearest but most controversial accomplishment of the UNF was to end Katanga's secession. This contributed to the political integrity of the Congo, but the political cost was high. UN authorities probably made an even more significant contribution when they closed the leading Congo airports in September 1960. This frustrated direct Soviet military assistance to the ousted Lumumba, and may have prevented a bloody civil war. But the UNF did nothing to protect Leopoldville from the rising rebel activity in late 1963 and 1964. Reflecting the prevailing view of its Afro-Asian supporters, the UN mission was far less concerned about the Peking and Moscow-supported rebels who threatened to overthrow the Central Government in the spring of 1964 than about secessionist Katanga in 1962 which sought only an unspecified degree of autonomy from Leopoldville. This split-level concern was due primarily to the unfounded view that Tshombe was simply the puppet of European economic interests and that Brussels was using him to reassert its authority.

At best the UNF served as a stopgap until the basic structure of central authority and internal security could be established. At worst the UN mission postponed effective assistance from Western states and complicated the resolution of major internal conflicts by internationalizing a largely local crisis. At the mission's end Secretary General U Thant soberly acknowledged its limited state-building and nation-building capacity: "The United Nations cannot permanently protect the Congo, or any other country, from the internal tensions and disturbances created by its own organic growth toward unity and nationhood."

The Tanganyika Crisis

The crisis in Tanganyika (now Tanzania) in January 1964, bears a striking resemblance to the Congo crisis in 1960. On January 21 and 22, two battalions of the Tanganyika Army mutinied against their British officers and demanded higher pay and total Africanization of the officer corps. This led to rioting in the streets of Dar es Salaam. President Julius Nyerere called for emergency military assistance from Britain, from whom his country had received independence just two years before, to halt the mutiny. Some 500 Royal Marine commandos were brought in from Aden and quickly restored order. The Tanganyika mutiny was followed by similar but smaller disorders in Uganda and Kenya. They, too, requested and received British military aid. In each case, the British were invited, did their job with almost no bloodshed (one man was killed and two were injured in Tanganyika), and left promptly. Eventually, Ethiopian and Nigerian troops replaced the British in Tanganyika and stayed about a year.

During the Tanganyika crisis, there is no evidence that Nyerere ever contemplated turning to the United Nations for emergency assistance. He wanted quick and reliable action and felt the former metropole could best provide the help. He knew that the UNF had made no progress in solving the mutinous Congolese army problem and probably regarded the multistate operation as a negative precedent.

There were obvious political differences between the Congo and Tanganyika mutinies, but in the first few days they were almost identical. In each case the soldiers sought better pay and some prospect of advancement. But in Dar es Salaam, the demands for Africanization of the officer corps were far more insistent and specific, and the crisis was related, at least psychologically, to concurrent political events in Zanzibar, including the involvement of Communist China and Cuba. In Leopoldville, the initial army protest was mild, unorganized, and apparently unrelated to outside political interests. This suggests that prompt and decisive disciplinary action against the mutinous soldiers at Camp Leopold II by their Belgian officers on July 4 at the first stage of the crisis might have nipped it in the bud and without bloodshed. The Belgian officers of the Congo army had the authority to discipline their troops without special permission from the government. Their indecisiveness encouraged the spread of the mutiny. To calm their demands Lumumba promoted all soldiers one rank. A few days later, he dismissed the Belgian officer corps. With this instant Africanization, the Congo army became the first army in history without privates or officers.

The second stage of the crisis was marked by panic in the European population. As a precaution, Brussels flew in paratroopers, but did not deploy them for several days while Belgian officers pleaded with Lumumba for permission to restore order. He refused. In desperation, the Belgians finally deployed paratroopers without his permission on July 10, but Foreign Minister Bomboko said the Belgian intervention took place at his request. This action, along with the efforts then under way to meet some of the soldiers' demands, would probably have restored order were it not for the exaggerated reports of a military clash in the port city of Matadi. A dozen Congolese were killed by Belgian troops on July 11 which sparked Tshombe's proclamation of independence. These two events transformed the crisis into its third and most critical stage.

Decisive Belgian action at the first or second stage of the crisis, with the quiet diplomatic support of Britain, France, and United States, as suggested by President Charles de Gaulle, might have been the best and least costly alternative, politically and morally, for containing the original mutiny. After the Matadi incident and Tshombe's secession, the only feasible immediate sources of external aid were Moscow, Washington, or the joint action of Britain, France, and the United States. Washington could have done the job and was invited to do so on July 12, but refused, mainly because the political cost of direct aid was overestimated in Washington. This miscalculation resulted in part from exaggerated reports of the disorder and the State Department's oversensitivity to charges of "neo-colonialism."

Stanleyville Rescue Mission

A quickly dispatched U.S. military presence in mid-July 1960 could probably have stopped the mutiny without killing a single Congolese. And the political backlash of such aid would have doubtless been less intense than the criticisms of the Belgian-American mission to rescue rebel-held foreign hostages in the Stanleyville (now Kisangani) area in November 1964. Washington diligently sought to have the hostages released through UN, International Red Cross, and Organization of African Unity channels, but when these efforts failed, President Lyndon Johnson authorized the U.S. airlift of Belgian paratroopers. Undertaken with the consent of the Congo Government, the operation "was carried out with restraint, courage, discipline, and dispatch," said Adlai Stevenson, U.S. ambassador to the UN. In four days some 2,000 people of nineteen nationalities—American, European, Asian, and African—were evacuated to safety. In a blistering attack, Communist and neutralist spokesmen accused Washington and Brussels of cynically supporting "imperialist Tshombe" against the "liberation fighters" under the cloak of a humanitarian mission. Critics accused the United States of genocide, "massive cannibalism," and "not being truly concerned with the lives of the hostages." For a variety of reasons, including a growing realization of the limits of UN intervention, Washington was prepared in 1964 to accept the flood of verbal abuse in New York and the physical attack against U.S. buildings in at least four capitals.

Crisis Management and State-Building

The entire Congo experience, illuminated by the Tanganyika crisis and the Stanleyville rescue mission, reveals a great deal about the limits of the UN as an instrument for crisis management and state-building. In crises between states that threaten the peace, a UN presence can be effectively deployed only at an early stage or after a settlement between the conflicting parties has been achieved. "Collective intervention," said a State Department spokesman, "is as uncertain a practice as collective security," and both are characterized by "delay, indecisiveness, vacillation, and erratic paralysis."

Peacemaking, a dynamic political process involving threats, bargaining, adjustment, and compromise, is also risky. A peaceful settlement can be achieved only by the conflicting parties or be imposed from without by a strong third party. A third party cannot force two adversaries to make peace against their will without violating the sovereignty and political integrity of one or both.

After a truce has been reached by peaceful or violent means, a UN observer group can play a useful role in patrolling a ceasefire line or a demilitarized zone. But its utility depends upon the temporary interest of each side in not pressing its claims by force. When either adversary concludes that the truce is no longer serving his interest, the UN observer group becomes obsolete. Such was the case in May 1967, when both Egypt and Israel preferred a military confrontation to a continuation of the uneasy truce. UN peacekeeping presence should not be sent to a theater of unresolved conflict between two states or between factions within one state.

The Congo experience demonstrates the severe limits of UN crisis intervention. Even with a legitimate invitation, substantial interference of this kind in the internal affairs of a desperate state can be construed as a violation of the spirit of the "domestic jurisdiction" clause of Article 2.

There are severe limits to what any outside agency can do to accelerate the long and painful process of developing a sense of national identity and loyalty in a state torn by tribal, class, or religious conflict. The task of state-building and state-maintaining cannot wait for the development of a cohesive nation. The rash of military coups in the Third World in the past few years indicates that the urgent problem of state-maintaining will be with us for a long time.

The Congo experiment makes it abundantly clear that the UN mission did not suspend internal or international politics. By internationalizing the Congo, the mission magnified the crisis and probably prolonged the conflict, while at the same time muting the violence of the adversaries. Designed to insulate the Congo from the Cold War, the mission insured that the Cold War would be waged there, but under constraints that furthered the interests of the United States and frustrated the objectives of the Soviet Union.

Given the inherent limitations of multinational intervention, UN emergency action in Third World crises should be regarded not as a first option, but as a last resort, to be undertaken only when the more traditional means of crisis management involve unacceptable costs or risks. The invited British assistance in Tanganyika and the invited Belgian-American rescue mission in the Congo in 1964 indicate how explosive situations can be dealt with quickly and efficiently, and with little lasting political cost.

35 The Illusion of Internationalizing Politics

Throughout Western history, men and women have dreamed of a Golden Age, an Eden where the lion will lie down with the lamb. In our time, this dream has taken the form of an idealized world where tribalism and nationalism would give way to a universal order—or at least to an international agency that would tame the external behavior of sovereign states. My address on this question at Notre Dame Law School was published in the school's Journal of Law, Ethics, and Public Policy *(Winter 1985).*

*   *   *

On December 31, 1984, the United States withdrew from UNESCO because that international body had become politicized and had lost sight of its original purpose of encouraging scientific, cultural, and educational advancement, primarily in the Third World. In mid-January of this year, the United States decided not to participate in the Nicaraguan case before the World Court because that case was, in the words of the State Department, "a misuse of the court for political and propaganda purposes." A department spokesman added: "We profoundly hope that the Court does not go the way of other international organizations that have become politicized against the interests of the Western democracies." The World Court, which the United States joined in 1949, decided in November 1984 by a vote of 15 to 1 to take up the charge of Nicaragua's Sandinista regime that the United States had violated international law by supporting anti-Sandinista guerrillas and mining a Nicaraguan port.

In an editorial criticizing the U.S. decision not to participate in the Nicaraguan case, the *New York Times* (January 20, 1985) said: "Strictly speaking, there being no world government, there's no such thing as world law. There is no parliament to write the law and no policeman to enforce it. Yet there sits this thing called the World Court, pretending for much of this century not only to adjudicate some disputes between governments but also to define some norms of international behavior. . . . " The editorial acknowledged that there is "legitimate doubt" whether this was an appropriate case for the Court (which was never intended to have jurisdiction over warfare) and "whether all the Court's judges are sufficiently independent of their government's policies."

Nevertheless, the *Times* inexplicably concluded that the United States is wrong for thumbing its nose at this "strange but real institution." The editorial reveals a persistent confusion between the realities of world politics and the dream of taming the perennial struggle of power by internationalizing the process for adjudicating, resolving, or preventing conflict among sovereign states. It is this confusion I wish to address.

Contemporary World Politics

World politics is a vast, unending drama with history as its stage. Its actors today are some 160 legally sovereign states, with the two superpowers as the chief antagonists. The UN Charter confers "sovereign equality" on all states, but some states are predatory; others are peaceful. There are live-and-let-live governments and even live-and-help-live governments.

World politics, like all politics, is a struggle of power and purpose. Morality or ethics is an inescapable element in all political behavior because such behavior, especially on the part of the superpowers, has consequences for good or ill. After World War II, Moscow incorporated Eastern Europe into its "evil empire." In contrast, the United States and its allies transformed Western Europe into a zone of freedom. President Truman's decision in 1950 to defend South Korea from Communist aggression succeeded in preserving the freedom and independence of more than 30 million people. Moscow's invasion of Afghanistan has brought death or destruction to millions. The less than adequate U.S. effort to defend the independence of South Vietnam led to its ultimate conquest by an ally of the Soviet Union with dire consequences for the Vietnamese people and for the people of Cambodia.

Those who seek independence, freedom, and genuine self-determination are threatened by both chaos and predatory states, the most powerful and brutal being the Soviet Union. There are also local conflicts that have little to do with vital superpower interests, but most regional conflicts involve the USSR and the United States. Since Hiroshima, there have been some 140 conflicts fought with conventional weapons that killed more than ten million people. Independent states are threatened by outright aggression as in Afghanistan, by externally supported subversion as in El Salvador, and by international terrorism.

The threat of nuclear war is often given center stage, but perhaps equally dangerous is capitulation to nuclear blackmail. For forty years the nuclear balance of terror has held firm in spite of the forward surge of Soviet nuclear might in the past fifteen years. The U.S. determination to offset partially the threat posed by Soviet SS-20 missiles targeted against NATO military facilities and cities has enhanced stability and made capitulation to Soviet political demands less likely.

Our most cherished values—freedom, order, justice, respect for human dignity—are threatened by chaos, local and regional conflict, and the predatory imperialism of the Soviet Union. It is not quite a Hobbesian world of a "war of every man against every man" because men are not totally selfish and there are historical forces of order and decency at work. These constructive forces must be harnessed to the power of governments if they are to make their full impact.

Rational Idealism vs. Historical Realism

The human drama is not without meaning. The Judeo-Christian tradition asserts that our worldly existence is characterized by struggle between good and evil. In political terms this means a struggle between freedom and tyranny, justice and injustice, human rights and oppression. Biblical religion declares both what *is* and what *ought to be*. It asks and answers two questions of central concern to understanding ethics and world politics: "What is the human situation?" and "What is the duty of man?" An understanding of what is is essential for understanding what ought to be.

Morally concerned persons in their zeal often become so preoccupied with the imperatives of human responsibility that they ignore the realities of human existence. This is especially true in the world arena where few people experience the limitations on human action they take for granted in their daily lives. Their moral fervor has often led to utopian crusades. The road from Versailles to Pearl Harbor is cluttered with causes that failed—the League of Nations, peace through economic planning, the Kellogg-Briand Pact, world peace through world law, and world government, to name a few. These crusades failed because the crusaders wanted to believe that morally desirable goals were politically possible because they were desirable. They misread the facts of current history and the possibilities of the future because they failed to understand the tragedies and contingencies of the whole realm of history. They misunderstood history because they did not understand the limits and possibilities of human nature. As James Madison put it in Federalist Paper 50: "If men were angels, no government would be necessary."

Madison and his fellow Founders were for the most part historical realists as opposed to rational idealists. Rational idealism is the child of the

Enlightenment and in its pure form it affirms the perfectibility, or at least the improvability, of man and the possibility, if not the inevitability, of progress in history. It has confidence in the triumph of man's nobler nature and tends to rely on reason as the redemptive agent that can save man and politics and eventually usher in an era of universal peace.

In contrast, historical realism emphasizes the moral limits of human nature and history and has its roots in St. Augustine, Martin Luther, John Calvin, Edmund Burke, and Madison, along with most classical Western thinkers.

There are few consistent rational idealists or historical realists, but we all tend to lean in one direction or the other. Most Americans appear to be more optimistic about the distant future than about the present where the problems and difficulties are more vividly perceived.

"Two Legs Bad, Four Legs Good"

Many rational idealists assume that international action and institutions are more noble or moral than unilateral actions by states. A brief glance at recent history will explode this assumption. The Communist International was hardly a benign force, nor is the Warsaw pact through which Moscow holds its "allies" in thrall and threatens the freedom of Western Europe. Conversely, many unilateral actions by states are constructive—ranging from self-defense to helping an ally to defend itself. The simple assertion that international action is better than national action reminds one of George Orwell's *Animal Farm*: "Two Legs Bad, Four Legs Good." It is the moral quality and political wisdom of behavior that counts, whether that behavior is expressed unilaterally, bilaterally, or through a regional or near-universal international agency.

There is little debate about the desirability of governments cooperating with other governments. The political and moral confusion arises when it is argued that state behavior has a higher ethical status or "does more good" when it is channeled through and disciplined by an organization like the League of Nations, the United Nations, or the World Court. The problem becomes even more serious when it is suggested that these universal agencies should be endowed with power and sovereignty to curtail the sovereignty of the participating states.

In grand structural terms, world politics can operate in only two ways—with one global government or with more than one government. From the beginning of history we have had the second system—more than one government, whether tribes, city states, territorial states, nation states, or empire states. Some rational idealists and many utopians believe that wars, conflict, aggression, and tyranny could be eliminated if we somehow could transform the multistate system into a one-state system. They believe world government would solve our problems. But as

Reinhold Niebuhr pointed out in his classic essay, "The Illusion of World Government" (Foreign Affairs, April 1949), an inclusive international government invested with sovereign power is neither politically possible nor morally desirable. Sovereignty is the right to act without asking the permission of any external agency. Would the Soviet Union, or for that matter, the United States, surrender this right to a higher authority without the assurance that its values and interests would be fully protected in the new arrangement? Neither the superpowers nor the lesser states are prepared to sacrifice their sovereignty to a superstate.

Even if it were possible, world government would not be morally desirable because one global authority would be tempted to become absolute and tyrannical. The new elite would enjoy a monopoly of the instruments of coercion. Since there would be no external foe, there would be no need for an army to protect the state against that danger. But there would be a world police force to deal with the dangers from within—insurrection, disaffection, secession, conflict, terrorism, and other challenges. Unless the citizens of the world state and the tribes, classes, and interest groups they belong to would be radically transformed into peaceful and benign persons and organizations, conflict would persist. The universal dream would probably become a universal nightmare. Niebuhr concludes his critique of world government: "We may have pity upon, but can have no sympathy with, those who flee to the illusory security of the impossible from the insecurities and ambiguities of the possible."

What Is Both Possible and Responsible?

Laying aside the illusion of world government, some idealists insist that we should develop "global systems of governance" (whatever that means) and as a first step strengthen and improve the United Nations. If by "strengthening" the UN is meant endowing it with a measure of sovereignty, this is by definition impossible. Sovereignty is not divisible. A state either has it or it does not.

When a state submits a dispute with another state for arbitration and is willing to abide by the result it has not surrendered its sovereignty, but affirmed it. Members of the Common Market in Europe have not given up their sovereignty; they are affirming it by voluntarily joining other states to achieve common objectives. When their vital interests are at stake, governments will withdraw from the jurisdiction of any agency that infringes on those interests, just as the United States has refused to acknowledge the jurisdiction of the World Court in the Nicaraguan case.

The complicated and confusing conglomeration known as the UN system that includes the World Court, Security Council, General Assembly, and a score of specialized agencies presents an interesting problem. As an historical realist and a student of world politics, I believe that no part of

the UN system can or should be given sovereign authority. In fact, no related agency claims to possess it. The UN is not a supernational entity
with a mind, will, and power of its own. It is a forum, a continuing conference for member states that can selectively use it as an instrument of
statecraft.

The World Court convenes only when two or more contending governments agree to submit to its jurisdiction, and its opinions cannot be imposed on any state. Decisions of the General Assembly are not binding.
The Security Council has a built-in veto; consequently any of the five permanent members can prevent action deemed inimical to its interests.

Because of the lofty aspirations articulated in its Charter and subsequent declarations on human rights, the United Nations is a symbol of
international cooperation and peace even as it reflects a dangerous and
divided world. There is little evidence to support the conclusion that either the Security Council or the General Assembly has made a contribution to peace or nation-building that could not have been made more effectively if there were no UN. All its peacekeeping efforts have been
carried out only with the consent of the states directly involved and the
support of other states that sought the same limited objective and could
have been conducted as well, or better, and with less political cost without the involvement of the Security Council.

The four-year UN expeditionary force sent to the Congo in 1960 to
maintain the peace and assist in strengthening a newly independent state
did not suspend either internal or international politics. By internationalizing the crisis, it magnified it and prolonged the conflict. Designed to insulate the Congo from the Cold War, the mission insured that the Cold
War would be waged there, but under constraints that, as it turned out,
furthered the interests of the United States and frustrated Soviet objectives. In retrospect, the goals of restoring order, consolidating the independence of the Congo, and thus serving the strategic interests of the
West could have been better served by a joint Belgian, French, British,
and U.S. peacekeeping effort.

On balance, the political UN since its creation in 1945 may have done
more harm than good. The one-state-one-vote character of the Assembly
both distorts political reality and subjects the members to bloc voting that
often results in resolutions that condemn responsible foreign policies
while overlooking irresponsible ones. As Ambassador Jeane Kirkpatrick
has said of the General Assembly, "selective name-calling is frequently
used against the United States while the Soviet Union goes unnamed." I
would anticipate no great harm to our national interest or to the cause of
peace, freedom, or justice were the UN to disappear. But as long as it is
with us, we should fight within it for honesty, fairness, and our interests
as Mrs. Kirkpatrick has so effectively done.

A Responsible U.S. Foreign Policy

Since the end of World War II, the United States has sought to defend its security and that of its allies through NATO and other alliances. It has pursued policies that respect the freedom and independence of all states and defined its national interest in terms broad enough to respect the legitimate interests of other states. Our policies have not been without flaws, but our shortcomings have been due more to innocence than to arrogance. The United States has been the major force for peace, freedom, and political development since the end of World War II, while the Soviet Union has been the major threat to peace and freedom with its messianic and expansionist policies.

The UN has not had a fundamental impact on the world struggle and has played virtually no role in curbing conventional conflict or in stabilizing the nuclear confrontation. If the UN has been a weak reed, or as some more severe critics would contend, a snare and a delusion, where can we turn for help in the unending task of seeking greater stability and freedom? How can we better curb aggression and subversion?

As the leader of the Free World, America must recognize the realities of power and assume the responsibility that history has thrust upon us. We must be true to our deepest values. At the same time, we must be strong enough militarily, economically, and politically to deter the Soviet Union from further expansion by outright conquest, subversion, or nuclear blackmail. This means that we must recognize the importance of maintaining a balance of power in favor of freedom. Responsible power must be arrayed against irresponsible power. We must work for peace through strength.

We do live in an interdependent world, but this interdependence cannot be expressed in an all-encompassing organization endowed with the power to suppress diversity and freedom in the name of a universal order. In a world of many states, America should strengthen its alliances with democratic and other states that pursue live-and-let-live foreign policies. By diplomacy, trade, investment, economic aid, and military assistance we should help Third World states to develop economically and politically.

The battle within history is never wholly won or lost. The struggle goes on. But we must turn our back on wishful thinking and utopian visions if our values and institutions are to survive. Winston Churchill introduced the final volume of his history of *The Second World War* with this theme: "How the Great Democracies Triumphed, and so Were Able to Resume the Follies Which Had so Nearly Cost Them Their Life." His grim warning is as valid today as it was in 1953 when he wrote it.

36 Is the United Nations Obsolete?

Shortly after the Persian Gulf War in 1991, the UN Security Council became involved in several smaller but highly controversial "peacekeeping" missions in countries torn by civil strife, notably Somalia, Bosnia, and Haiti. In each, there was no peace to keep, no clear-cut lines to patrol. Consequently, U.S. forces serving under a UN mandate inevitably become involved in state-building and nation-building, as well as in humanitarian services. My views on UN intervention (Foreign Affairs, *Summer 1993) and on UN Secretary General Boutros Boutros-Ghali* (Wall Street Journal, *September 19, 1995) are excerpted here.*

*　　　*　　　*

The United Nations is not and cannot be a political actor in a world of sovereign states. Despite the successful Persian Gulf War coalition, the Security Council is no substitute for alliances, ad hoc great power coalitions, or unilateral U.S. foreign policy initiatives. The UN on occasion may be a useful instrument to serve the parallel interests of the United States and other major powers in addressing specific crises. But this consequential difference between actor and instrument has been frequently confused, especially since the Cold War's end.

One should not be surprised if UN Secretary General Boutros Boutros-Ghali considers the UN, indeed the position of secretary general itself, as an international actor with the power to make and maintain peace in troubled regions. Critics more modestly accept the notion that UN-authorized troops may have a "moral legitimacy" that allied or unilateral military actions do not. Both claims reflect a persistent Wilsonian idealism that has been rejuvenated in the wake of the Security Council–blessed Gulf War. Woodrow Wilson's League of Nations was designed to sanitize and order world politics. At the dawn of the United Nations in 1943, Secretary of State Cordell Hull predicted that "there will no longer be any need for spheres of influence, for alliances, for balance of power . . . by which in the unhappy past the nations strove to safeguard their security or to promote their interests."

The League could not stop Mussolini or Hitler or prevent Japan from rearming. The symbols and machinery of international cooperation were tragically irrelevant as the world was racked by tyranny, aggression, and civil conflict. The juggernaut of war rolled on.

The secretary general has claimed that the UN "invented peacekeeping." Hardly. Usually peace has been created and maintained by the action of independent states to curb turbulence or to deter expansionist powers. The decisions of the United States to enter the world wars were unilateral and contributed mightily to world peace. In World War II the U.S. effort, alongside that of its allies, led to the defeat of Hitler's Germany and of Japan. Five years later, President Truman's move to counter North Korean aggression was also unilateral. But due to a fluke—the Soviet delegate was absent from the Security Council—Truman's initiative received a retroactive UN fig leaf. In 1962, President John Kennedy acted unilaterally to have Soviet missiles withdrawn from Cuba, though he kept America's European and Latin American allies informed.

The most consequential decisions are still made by the major powers. Internal factors aside, the downfall of the Soviet empire can be attributed in part to President Ronald Reagan's unilateral decision to deploy medium-range Pershing II missiles in Europe to counter Soviet SS-20s, and to pursue a space-based missile defense system. Those actions resulted not only in the eventual elimination of all intermediate-range nuclear weapons but also helped convince Mikhail Gorbachev that the USSR could no longer compete militarily with the United States. Along with other unilateral actions, such as military aid to anti-Communist forces in Afghanistan and Nicaragua, those decisions helped alter the "correlation of forces" that led to the fall of the Berlin Wall and the dissolution of Soviet power in Eastern Europe.

Judging What Is Just

Whatever one may think of the Gulf War, it must ultimately be judged by what it accomplished and failed to accomplish and at what human and political cost, not by the fact that it was a U.S.-led coalition sanctioned and constrained by the Security Council. All military action, indeed all foreign policies, should be subjected to the traditional just war criteria: Is the intention just? Are the means just and proportional? And, if the effort succeeds, will the chances for justice and peace be enhanced?

Notwithstanding reservations about how President Bush conducted the Gulf War, the U.S.-led coalition met these just war criteria. But this conclusion would have been equally valid if the United States had acted unilaterally or in concert with Britain, France, and Saudi Arabia.

International action enjoys no special moral status over unilateral action. The twentieth century has seen many examples of destructive multinational behavior, from the League of Nations' flaccid and ineffectual effort to stop Mussolini's rape of Ethiopia in 1935, to the Warsaw Pact's crushing of the Hungarian uprising in 1956 and the Prague Spring in 1968. The number of actors is morally irrelevant. It is the intention and consequence of the action that counts.

Wilsonian idealists persist in attributing intrinsic merit to multinational action, an ideal rooted in the democratic concept of majority rule. That notion is quite appropriate for a democratic community that shares a common moral heritage and political culture. But a world of highly disparate states is neither democratic nor driven by common values. The actors are governments with different interests and expectations, and led by men with varying degrees of moral rectitude and political responsibility. Under a one-government one-vote scheme, Libya's Muammar Qadhafi and Zaire's Mobutu Sese Seko would have an equal voice with the United States and Britain.

A unanimous Security Council vote authorizing measures to deal with a threat to or breach of the peace does not necessarily mean that these measures are right or just. Such a vote may reflect a temporary and fragile concurrence of interests, or far more serious, a least-common-denominator consensus that compromises or undercuts responsible action.

The all but forgotten UN debacle in the Congo in 1960 is a good example of the ineffectual multilateral policies and should stand as a timely warning to those calling for UN military intervention in the former Yugoslavia and other conflicts. Secretary General Dag Hammarskjold had persuaded the Security Council to dispatch a peacekeeping force to quell the local mutiny of Congolese soldiers that occurred in the wake of independence from Belgium. But that conflict was no threat to neighboring states. The secretary general acted too hastily when Congolese politicians appealed to him and the United States for military assistance to frustrate alleged "colonialist machinations" by Belgium. As the Congo descended into chaos, there was no peace to keep, no line to be patrolled.

The political and moral cost of the deeply flawed UN Congo mission stands in sharp contrast to the success and low cost of unilateral British intervention in Tanganyika in 1964. (See Chapter 34.)

Acting Judiciously in Bosnia

How should the United States respond to those urging support for major UN peacekeeping operations in Bosnia and elsewhere? Certainly President Clinton should heed the lessons of the Congo and Tanganyika experiences, especially the risks of internationalizing a local crisis. Of course, each crisis is different and the extent of national interests will vary. In most cases the United States should act alone or with close allies. There may be a few crises where it is prudent for Washington to turn to the Security Council. It is no small matter for the United States to invest money, troops, and prestige in an international effort in which it surrenders a measure of control. During the Gulf War, President Bush repeatedly invoked the constraints of Security Council resolutions to justify his military strategy and restraint.

Perhaps the greatest peril in relying on a UN sanction is the abdication of moral responsibility. There is no honorable way for the United States to turn over its foreign policy burdens to an international body, however appealing that may seem to those Americans who feel guilt over their power and wealth and think that somehow a UN fig leaf will sanctify the use of military force. But a sovereign state, like a free human being, is responsible for its actions.

When U.S. interests are clearly involved in a crisis—whether in the Middle East, Central Europe or Asia—and America has the necessary military assets and public support to act, it should act. On occasion, it may act in concert with allies who have parallel interests; in rare instances, such as Iraq's aggression against Kuwait—which threatened vast oil reserves vital to this nation and its allies—the United States may seek support from other governments through the UN Security Council.

Boutros-Ghali's Hubris

Despite the disasters in Somalia and Bosnia, Boutros Boutros-Ghali claims that all UN peacekeeping operations "have been cost-effective" because they "prevented more costly wars." In February 1994, he said that the UN had "negotiated 172 peaceful settlements to regional conflicts. It has used quiet diplomacy to avert 80 imminent wars." His aides were unable to document this startling claim. At the same time, he failed to mention the scores of regional wars in Asia, Africa, and the Middle East that the UN failed to prevent—conflicts in which millions have died and millions more uprooted from their homes.

Recently, Mr. Boutros-Ghali wrote in the *Washington Post* that the UN provides the "only machinery we have for collective cooperation among nations. It is the only global tool for promoting peace and security, furthering development, protecting human rights, and strengthening international law." This simply is not true. Since the mid-18th century there has been a more comprehensive instrument for pursuing peace and human rights—it is called international diplomacy.

His extravagant claims reflect a naive (or cynical) view of the UN and world politics, ignoring the many UN member governments that abuse their citizens, prey on their neighbors, foment revolution, or otherwise flout the UN Charter. Mr. Boutros-Ghali also fails to acknowledge that the UN is only a symbol of peace and an instrument, not an independent actor on the world stage.

Ignoring the fundamental problems, he focuses on their symptoms. The UN is in trouble, he says, because "national budgets are shrinking," promising that the UN can fulfill its mission by cutting the size of its staff, monitoring corruption and wrongdoing within its bureaucracy. (As of June 1994, the staff of UN Secretariat and related organizations numbered 33,967 from 150 countries.) He says members should pay their assessments, noting that as of May 1995, member states owed $2.7 billion, of which Washington owed $1.1 billion.

His band-aid approach to fixing the gargantuan UN bureaucracy is an escape from the real problems of peace and freedom in the world, which at the bottom must be addressed by the great powers, and uniquely by the United States. Depending on circumstances, Washington will and should act unilaterally, bilaterally, or in concert with other powers.

On occasion the Security Council has provided a useful forum or channel for U.S. policies, but the ultimate political and moral responsibility lies with our government. We should never surrender our sovereignty—or even less, an endless flow of dollars—to a majority vote of the UN Security Council or to the whims of an overly eager secretary general.

37 *Perilous Crusades*

U.S. foreign policy, especially since Wilson, has been strongly influenced by American exceptionalism—the view that as a city set on a hill, America is an example and a beacon to the world. There is merit to the concept, but the problem is how to honor this notion and at the same time pursue realistic policies to advance peace and stability. Promoting democracy and human rights in other people's countries can be arrogant and counterproductive. The Carter and Clinton administrations were accused of looking upon aspects of foreign policy as "social work." This selection (National Review, *June 10, 1991) examines the argument of one scholar who insists that promoting democracy abroad "can be America's most effective foreign policy."*

*   *   *

Some Americans believe that a major objective of U.S. foreign policy should be to promote democracy throughout the world. In 1991, Joshua Muravchik called for America to fulfill its destiny by "exporting democracy" in his book with that title. His argument has added fuel to the spirited debate over America's purpose in the post–Cold War era. The continuing ambiguity of U.S. policy toward Iraq has sharpened the issue over what America should do in other people's countries. What, if anything, should Washington do to depose Saddam Hussein or to establish an autonomous Kurdish state?

The debate is rooted in the protracted dispute between interventionists and non-interventionists, "idealists" and "realists," and combinations of these slippery camps, each claiming a harmonious blend of realism and the American dream.

Mr. Muravchik presents a clear and detailed case for an updated Wilsonian vision. He believes that America should export democracy everywhere and that this will serve our national interests and fulfill our moral destiny. He also supports a strong military posture.

He believes that a world hungering for freedom is ripe for democracy. "Democracy in China and the USSR may not be easy to achieve, but it is not much more far-fetched than the idea of democracy in India or Japan had been at one time." In blunt fact, it is much more far-fetched. India had a century and a half of British rule and Japan had Douglas MacArthur.

Going beyond Henry Luce's vision of an American Century, Muravchik foresees a "Pax Americana unlike any previous peace, one of harmony, not of conquest . . . by virtue of the triumph of the human idea born in the American experiment." He asserts that a rich and powerful America has the political, economic, and moral resources to do the job. And the tools—foreign aid, the Voice of America, and the National Endowment for Democracy.

Few will take exception to Muravchik's view that we Americans are an idealistic people who wish all peoples could enjoy the blessings of liberty. But many will take exception to his version of American exceptionalism—that we have a unique responsibility to make the world over in our own image.

Muravchik's beguiling ideals keep bumping into uncomfortable realities, including the limits of ideology, the perils of crusades, and the irascibility of human nature.

In 1934, William Graham Sumner said: "If you want war, nourish a doctrine," noting that doctrines driven by crusades become "frightful tyrants." Obviously, evil doctrines like Aryan supremacy lead to evil consequences, but seemingly benign doctrines like " manifest destiny" can also be dangerous. Is it not arrogant to attempt to impose democracy on the people of another sovereign state in the absence of an occupation statute?

This doesn't mean that America cannot help to nudge history in a humane direction. U.S. foreign policy since World War II has done precisely that. Perhaps the single most telling contribution to freedom and human dignity has been our strategic arms policy that prevented nuclear war and eventually forced Gorbachev to surrender his medium-range missiles and Eastern Europe.

Mr. Muravchik overestimates the potential for democracy, not only in China and Russia, but also in the Third World. He seems to see Asia, Africa, and Latin America through Wilsonian lenses. During my visits to some fifty Third World countries, I encountered little to suggest that democracy as we Americans know it is about to take root, even with all the nurturing we might provide. In most of the countries that he lists as democratic—India, Pakistan, the Philippines, Brazil, Botswana, and many others—the fledgling institutions for translating the popular will into policy are fragile and human rights are frequently violated. Their political culture is characterized by kinship groups that have little sense of responsibility for persons outside their group. Corruption is rampant. Hardly fertile soil for a pluralistic democracy.

Muravchik fails to make the crucial distinction between nation-building and state-building. A state can be quickly established by military conquest or even by fiat. In contrast, building a nation—a cohesive people with a common historical memory—takes generations. Most states in the world are not nation-states, but artificial political structures attempting to rule diverse tribes and classes that have conflicting customs and interests.

The first task of any government is to govern, the second to govern justly, and the third to govern democratically. Few Third World regimes are capable of performing the first two tasks, much less the third. To expect too much is to invite disillusionment and cynicism.

Muravchik may not suffer from the illusion of American omnipotence, but he may reflect a more serious flaw, the illusion of American virtue. As countries and peoples go, America has many virtues. But one of its virtues is or should be humility—a "city on a hill" serving as a quiet example rather than a noisy preacher or imperious crusader. He quotes and then seems to dismiss Reinhold Niebuhr's view: "We are not a sanctified nation [and weaker nations will resent] our pretensions of superior virtue." George Will has called persons who hold Muravchik's views "imperial conservatives" who "want America to do for the world what Lyndon Johnson's Great Society was supposed to do for America: fix it."

A more modest appreciation of what America can do in the larger world can be gained by recognizing political realities and by accepting the Judeo-Christian understanding of human nature and history. Slighting this understanding, Muravchik sides with the rational idealists who dream of a new world order, and against the historical realists who reject all religious and secular utopian schemes. These realists, who also share Muravchik's ideals, insist that their achievement is limited by man's arrogance and self-interest. They argue that perfect justice, freedom, and democracy are not universally achievable, though approximations of these lofty goals are not beyond human grasp.

PART EIGHT
The God That Failed

As early as 1951, I wrote that Communism as a secular religion was morally bankrupt and that the Soviet system was doomed by its hubris and failure to comprehend man's unquenchable thirst for freedom and dignity. (See Chapter 16.) I also said that "American Communists were strangers in their own land," and I criticized Communist apologists, especially those who espoused moral symmetry between the Soviet Union and the United States. This was more than a decade before the term moral equivalence was coined. I knew then that the hypnotic dream of the true believers would be betrayed by their false gods and that the "evil empire" would be destroyed by its crippling contradictions. But I didn't know when.

In 1960, during my first visit to the USSR, I became convinced that the Communist system would collapse in my lifetime. Rejecting a holy war against "godless Communism," I supported a strong nuclear deterrent to contain the Soviet Union and intellectual efforts to lay bare its religious pretensions. I later joined the Committee on the Present Danger and the Committee for the Free World.

In mid-November 1989, at the annual Ethics and Public Policy dinner, I said the Berlin Wall "has been consigned to the dustbins of history, but the long-suffering people of the Soviet Empire are still yearning to be fully free. . . . The utopian creed of the totalitarians is dead. Administered economies lie in ruins. The rigid structure of tyranny built on lies has cracked, but it has not yet crumbled. In this hour of dangerous opportunity, we as a nation must remain morally and militarily strong."

Two years later, I went to Moscow to celebrate the imminent collapse of the Soviet Union. The hammer and sickle would soon be replaced by the Russian flag. But as I rejoiced, I knew that the totalitarian temptation was not dead and that new secular messiahs would again arise. The struggle for freedom and justice would never end.

38 *Treason of the Intellectuals*

Marx and Lenin denied man's sinful nature and his God-given thirst for free-dom, concepts that lie at the heart of the Judeo-Christian religious heritage. Con-sequently, Marxist eschatology was fatally flawed from the start. Why, then, did it take so long for thousands of Western church leaders and intellectuals to com-prehend that Soviet totalitarianism was the antithesis of all that we hold dear? I addressed this question in "The God That Failed" (The World and I, *October 1989), a review of* The Grand Failure: The Birth and Death of Communism in the Twentieth Century *by Zbigniew Brzezinski. Both that book and my re-view were written before the Berlin Wall fell. Several paragraphs on the treason of Western intellectuals have been added.*

*   *   *

To understand the long-delayed but sudden collapse of Communism, it is instructive to consult the anguished writing of former Western Marx-ists and apologists for the Soviet Union published in the late 1940s. In his introduction to *The God That Failed* (1950), Richard Crossman, the vol-ume's editor, says the book was conceived in the heat of an argument he had with Arthur Koestler on political philosophy and the Soviet Union. He quotes Hungarian-born Koestler as saying in desperation to his well-bred British companion: "Either you can't or you won't understand. It's the same with all you comfortable, insular, Anglo-Saxon anti-Commu-nists. You hate our Cassandra cries and resent us as allies—but, when all is said, we ex-Communists are the only people on your side who know what it's all about." This exchange led to a collection of essays by six ex-Communist writers who explain why they became disillusioned with a dogma and a system they previously had venerated—Koestler, Ignazio Silone, Richard Wright, Andre Gide, Louis Fischer, and Stephen Spender.

Koestler is right. Those who have experienced Marxist-Leninist realities face-to-face are far more likely to become anti-Communist and pro-free-dom than those who view the phenomenon from afar and tend to exaggerate the blemishes of Western societies. This was indeed true of Richard Wright, who was born in Mississippi and endured racial discrimination, and who first turned to Communism as a haven from such abuse. After his Communist god had failed, he saw America's flaws from a different perspective and recognized that they were potentially correctable.

The God That Failed first appeared forty years ago. Its contributors condemn Marxism-Leninism as a utopian secular religion whose dream of a classless society and a warless world has been twisted by Stalin and other Soviet leaders into a nightmare of terror at home and a multipronged assault against peoples beyond Soviet borders. In his book, *The Grand Failure* (1989), Zbigniew Brzezinski rightly sees Communism as a vital political religion in lively competition with other faiths for the loyalty of men.

Gorbachev and the Future

He recognizes that Gorbachev's demands for openness and restructuring represent something quite different from Stalin's terror, Nikita Khrushchev's bluster, and Leonid Brezhnev's arrogance. But he is not impressed by Mikhail Gorbachev's charm offensive. Even before Gorbachev took over in 1985, it was widely recognized outside the Soviet Union that the Communist god had failed, that Communist economies were in shambles, and that the Soviet imperium was in trouble in Eastern Europe, Afghanistan, and southern Africa—thanks in part to President Reagan's military pressure in Europe and assistance to Third World freedom fighters.

As Brzezinski looks at the past, present, and future of Communism, he is instructed by a quiet realism as well as by his heritage as a son of Poland and his experience as President Carter's national security adviser. He is skeptical, but not cynical. His earlier characterization of Soviet evils was decried by some Western intellectuals as the understandable exaggeration of a Pole, but recent revelations during the Gorbachev regime have underscored his prescience.

One need not have a Polish, Baltic, or Ukrainian heritage to recognize the persistence and portent of national identity and pride in the unfolding drama of Soviet politics. The ideological dissolution of Communism under Gorbachev, says Brzezinski, has inevitably intensified "national tensions within the Soviet Union, while strengthening separatist aspirations." This has spurred a "revival of Great Russian nationalism" and, even more so, "the self-assertion of the non-Russian nationalisms. As a result, Gorbachev has unintentionally placed on history's agenda the possibility of the actual dismantling of the Soviet Union." Brzezinski notes that demands for sovereignty are already being made in Estonia, Latvia, and Lithuania. Nationalist dynamism and self-assertion will play an increasing role in the transformation of Eastern Europe and the post-Communist balance of power in the larger world.

Although World War II ended with only one totalitarian system in place, Brzezinski suggests that it is not exaggeration to assert that Hitler was as much a Leninist as Stalin was a Nazi. Since 1945, the conflict between the Soviet Union and the United States has been fought on the ideological, diplomatic, political, and military fronts. The Cold War has not ended, but its rules of engagement are changing because Communism is in a terminal crisis.

The Marxist god has failed; the dogma is in its death agony. The classless society and the new Soviet man have not materialized. True, the Soviet Union has become an industrial power and has built a mighty military machine and an impressive space program—based in large part on technology stolen from the West—but it is not able to feed itself or provide other necessities. More important, neither the people of the Soviet Union nor of its client states enjoy the elementary human rights that citizens in democracies take for granted.

Assessing this bleak picture, Brzezinski concludes that by the beginning of the twenty-first century, "Communism's irreversible historical decline will have made its practice and its dogma largely irrelevant to the human condition. . . . Communism will be remembered largely as the twentieth century's most extraordinary political and intellectual aberration." Brzezinski's central thesis is true. Communism is a grand failure, but discredited ideas have a way of rising again from the ashes. And power-hungry men will again invoke utopian dreams to impose their tyrannies.

Treason of the Intellectuals

Why did the Soviet Empire survive for seventy years while Hitler's Third Reich lasted only twelve? The obvious cause was Germany's defeat in World War II. A less obvious reason is that virtually everyone in the West saw Nazism as an unambiguous evil.

That Communism was not so perceived reflects a dogged mindset among Western intellectuals—danger always came from the political Right, not from the Left. Hitler was an extreme rightest, glorifying his nation, his race, and his military might. Hence, he was seen as a clear threat to Western democracy, while Stalin, who personified the Left, was not. Stalin spoke of justice and equality. In 1929, Albert Einstein, while still an honored German citizen, said he had no use for dictatorships anywhere, but at least Russia's dictatorship was established by men with pure motives. This is not the only example of Einstein's political naiveté.

Hitler was alarmingly honest about his ideology and matched his words with deeds. Openly racist and virulently antisemitic, he despised democracy as effete. In contrast, the Marxists claimed to be true democrats, and Stalin hid his racism under lofty slogans about a classless society and a New Soviet Man.

Some apologists went so far as to believe in the immaculate conception of the 1917 revolution, even justifying the Stalin-Hitler pact in 1939. Utopians all, they were not chastened by the reality of original sin—the serpent in the garden. Their fixation on equality subverted individual freedom. An idealized Marxism became their opiate. Some became itinerant fellow-travelers. When their revolution of choice—Russian, Chinese, or Cambodian—turned sour and became too bloody, they moved blithely on to the next promised land or called for a return to "true socialism."

Among those who saw promise in the promised land were Theodore Dreiser, W.E.B. DuBois, Harold Laski, George Bernard Shaw, Upton Sinclair, Anna Louise Strong, H.G. Wells, Beatrice Webb, and later Jean-Paul Sartre. In America, Lillian Hellman's lifelong infatuation with Soviet Communism and her dishonesty about her beliefs, nourished the illusions of thousands of leftist intellectuals and liberals. Bedazzled by an unrealizable dream, these utopians couldn't see what was in front of their noses, much less discern the signs of the times.

Consequently, the tragic delay in recognizing the evil of Communism was due in no small part to Western liberals with a utopian streak. In their obsession with a new Eden—with solving once and for all the human predicament—they rejected the historical realism of the Judeo-Christian heritage. Most apologists were elitists who looked down on ordinary mortals while claiming to speak for them. Lofty slogans became a substitute for compassion. Arrogant and self-serving rationalizers, they were as wicked as the totalitarians they praised or absolved.

This, then, was and is the treason of the intellectuals.

There were, of course, responsible Western thinkers, including the early "god that failed" writers, who contributed to Communism's final collapse by exposing its pretentions and peeling off the Potempkin facade of the system to reveal its festering sores. The voices of the ex-Communists like Whittaker Chambers, Stephen Spender, Malcolm Muggeridge, and Freda Utley were amplified by a few "liberal" thinkers who had been briefly infatuated with socialism, but not with the Soviet Union. Among them were Reinhold Niebuhr, George Orwell, and Sidney Hook.

There were also conservatives who had never been beguiled by utopian fantasies and thus never suffered the anguish of conversion, nor basked in the glow of a repentant sinner. The most influential included Russell Kirk, John Chamberlain, William F. Buckley Jr., and George Will. Neoconservatives like Irving Kristol, Jeane Kirkpatrick, and Norman Podhoretz also helped lay the conceptual foundation for a revived American conservatism.

39 *How New Is the New World Order?*

The crumbling of the Berlin Wall and the collapse of the Soviet Union were greeted with euphoria and a sense of relief. Since the United States and the West had won the Cold War without firing a shot, many Americans thought we would face a more peaceful and less demanding world. But the old Wilsonian hopes were soon dashed by new conflicts and old realities. The following excerpt is from "How New Will the Better World Be?" published in National Forum, The Phi Kappa Phi Journal *(Fall 1992).*

*   *   *

In October 1991, I visited Moscow, East Berlin, Prague, Budapest, Warsaw, Kiev, and the Baltic States. My hosts pointed to vacant pedestals where Lenin's statue had stood—symbolic evidence that Communism as an idea and a system had failed.

The twentieth century has produced the three most monstrous tyrannies in history—the USSR, Nazi Germany, and Communist China. Each had killed millions of its own citizens and conquered or attempted to conquer neighboring states. Two have fallen, and one seems to be mellowing. Though the Soviet Union is no more, two outposts of its former empire are still hanging on—Kim Il Sung's North Korea and Castro's Cuba.

In Germany, Hitler's touted Thousand-Year Reich was crushed after only twelve years in a mighty war by the democratic Western allies and, ironically, the totalitarian Soviet Union.

Yet the totalitarian idea and the totalitarian temptation have not been eradicated from the human drama. Out of the rubble of failed systems, the chaos of defeat, and the agony of alienated peoples, a new totalitarian savior could arise again, proclaiming a new secular utopia.

For the immediate future, the totalitarian menace has passed and its dangers have been eclipsed by less momentous threats. The Cold War has ended, but the never-ending struggle of power and purpose among men and nations goes on. The lower-case cold war will always be with us.

We continue to live in a dangerous world in which fanatic Muslims call us "the Great Satan," where Iraq's arrogant Saddam Hussein threatens again to invade oil-rich Kuwait, and where in the former Yugoslavia innocent persons are murdered or allowed to starve in the name of "ethnic cleansing."

And within the former USSR serious conflicts continue among hostile nationalities. Russia and the Ukraine are fighting over who is to control nuclear arms, warships, and other military assets.

Add to this the unsettled conflicts between Israel and its Arab neighbors, massive tribal slaughter in tropical Africa, and the ongoing chaos in many other parts of the Third World.

A Better World?

In the wake of Communism's collapse and the success of the American-led coalition in driving Iraq out of Kuwait, President George Bush has spoken out for a "new world order." His noble aspiration recalls Carl L. Becker's prophetic book, *How New Will the Better World Be?* (1944). Becker argued convincingly that the post–World War II world would probably be more like the world before the war than different from it.

After all, history is characterized by continuity rather than radical discontinuity. This is so because the raw stuff of history is human nature, and human nature has not fundamentally changed over the millennia. There will always be evil men who will resort to tyranny over their people or conquest over their neighbors to satisfy their hunger for power and dominion. They cannot be stopped by gentle persuasion or UN resolutions. They can, however, be deterred or thrown back by responsible power arrayed against them.

The United States remains the strongest power on earth and the leader of the free world. We are far from being omnipotent, but we have a unique responsibility in this new and dangerous environment. Settling for a great deal less than "a new world order," and without attempting to police the globe or put out every brushfire, we can nevertheless continue to strengthen peace and encourage freedom. Sometimes we will succeed, and sometimes we will fail. But we must try.

Our chief asset, as President Bush demonstrated in the Persian Gulf War, is our capacity to build coalitions with other governments with parallel interests to confront egregious breaches of the peace. To this end, we should maintain a strong North Atlantic Alliance, provide mutually beneficial support to Russia and other republics in the former USSR, foster openness in the People's Republic of China, encourage Israel to become economically self-sufficient, and intensify efforts to control weapons of

40 *Reassessing Vietnam's Legacy*

The Vietnam War was the longest armed conflict in the nation's history. For Americans, it was the most heart-wrenching war of the twentieth century, just as the more deadly Civil War was for the nineteenth. In 1861, on the eve of the Civil War, Abraham Lincoln spoke hopefully of the need for healing after the conflict: "The mystic chords of memory, stretching from every battlefield and patriot grave to every living heart [will eventually yield to] the better angels of our nature." For America, the Vietnam War ended when the last U.S. troops pulled out of Saigon in April 1975, but our national memory is still split over the war's larger meaning and consequences. The following essay, "Vietnam's Ghosts," appeared in the Wall Street Journal *on May 21, 1997, just before Memorial Day.*

*   *   *

Who controls the past, controls the future.—George Orwell

Vietnam won't go away. Its ghosts still haunt the American psyche like fragments of a twisted nightmare.

Last March, six U.S. senators who had fought in the Vietnam War met in Washington to observe the 15th anniversary of the Vietnam Veterans Memorial. Standing before the Wall with its 58,196 names of dead and missing chiseled in black granite, Senator John McCain from Arizona, who was tortured and held prisoner by Hanoi for seven years, called it "a wonderful place of healing." His wishful sentiments were echoed by his colleagues.

But the Wall has not, and cannot, heal the painful breach in America's historical memory until we recognize that the tragic Vietnam War was not fought in vain.

"We killed. We died. We died for less than nothing," cried a protester at the Memorial's dedication in 1982. President Reagan offered a different assessment: "Who can doubt that the cause for which our men fought was just? It was—however imperfectly pursued—the cause of freedom."

These two dramatically opposed interpretations of Vietnam are vying for acceptance in America's consciousness. If our collective memory of pivotal events—like the Civil War or Vietnam—is split on ideological fault lines, it bodes ill for the future. A common understanding of such events allows history's wounds to heal, creating a cohesive national psyche equipped to grapple with future crises. But when a vocal minority holds views contrary to those of the less articulate majority, confusion and mischief follow.

The Vietnam Syndrome

The cynical view of our involvement became a part of a larger culture of shame, guilt, and self-flagellation that erupted in flag burning and other attacks on our traditional institutions. It also helped spawn the Post-Vietnam Syndrome that all but paralyzed America from using military force abroad. Thus, after the fall of Saigon, Leonid Brezhnev stepped up Soviet subversion in Africa and Central America and in 1979 brazenly invaded Afghanistan confident that Washington would not act.

The Vietnam Syndrome was partially exorcised by Ronald Reagan's mini-invasion of communist Grenada in 1983 and by George Bush's leadership in the Gulf War seven years later. But we have yet to recover fully our pre-Vietnam confidence and willingness to shoulder the heavy burdens of a humane superpower.

And that will not happen until we openly acknowledge the contribution of the Vietnam War to peace and freedom, along with admitting our faults and miscalculations. The most pernicious demon to exorcise is the charge that Lyndon Johnson and Richard Nixon waged a racist, imperialist, and thoroughly unjust war against a poor, nonwhite people. In truth, their purpose was noble and just—to prevent communist North Vietnam from conquering the South, just as Harry Truman had stopped the communist North Korea from swallowing the South.

Too late, we learned that Vietnam was not as vital strategically as Korea, which is located in the vortex of three great powers—Japan, China, and Russia. This strategic confusion was reinforced by the zero-sum assumptions of the Cold War, stemming from George Kennan's containment doctrine (which, incidentally, worked well enough in Europe).

And we were too often arrogant and overconfident in dealing with South Vietnam. Perhaps the worst blunder was John Kennedy's complicity in the 1963 coup that killed Ngo Dinh Diem, the authoritarian but able civilian president. LBJ later admitted that ousting Diem was "the worst mistake we ever made." The power vacuum created by Diem's violent death led to protracted instability and hogtied Washington to Vietnam's future.

A Contribution to Peace and Freedom

But this is not the whole story. For despite political misperceptions and seriously flawed tactics, our involvement made a positive contribution to peace and freedom. Had we prevailed, or even held the line at the 17th parallel, a million or more lives might have been saved and tens of thousands of boat people spared the anguish of being cast adrift.

The fall of Saigon in April 1975 precipitated the Cambodian holocaust—the Khmer Rouge killed an estimated one million out of the nation's seven million people. The horrific bloodbaths there and in Laos, and the purges and concentration camps in South Vietnam, confirmed the much-maligned domino theory. Looking back, Norman Podhoretz said the "moral soundness" of our "imprudent idealism" was "overwhelmingly vindicated by the hideous consequences of our defeat." But despite defeat, our involvement did strengthen security and freedom in three significant and largely overlooked ways.

First: Johnson and Nixon's firmness under relentless and often cynical domestic attack reassured our allies around the world. An America that would not cut and run in far-off Vietnam would hardly abandon its key allies in Europe and the Pacific. Given the poisoned intellectual climate of the time, these sentiments were rarely expressed in public, but in retrospect we can see their crucial importance.

Second: our steadfastness in Vietnam strengthened nationalist and anticommunist forces elsewhere in Southeast Asia and the Pacific—notably in Indonesia, Malaysia, the Philippines, Singapore, and Thailand, all of whom have remained free and independent.

Third: holding the line in Indochina as long as we did eventually led to a balance of power favorable to the states in the region and to us, a point Prime Minister Lee Kuan Yew of Singapore repeatedly emphasizes. Last December in Washington, he said that "by fighting and negotiating with the North Vietnamese, [the United States] enabled Southeast Asia to get its act together." Without America's intervention in Vietnam, Mr. Lee added, today's "flourishing East Asia" would not have been possible.

The two diametrically opposed interpretations of Vietnam continue to vie for the American psyche. Until the issue is resolved, we will suffer from a kind of historical schizophrenia. To be healthy and courageous in facing the external world, we need to forge a more cohesive national memory of Vietnam approximating that of our three victorious wars of this century: World War I restored peace to Europe, World War II stopped

Nazi and Japanese conquest, and the Korean War prevented the North from overrunning the South.

If the more positive and nuanced view prevails—that our cause was eminently just though "imperfectly pursued"—America will be better prepared to accept its heavy tragic and ironic elements. Vietnam helped us better understand our limitations by dispelling what Denis Brogan once called "the illusion of American omnipotence"—and, I would add, the illusion of American innocence.

Epilogue:
The Last Days of Rome?

This concluding essay defines briefly my concept of the American idea and experience—views implicit in the foregoing pieces. It then raises three questions facing an America on the threshold of the twenty-first century: Will the American idea survive the challenges it faces at home and abroad? What are America's external responsibilities as the only superpower and leader of the free world? As a people, do we have the crucial material and spiritual resources to shoulder the burden that history and the American idea have thrust upon us? These questions are further explored and argued in my forthcoming book, tentatively titled Ethics and Empire: America's Imperial Dilemma.

* * *

As the world enters the third millennium, America stands proud, trembling, and perplexed before the bar of history. Though the United States is the sole undisputed superpower, we Americans are confused about our role in the vast but interdependent external world. We are also confused about who we are as a people, what we stand for, what our government should and should not do. From its exceptional birth, the American experiment has survived wrenching internal crises, notably the Civil War, and demanding external challenges—two world wars and the Cold War. In the face of grave new problems at home and abroad, can the American idea survive and prosper? Do we have the right stuff to continue as the vanguard of peace and freedom?

We cannot know precisely what the next century will yield, but we can be certain it will be fraught with danger. Empires and nations will rise and fall. Peace will be shattered by wars of conquest. Freedom will be menaced by tyrants, terrorism, and tribal conflict. Old alliances will give way to new. The next century will be much like the present one, which, alas, humanity has had to share with the likes of Hitler, Stalin, and Mao.

The American Idea Under Siege

The American idea is anchored in the Judeo-Christian respect for every human being as a creation of God and in the political heritage of the West—Roman law, the Magna Carta, the Mayflower Compact, and the Declaration of Independence. It is a commitment and a promise, not an airy abstraction or an ideology. America is rooted in an unsentimental understanding of human nature and history. The founders of our nation were not utopians, but they had a transcendent vision—"the Laws of Nature and of Nature's God." They believed that men, though flawed, were capable of achieving a tolerably just and peaceful society. Their vision provided a moral compass, democratic checks to curb tyranny, and freedom to pursue happiness.

Jefferson saw the new nation as innocent, purged of Old World vices, but Madison emphasized the tenacity of original sin. Madison was right. America was never innocent. No nation ever was or is. At the same time, America was not conceived in sin and brought forth in iniquity.

In 1821, Jefferson was optimistic about America's future: "Should the cloud of barbarism and despotism again obscure the science and libraries of Europe, this country remains to preserve and restore light and liberty to them." A century after he died, the "cloud of barbarism" did descend on Europe, far more savagely than he could ever have imagined. Nazi totalitarianism plunged the continent into darkness and despair. Just before midnight, America entered the struggle and, with the help of allies, threw back German and Japanese imperial conquests. Then, America led the protracted peaceful conquest that helped bring about the collapse of the Soviet Union.

Since the countercultural 1960s, America has been assailed by voices in the academy, church, media, and Hollywood that ignore or twist the spiritual and political premises of the founders and belittle or distort our accomplishments as a nation.

The multicultural elitists undercut *e pluribus unum* and sponsor a tribalism that divides Americans into victims and victimizers. The assault on "dead white European males" attempts to marginalize Western culture. Two decades ago, Malcolm Muggeridge saw it coming: "It is difficult to resist the conclusion that Western man, wearied of the struggle, has decided to abolish himself."

In 1996, Billy Graham declared that "the greatest nation in history stands on the brink of self-destruction," and Robert H. Bork, in his *Slouching Towards Gomorrah*, seemed to concur. Bork laid much of the blame on a "modern liberalism" rooted in the Enlightenment's emphasis on unaided reason and the French Revolution's demand for "radical egalitarianism." This, along with a "rampant individualism," he said, erodes the social obligations and restraints essential to a good society.

Muggeridge, Graham, and Bork may well exaggerate the erosion of the American idea and underestimate the devotion of the American people to their core values, as well as the resilience of the American family, religious institutions, and communities. But they are not alone in raising the fundamental question—is America living in the last days of Rome or the twilight of the British Empire? Or by calling on "the better angels of our nature" and with the help of God, can America approximate Lincoln's "last best hope of earth"?

Our Inescapable Imperial Burden

On the cusp of a new century, Americans face two formidable challenges—how to survive with the American idea intact and how to discharge our imperial responsibility without imperiling our soul. If we fail in the internal task of renewing the American idea, we will also fail in bearing with honor our imperial burden.

The dimensions, strategies, and costs of that burden remain to be defined. Most political leaders and academics who worry about such things find themselves somewhere between two extremes—erect-the-ramparts neoisolationism and neo-Wilsonian interventionism. The neoisolationists insist that the post–Cold War world is more benign than the era of the "evil empire" and contend that America should reduce its foreign commitments accordingly. We should eschew tangling alliances, they assert, and use military force abroad only when our tangible national interests are directly threatened. Defense expenditures should be substantially cut.

At the other extreme are the neo-Wilsonians who insist that America use its influence intrusively, even punitively, to promote democracy and human rights in other countries. Some Americans are both military isolationists *and* ideological interventionists. Others support our strategic role but insist that we actively oppose all repressive regimes.

From Harry Truman onward, all our presidents, supported by the great majority of the American people, have pursued realistic and prudent policies that have rejected both craven isolation and crusading intervention. This responsible mainline approach embraces a firm commitment to global stability, a decent respect for the interests of other states, and a recognition that, as a humane superpower, America can, mainly by example, nudge history in the right direction.

If such leadership falters, the world will become more dangerous— peace will suffer, predatory tyrants will rise and threaten, and the virus of tribalism and terrorism will spread. And our own survival as a free people will be imperiled. Even a great superpower cannot be an island of serenity in a sea of chaos.

As the preeminent power, our most vital external task is to maintain strategic stability—to preserve the ever precarious balance among the great powers. This requires a strategy to restrain the expansionist ambitions of the other major nuclear powers—China and Russia—while at the same time continuing our alliance with the two other great industrial powers—Germany and Japan. As the crisis-ridden 1930s and 1940s demonstrate, the alternative to a balance among the great powers is conquest and war.

Do We Have the Right Stuff?

In the face of daunting responsibilities abroad, do we Americans have the material and spiritual resources to be an effective and respected leader of the free world? Is our economy dynamic enough to compete with Japan, Germany, and other industrial powers? Or has America reached "imperial overstretch" with "global interests and obligations" far greater than our "power to defend them all simultaneously," as Paul Kennedy asserted in his *The Rise and Fall of the Great Powers* (1987)?

Kennedy's appraisal tends to overlook the dynamic, if less tangible, components of power and leadership recognized by philosophers from Aristotle and Thucydides to Madison and Reinhold Niebuhr. The driving force of world politics is political power, the capacity of a state to move men and nations. And that capacity ultimately depends upon our character as a people—our will, morale, education, and spiritual vitality.

Our future is not foreordained. In my darker moments, I worry about the fate of America and think of Western civilization as a shrinking island in a raging sea of barbarism. I agree with those who see contemporary America in moral decline, but disagree on the pace of descent and the outcome, preferring the tentative mood of an old limerick:

> God's plan made a hopeful beginning
> But man spoiled his chances by sinning.
>   We trust that the story
>   Will end in God's glory,
> But, at present, the other side's winning.

America is still dynamic and this dynamism is a source of hope. But there is no easy way to reinvigorate the American idea which has been eroded both in theory and practice. The government is not the answer. It cannot rekindle the flame or build character, but it can safeguard the freedom of society's character-building institutions—the family, church, school, and neighborhood. Washington cannot impose civic virtue, but it can take measures to encourage it.

At the very least, alienated academics, journalists, artists, and entertainers should acknowledge the historical fact: that America was founded on a belief in the majesty and sovereignty of God and that our world is a small part of the endlessly awesome mystery of creation. Certainly, our ongoing exploration of the moon and Mars ought to give us pause.

To survive and prosper, we Americans must recapture the vision of our almost miraculous beginning and our unique heritage of freedom and democracy. We must reaffirm this common heritage—including never ending efforts to mend our flaws—if we are to forge a coherent national purpose for ourselves and for our role in the world.

Recapturing a clear sense of purpose in the post–Cold War era is difficult because we no longer face a great and unifying national challenge. In the 1860s, it was saving the Union; in the 1930s, it was eliminating stark poverty; in the 1940s, it was winning the war; and for four decades, it was facing down the Evil Empire.

The foundations of Western civilization are still being shaken, but they have not crumbled. They can be shored up. And despite the siren calls of isolationists and crusaders, I believe most Americans are prepared to accept the costs and risks of world leadership. Edmund Burke warned imperial Britain in words applicable to us: "I dread our own power and our own ambition; I dread our being too much dreaded . . . we may say that we shall not abuse this astonishing and hitherto unheard-of power. But every other nation will think we shall abuse it." We must resist the temptation to be loved and cultivate instead the disciplines that earn us respect.

I want to believe that America still has the material and spiritual strength to shoulder its imperial burden without yielding to paternalism or hubris. The American idea is still vibrant and our nation can continue as a city on the hill. To accept with honor our imperial responsibility, we must recognize our limits, neither exaggerating our virtues nor underestimating our vices. With justifiable pride in our past accomplishments, we should shrug off both self-flagellation and arrogance. In this spirit, we have a fighting chance of renewing the American idea at home and fulfilling our responsibilities abroad.

Index